Who Do You Say I Am?

Who Do You Say I Am?

On the Humanity of Jesus

Edited by

George Kalantzis
David B. Capes
and **Ty Kieser**

CASCADE *Books* · Eugene, Oregon

WHO DO YOU SAY I AM?
On the Humanity of Jesus

Cascade Books
An Imprint of Wipf and Stock Publishers
199 W. 8th Ave., Suite 3
Eugene, OR 97401

www.wipfandstock.com

PAPERBACK ISBN: 978-1-7252-6292-8
HARDCOVER ISBN: 978-1-7252-6293-5
EBOOK ISBN: 978-1-7252-6294-2

Cataloguing-in-Publication data:

Names: Kalantzis, George, editor. | Capes, David B., editor | Kieser, Ty, editor.

Title: Who do you say i am? : on the humanity of Jesus / edited by George Kalantzis, David B. Capes, and Ty Kieser.

Description: Eugene, OR: Cascade Books, 2020. | Includes bibliographical references and index.

Identifiers: ISBN 978-1-7252-6292-8 (paperback) | ISBN 978-1-7252-6293-5 (hardcover) | ISBN 978-1-7252-6294-2 (ebook)

Subjects: LCSH: Jesus Christ—Humanity. | Jesus Christ—Person and offices.

Classification: BT218 W56 2020 (print) | BT218 (ebook)

Manufactured in the U.S.A.   FEBRUARY 21, 2020

Cover image: *The Luminous One* 2015–17, for the Wheaton College President's Art Commission, designed by Jeremy Botts, mosaic facilitated by Leah Samuelson.

For Daniel Ryan Capes (1983–2019)
in loving memory

Contents

That Which was Testified to: History and the Humanity of Jesus

And Which We Proclaimed to You: The Contemporary Church and the Humanity of Jesus

Illustrations

Fernando Yáñez de la Almedina, "Head of Christ," 1506. Now in the Metropolitan Museum of Art, New York. Public Domain (open access for scholarly publishing). | 84

Early Christian Sarcophagus with scenes of Christ and Peter, ca. 325–50. Now in the Museo Pio Cristiano, Vatican. Photo credit: Vanni Archive, Art Resource, NY. | 90

Detail from an icon depicting the Story of King Abgar receiving the Mandylion, ca. 940 CE, from the Monastery of Saint Catherine, Sinai, Egypt. Photo credit: DeA Picture Library/Art Resource, NY. | 91

Icon of Christ, Pantocrator. Sinai, Monastery of St. Catherine, Egypt. 6th cen. Image from Wikimedia, Creative Commons: https://commons.wikimedia.org/wiki/File:ICONS,_Sinai,_Christ_Pantocrator,_6th_century.jpg. | 92

Belvedere Apollo, Roman, ca. 120–40 CE., now in the Vatican Museum. Photo Credit: Wikimedia Creative Commons: https://commons.wikimedia.org/wiki/File:Apollo_of_the_Belvedere.jpg | 93

Early Christian sarcophagus with Christ giving the New Law to Peter and Paul, mid-fourth cen. Now in the Musee de l'Arles antique. Photo credit: Erich Lessing/Art Resource, NY. | 94

Jesus as Teacher Surrounded by His Apostles. Mosaic apse from Sta. Pudenziana, Rome, ca. 400 CE. Photo credit: Robin M. Jensen. | 94

Jesus Healing the Paralytic, mosaic panel from Sant'Apollinare Nuovo, Ravenna, ca. 500 CE. Photo credit: Robin M. Jensen. | 95

Bronze statuette of Jupiter, second half, second century, Rome. Now in the Metropolitan Museum of Art, public domain (open access for scholarly publishing). | 95

Last Supper, mosaic panel from Sant'Apollinare Nuovo, Ravenna, ca. 500 CE. Photo credit: Robin M. Jensen. | 96

Acknowledgments

Our existence is a bodily existence. Because we experience the world and one another through our bodies, a first principle of historic Christianity has been that, in order that God may redeem all of our existence, Jesus assumed our humanity in its fullness. Yet, in our discussions about Jesus's person and work, and our relationship with the triune God, Christians have sometimes presented Christianity as a religion concerned exclusively with the afterlife, neglecting the importance of present realities. We invited our speakers and audiences to explore with us why the humanity of Jesus is central to the Christian understanding of salvation. Over the span of two days we explored how the reality of the Incarnation challenges and redeems our broken social structures, including racial and ethnic divisions, economic systems, and sexuality.

Modern Christians regularly confess the deity of Christ and situate him at the center of their worship. They offer him prayers, sing him hymns, listen intently to his words and deeds, and feast deeply at his table. Acknowledging his unity with the Father shapes much of what Christian believe and practice. Seldom, however, do most Christians reflect upon the humanity of Jesus and why it matters. In 2019 the Wheaton Theology Conference gathered scholars and leaders towork through the theme: "'Who Do You Say That I Am?' Why the Humanity of Jesus Matters."

We wish to thank all of our presenters for joining us and bringing their best ideas to the conference on our theme. Most were willing and able to turn their public lectures into essays for this book. We appreciate the faculty and staff of Wheaton College who supported and helped run the conference. In particular, Ms. Krista Sanchez, Office Coordinator in the Graduate Biblical and Theological Studies at Wheaton College, brought her enormous energies and talents to plan, organize, promote, and execute the conference. She assembled a talented staff of students from the college to ensure that all would go well. Throughout her tenure she has been a steady advocate and ally of the School of Biblical and Theological Studies at Wheaton College.

We were fortunate to have Dr. Tony Payne, Associate Professor of Music and Director of Special Programs & Artist Series, planning and performing the worship for the conference. His artistry at the keyboard and in leading worship set a beautiful tone for everything that transpired during the conference. His generous spirit always pervades everything he touches.

We wish to express our gratitude to Dr. Margaret Diddams, Provost and Professor of Psychology at Wheaton College, and Dr. Philip Ryken, President of Wheaton College, for their tireless support of the School of Biblical and Theological Studies, its mission, and this conference, which has been a part of the rhythm of Wheaton College for twenty-nine years.

Over the years InterVarsity Press has been a gracious partner in helping the faculty and staff of Wheaton College design and execute this conference. Our liaison, the Rev. Dr. David McNutt, has been present from the first as we imagined and brought this conference to reality. It has been a valuable partnership over the years.

We are grateful this year to Michael Thomson and the good people at Cascade Books of Wipf and Stock Publishers who have worked tirelessly to bring this volume to print. It has been exciting to watch as Wipf and Stock has grown and developed over the years into one of the premier presses in North America for theological studies. Strong leadership and vision continue to mark their organization and we are thankful for their support.

A few weeks before the conference opened, David and Cathy Capes received news that their middle son, Daniel, had a serious health problem. He had a rare and aggressive form of cancer that was incurable. Daniel Ryan Capes died in early August 2019 surrounded by his wife, Jenel, Tobias, his four-year-old son, and his family. He was 36 years old.

It is to Daniel that this book is lovingly dedicated.

George Kalantzis, David B. Capes, Ty Keiser,
Feast of the Epiphany, 2020

List of Contributors

Milton Acosta Benítez (PhD Trinity Evangelical Divinity School) is Professor of Old Testament and researcher in the *Theology and Forced Displacement Project* at the Fundación Universitaria Seminario Bíblico de Colombia in Medellin.

Darrel Bock (PhD University of Aberdeen) is the Executive Director of Cultural Engagement and Senior Research Professor of New Testament Studies at Dallas Theological Seminary.

David Capes (PhD Southwestern Baptist Theological Seminary) is Senior Research Fellow and former Dean of Biblical & Theological Studies and Professor of New Testament at Wheaton College.

Lynn Cohick (PhD University of Pennsylvania) is the Provost and Professor of New Testament at Denver Seminary.

Brian E. Daley, SJ (DPhil University of Oxford) is Catherine F. Huisking Professor of Theology at the University of Notre Dame.

Dana M. Harris (PhD Trinity Evangelical Divinity School) is Associate Professor of New Testament at Trinity Evangelical Divinity School and the editor of *Trinity Journal*.

Christopher M. Hays (DPhil University of Oxford) is Associate Professor of New Testament at the Fundación Universitaria Seminario Bíblico de Colombia in Medellín, and director of *Theology and Forced Displacement*, the seminary's institutional research project on forced migration.

David Hooker (MFA Kent State University) is Professor of Art at Wheaton College.

Robin M. Jensen (PhD Columbia University) is the Patrick O'Brien Professor of Theology and Professor of the History of Art at the University of Notre Dame.

George Kalantzis (PhD Northwestern University) is Professor of Theology and Director of *The Wheaton Center for Early Christian Studies* at Wheaton College.

Ty Kieser (PhD Wheaton College, cand.) is Guest Assistant Professor at Wheaton College.

Esau McCaulley (PhD University of St. Andrews) is Assistant Professor of New Testament at Wheaton College.

The Rev. Fleming Rutledge (MDiv Union Theological Seminary), one of the first women to be ordained to the priesthood of the Episcopal Church, is well known in the United States, Canada, and the UK as a lecturer, preacher, and teacher of other preachers.

Abbreviations

ANF   *The Ante-Nicene Fathers*. Edited by Alexander Roberts and James Donaldson. 1885–1887. 10 vols. Repr. Peabody, MA: Hendrickson, 1994.

BDAG   Walter Bauer, Frederick W. Danker, W. F. Arndt, and F. W. Gingrich. *Greek- English Lexicon of the New Testament and Other Early Christian Literature*. 3rd ed. Chicago: University of Chicago Press, 2000.

LNST   The Library of New Testament Studies

NPNF   *A Select Library of Nicene and Post-Nicene Fathers of the Christian Church*. Edited by Philip Schaff and Henry Wace. 28 vols. in 2 series. 1886–1889.

SNTSMS   Society for New Testament Studies Monograph Series

WUNT   Wissenschaftliche Untersuchungen zum Neuen Testament

Introduction

As one walks into the Billy Graham Center at Wheaton College one is immediately met by a 15-foot-wide mosaic composed of 63,000 ceramic, marble, and stone tiles that depicts Jesus's encounter with the Samaritan woman. Set in front of a sprawling landscape with wheat fields and wildflowers, Jesus extends his hands toward the woman who is holding a bucket as water springs from his hands into the bucket, and overflows onto the ground toward the viewer. A peacock, symbolic of life eternal, stands at the edge of the frame as the terminus of the overflow of water provided by the hands of Jesus. Full of imagery that is both ancient (i.e., an olive tree, sheep, a wave border) and contemporary (i.e., Wheaton College buildings among Midwestern US landscape), this mosaic captures something of the purpose of this book. Like the mosaic, this book seeks to present the beauty of the offer of life that Jesus brings by looking at the significance of his humanity. Like the mosaic, this book attends to Jesus's humanity in Scripture and its reception in the Christian tradition. The mosaic captures Jesus's embodied work in its contemporary receptivity by the use of the square halo that surrounds the head of the Samaritan woman, an iconographic convention indicating the saints who were still alive at the point of the artist's depiction; likewise, this book seeks to attend to the contemporary significance and pastoral implications of Jesus's humanity. Finally, like the mosaic, this book is itself a whole composed of various parts with various points of emphasis and perspectives from the various authors in various disciplines.

As such, this book confronts what Charles Taylor calls the "excarnation" of Christianity—"a transfer out of embodied, 'enfleshed' forms of religious life, to those which are more 'in the head.'"[1] "Excarnation" reverses the

---

1. Taylor, *Secular Age*, 554. As an example of the influence of Taylor's book, *Modern Theology* 26 (2010) included five articles by prominent theologians (e.g., Stanley Hauerwas) interacting with his work. This is evident in broadly evangelical circles as well; see,

1

central Christian doctrine of the "incarnation" of the Son of God, whereby the Word "took on flesh and dwelt among us" (John 1:14).[2] "Excarnation" puts off the flesh and rejects the human body as a good created by God—a good that the Son of God was "not ashamed" to take upon himself so that he might call us brothers and sisters (Heb 2:11).

The pervasiveness of excarnational thought has had adverse effects on contemporary Christian theology and practice. It is the contention of this book that these negative effects can be, and ought to be, addressed from the perspective of the doctrine of the person and work of Christ, Christology. These essays, therefore, attempt to address the problem of excarnation from various perspectives on the incarnation.

In order to prepare the way for the essays that follow, we will present a few of the negative effects that excarnation has brought about in the church today. Then we will propose the incarnation of Christ as a viable and valuable foundation from which to address these concerns. Finally, we will outline how each of our contributors brings the humanity of Christ into conversation with contemporary questions of Scripture, culture, and theology.

THE CELESTIAL "CANDY-MAN" OR THE PROBLEM OF TRANSACTIONAL CHRISTIANITY

The development of excarnation, at the expense of the incarnation, has led to consequences that reach all the way into contemporary doctrines of God. That is, rather than allowing our view and vision of God to be drawn from that which he has revealed of himself through his encounters with humanity in the history of redemption, many modern Christians draw our ideas of God from our ideals. Rather than coming to know God as the one who makes and keeps covenants with particular humans in history, we prefer to think of him as the celestial candy-man, cheerfully distributing good things to people who ask politely.[3] As such, we prefer to conceive of God in our

---

for example, Root's *Ministry in a Secular Age* trilogy; Smith, *How (Not) to Be Secular*; and Hansen, *Our Secular Age*.

2. Taylor, *Secular Age*, 614.

3. For another example of this critique see Long, "God is Not Nice," 39–54. See also Smith and Denton, *Soul Searching* for what they term Moralistic Therapeutic Deism (MTD).

image, rather than receive the revelation of God in the flesh of Jesus Christ, who is the exact imprint of the divine nature (Heb 1:3).

Similarly, and likely as a consequence of such a theology, we are often tempted to conceive of the Christian life in unembodied terms and seek unembodied means of life with God. We need not look beyond many Sunday morning services in order to see the way that excarnation has taken root in contemporary (especially American) Christianity. Rather than encountering God in the physical and concrete, many churches turn the lights down low so that parishioners can feel like it is just "me and Jesus." We encourage spiritual practices that are "in our heads" and often neglect those which are in our bodies. For instance, churches (rightly) encourage the practice of regular Scripture reading and individual prayer. However, it is (sadly) often seen as "extraordinary" to practice fasting, service of the needy, and sabbath rest.[4]

This excarnational view of spirituality lends itself to individualistic, primarily intellectual, and exclusively propositionally-focused modes of the Christian life. The individualism and intellectualism of the Christian-life may be seen in an earlier generation's default-spirituality-question, "how's your walk?" and a younger generation's default, "how are you . . . really?" The expected answers to these questions are primarily individual, intellectual, and emotional. Why can we not follow up those questions with a more embodied question like: "how's your walk with your neighbor?" Likewise, we can see the intellectual and propositional emphasis in the way we think about living the Christian life and ethics. Returning to Charles Taylor, he laments that ethics has come to be defined as a list of dos and don'ts—derived from calculations of the utility of various consequences or universalization of maxims—rather than attention to the embodied affections of love and joy in God and with others.[5] Additionally, we regard the Christian life as a sequence of propositions learned about God and about ourselves. For example, countless stories of personal and collective suffering include the line, "but through this hardship God has taught me _____." Does God "teach people lessons" and want us to "learn from various experiences?"

---

4. One might be surprised to see fasting (which seems like an unembodied practice) on this list since it is the cessation of a bodily activity. However, for fasting to occur one needs to recognize the body as valuable, because "sacrifices" only involve that which we consider of value to us. It is never a "sacrifice" to give up something you don't value. So, fasting requires a value on the body and its ordinary operations in order to be sacrificial and, therefore, beneficial.

5. See Taylor, *Secular Age*, 615.

Certainly! But when we prioritize learning a lesson over communing with God and being conformed into God's image, we prioritize a proposition over the Lord of all propositions. We come to think of the Christian life in terms of moving from point A to point Z by accruing "lessons," rather than embracing the abundant life of wholistic obedience and dependence, joy and lament.

Additionally, we see the negative consequences of excarnation in our ecclesiology (i.e., what the "church" is, who composes it, and how it works). For example, Americans can attend "online churches" without ever leaving their homes or meeting another person. When we do step into a church building, we might consume a sermon that is delivered via live stream from our "video pastor" who proclaims the word of God through a larger-than-life screen.

The adverse effects of excarnation are often felt most by the most vulnerable in churches today. When Christians neglect the importance of the body, we erect barriers for those whose bodies do not function the same way as others, making it difficult for persons to participate properly and fully in the body of Christ.[6] Likewise, when Christians dismiss the value of the body in regards to race and ethnicity—perhaps in an attempt to be "color-blind"—we not only disregard the value that every tribe, tongue, peoples, and nation (Rev 7:9) has to contribute, but also disqualify the concerns of personal and system injustice raised by our brothers and sisters.[7] It is not surprising, therefore, that the call to recognize embodiment, and particularly the embodiment of God in Jesus Christ, is often most loudly proclaimed by theologians who represent the underrepresented.[8]

This phenomenon of excarnation is not, however, novel or exclusive to twenty-first-century West. Various iterations of Gnosticism (the belief that humans are primarily immaterial souls who need to escape the prison of the physical body) have plagued the church nearly since its inception.[9] Gnosticism not only denigrated the physical, but elevated the intellectual capacity to overcome the physical, a knowledge which only a select few possessed. They elevated the claims and statuses of these special individuals

6. For an articulation of the need for a better theology of disability and one prominent proposed solution see Yong, *Bible, Disability, and the Church*.

7. See, for example, the monumental work by Jennings, *Christian Imagination*.

8. For example, see Douglas, *Black Christ*, 19–21 claim that the humanity of Christ and his human actions is a central emphasis of Black and Womanist Christologies.

9. For example, Irenaeus's *Against Heresies* (written circa 180) and even the anti-proto-gnostic tendencies of the epistle of 1 John.

in ways that are reminiscent (or, rather, foreshadowing) of the American elevation of the "celebrity pastor." These are our contemporary enlightened gurus who have all the answers and whom we follow indiscreetly.

Yet, the above critique of excarnation need not mean that all things "immaterial" are bad, nor that all things "material" are good. As with most things, the reality is more complex than it first seems. On the one hand, there is an insistence upon the invisibility and non-materiality of Christian hope (Rom 8:24; Heb 11:1).[10] On the other hand, the embrace of God's physical creation as a good ought not be taken as a rejection of prayer, the intellect, or propositions; rather, this is the rejection of the exclusive employment of unembodied humanity toward self-determined ends. Prayer, for example, can and ought to be both individual and communal. As we gather with believers, joining our hands and voices in prayer, we are living an embodied faith that links us with other members of Christ. Likewise, the study of Scripture is not merely a personal act. Whenever we open the Scriptures and read them, we join a stream of tradition that extends over thousands of years of people who have meticulously read, interpreted, and transmitted them faithfully. Every period, paragraph, chapter, and verse represent the judgments of scholars who labored long over texts. Just by reading the Scriptures we become part of that stream. Plus, we may be at our best when we read Scripture within a community of faithful women and men with whom we act and interact throughout the week. In the end, the church needs more prayer, not less. We need robustly embodied disciplines and practices.

"CHRIST THE KEY"

This book is not the first to note such a concern in the contemporary church, nor will it be the last. Contemporary literature presents solutions to the lack of attention to human embodiment, the goodness of creaturely finitude and particularly, the value of humanity from various theological corners and perspectives (especially in accounts of the doctrine of creation

---

10. For example, Michael Allen critiques a trend in contemporary Christianity which, in an attempt to appreciate embodiment in the eschaton, has overcorrected and lost "sight" of the centrality of God in the restoration of heaven and earth in the last days (*Grounded in Heaven*). For an account of the pairing "embodiment" and the "beatific vision" see Cortez, "Body and the Beatific Vision."

and theological anthropology).[11] These developments are evident in the numerous discussions of embodiment and particularity throughout contemporary conversations on sexuality, race gender, disability, pastoral ministry, the Christian life, etc. However, this book seeks to approach the question from the perspective of Christology and ask, "Why does it matter that God the Son took on *humanity*?"

We turn to Christology not merely as an intellectual discipline that contemplates the ontological coexistence of divinity and humanity in a single person, but as a communal discipline which (when understood correctly) is employed and practiced in the lives of everyday Christians. The Synoptic question, "Who do you say that I am?" (Mark 8:29 and par.) is asked of all people individually and collectively. Our response comes as the "body of Christ" (1 Cor 12:27). And our response comes not merely with words but with our lives, with a humble posture toward God and our neighbor. As Rowan Williams says,

> Christology, in short, is 'done' by the Church; it is done in the practice of a community that understands itself to be the Body of Christ, a group of persons living and acting from the conviction that human community is most fully realized in the unconditional mutuality which is represented by the language of organic interdependence. Christology is done in the practice of lives that embrace their finitude and materiality without fear, lives that enact the divine self-identification with those who endure loss, pain and contempt. Christology is done in a practice of prayer and worship that does not approach God as a distant and distinct individual with a will to which mine must conform—as if in a finite relation of slave to master—but acts out of the recognition of adoptive filiation and the intimacy that flows from this. . .christology in this vein is the impetus for both the stillness and expectancy of prayer and the risk of action on behalf of the neglected or oppressed other.[12]

Williams's claims here sum up much of the task of this book. Christology seeks to be a churchly exercise. That is why we have gathered together various voices from the church to contribute to this discussion. Christology embraces the "finitude and materiality" of humanity "without fear." That is, we recognize the creaturely goods of being limited in our abilities and the

---

11. Among others, good examples of this kind of work can be seen in Kapic, *Embodied Hope*; Cortez, *Theological Anthropology*; Levering, *Engaging the Doctrine of Creation*; Crisp and Sanders, *Christian Doctrine of Humanity*.

12. Williams, *Christ The Heart of Creation*, 250.

consequent dependence on the God who "acts on behalf of" his people (Isa 64:4). Christology is "practiced" in the Christian life and it is practiced from an understanding of God as gracious and ourselves as adopted children.[13] As such, Christology seeks to address the problems of excarnation through the doctrine of the incarnation of God. From an "enfleshed" understanding of Christology, we come to see everything (i.e., God, creation, ourselves, one another, etc.) in its proper and clearer light.

Through the humanity of Christ, we come to know God as he has revealed himself to be—as he has revealed himself to particular people in a particular place at a particular time by means of particular flesh and blood. The one who is the image of the invisible God and the exact imprint of God's nature (Heb 1) became flesh and dwelt among us (John 1) so that we might see the Father (John 18). God does not reveal God's self from a distance, but instead makes himself known through the human Jesus. God makes the divine self known not only as the God who thunders from Sinai, but also the God who washes the feet of his unfaithful friends. Likewise, we come to know the identity of Jesus as God not merely by virtue of his propositional articulation of his status, but also by virtue of his revelatory works as a human amongst other human beings.

As we come to know God in the humanity of Jesus, so too we come to understand humanity fully in the incarnation of God; or, as Karl Barth put it, "Jesus Christ, as this Mediator and Reconciler between God and man, is also the Revealer of them both."[14] That is, in Jesus we come to know what it means to be truly human. Jesus, in his humanity, reveals for us the way of the abundant life and he embraces it on our behalf. In Jesus's humanity we see the value of service; we see the value of prayer; we see dependence upon the Spirit of God; we see the proper definition and use of power.

As the true revelation of God and humanity, we come to know ourselves within the story God tells through the humanity of Jesus. As such, we come to understand salvation as an embodied reality. Christ, in his humanity, saves us through his bodily death and resurrection. Salvation does not come through mere divine fiat, but is accomplished because Jesus "was delivered up for our trespasses and raised for our justification" (Rom 4:25). Likewise, we can look forward in hope not because "he lives within my

---

13. On the importance of "practicing doctrine" see Jones, *Practicing Christian Doctrine*.

14. Barth, *Humanity of God*, 47.

heart," but because Jesus was bodily raised as the "firstfruits" of the resurrection (1 Cor 15:20) and the "firstborn" of the dead (Col 1:18).

The church, the "body of Christ," knows itself and functions according to this gospel of embodied salvation. As the church, we operate in the freedom that Christ accomplished on our behalf and we follow his example. Truly human, Jesus directs his attention and time toward those in need, to the outcast and the discounted. Jesus encounters the other, and goes "outside" the gate for our good. In doing so, Jesus shows us the dignity of all humanity. He is not infatuated with the social influence of the Pharisees, but instead recognizes the dignity of the prostitute, tax collector, and Samaritan. Likewise, he does not laud the extraordinary acts of superficial service, but instead praises the ordinary, everyday, obedience of the widow with her two coins (Luke 21:1–4).

Likewise, Jesus does not shirk his Jewish and Galilean identity. Instead, he shows us the value of affirming racial and ethnic diversity. He affirms the unity of the body of Christ from diverse parts and the value of each part (1 Cor 12:12–31). Therefore, we come together regularly as a church (Heb 10:25), we celebrate that which the Lord accomplished in his humanity and thereby recognize the dignity of humanity in each of us. We appreciate the gifts of various parts of the body and we seek to appreciate the goodness of embodied life with God. If God was "not ashamed" to take on flesh, we need not be ashamed of our own. Instead, we can celebrate the gifts of God to the church through particular people, in particular places, at particular times, and we can rest our finite lives in the infinite life of God.

ACROSS SPACE AND TIME: AN ONGOING REORIENTATION

The essays that follow represent an attempt to appreciate the embodiment of God in Jesus and they do so from the perspectives of the contemporary church, history, art, and Scripture. We gathered in the Spring of 2019 for the 28th Wheaton Theology Conference and engaged in vigorous, challenging, and life-giving discussions with scholars, artists, students, pastors, and laypersons and the essays in this volume represent parts of our time together. In planning for the conference, we wanted to hear from theologians, New Testament scholars, experts in the history of the church, social scientists, artists, and art historians. We encountered fresh sounds of music that reminded us of the great traditions; and we worshiped together.

The book's structure is largely drawn from the introduction of 1 John 1, especially verse 2. It begins with Fleming Rutledge's introductory essay, which opens with a treatment of 1 John 1:1–4 and exemplifies the method and message of much of the book. The book then follows 1 John 1 in four sections that orient our study of the humanity of Christ. At the beginning of 1 John 1 the reader is reminded of the "Word of Life" and the audience's experience of hearing, seeing, and touching the Word enfleshed. 1 John 1:2 then describes the eternal Word of life, Jesus, as that which was "revealed . . . , seen . . . , testified to . . . , and proclaimed." These four verbs from 1 John 1:2 represent the four sections of the book. We examine the humanity of Christ as it is revealed in *Scripture*, seen in *art*, testified to throughout the *history* of the church, and proclaimed to us as members of the *contemporary church*.

The vision for the book comes, in part, from the questions that Jesus asked of his disciples throughout his life. He asked the Samaritan woman, "Will you give me a drink?" and asked Peter, "Who do you say that I am?" Jesus encounters us today with similar questions. Each chapter raises some of these questions and asks us to consider ourselves before the Christ who took on our humanity.

In the first essay, Fleming Rutledge encourages us to consider, "How do we receive the embodied Word in our embodied lives?" Rutledge treats 1 John's claim of Christ as the one whom "we have heard, which we have seen with our eyes, which we have looked upon and touched with our hands" and expounds the significance of the humanity of God in terms of God's embodied activity and the hope that the Word brings to those who (like Jesus) suffer in their bodies.

The section on the humanity of Jesus in Scripture asks, "Who does Scripture say that this man Jesus is?" Lynn Cohick delves deeply into Jesus's encounter with the Samaritan woman in light of the expectations of women in the first century. Rather than being a "crafty" or "immoral person," the unnamed woman in John 4 is shown to be an inquisitive interlocutor of Jesus, exhibiting "typical" as well as extraordinary qualities in her encounter with Jesus, qualities that highlight the "atypical" character of Jesus as the savior of the world. Dana Harris examines the humanity of Christ in Hebrews 2, 4, and 5. From a close examination of various texts in these chapters, she draws our attention to the interrelated themes of suffering, solidarity, and salvation. Darrell Bock investigates the Gospel's presentation of Jesus's humanity "from the earth up," and seeks to understand Jesus's identity from the embodied and seemingly earthly actions of the incarnate Christ.

The next section asks us to consider how visual representations of the humanity of Jesus engage and form our understanding of "the man Jesus Christ" through the work of an art historian and a practicing artist. Robin Jensen narrates the history of depicting Jesus's humanity throughout the history of art. She considers the theological significance and underpinnings of trends in artists' depiction of Jesus from the period of the church fathers through today. Next, David Hooker narrates the story of *Corpus,* one of his pieces of art that is part of the permanent exhibits in the Billy Graham Center.

The third section considers the testimony of the Christian church to the significance of the humanity of Jesus to our sisters and brothers of the past. George Kalantzis recounts two stories of martyrs of the early Church (Belinda, Perpetua, and Felicity) who suffered in their bodies in imitation of Christ, transforming the socially prescribed gender norms of their times, and testified to the "unruly God." This God took on humanity in order to redeem not only souls but also systems, raising the marginalized, and inaugurating the kingdom of God as a new reality superseding the temporal one. Brian Daley examines the thought of Irenaeus and Origen in order to show that Christian theology rests upon the paradox that the God who is eternal, invisible, creative, in the person of Jesus, has "become flesh and dwelt among us" (John 1:1–2, 14–18)—temporal, visible, created. Because of this paradoxical foundation, humans can behold, receive, and participate in the life of the God of love.

The final essays ask what Jesus's humanity means for the way that we view our own humanity and how we relate to our (geographic, ethnic, and economic) neighbor? Treating the significance of the humanity of Christ for the contemporary church, the first section begins with Esau McCaulley's account of Jesus's Jewishness as embracing human ethnicity. Within the broader Christian story of Jesus as the messianic king of Israel, the particularity of Jesus's person and work bring about God's intention to create a people from every tribe, tongue, and nation who will reflect him in the world. Milton Acosta and Christopher Hays consider the significance of Jesus's human life for a contemporary account of immigration. They examine the biblical testimony of Jesus as our migrant messiah and the shape of the "migrant church" that he establishes.

"WHO DO YOU SAY I AM?"

These essays bring to the fore questions about God, Jesus, humanity, and the good life. Here we encounter the reality of God becoming human in a way that shapes our understanding of God, ourselves, and the world around us. If Taylor is right to suggest that we live in a world where excarnation reigns and that by accepting this excarnational premise, Christianity "is denying something essential to itself," then we must turn to the God who is incarnate. As Taylor says, "We have to struggle to recover a sense of what the Incarnation can mean."[15] Notice that he does not say "fully recover" or "fully appreciate" (a task that is likely impossible on this side of the *eschaton*), but to "struggle to recover." This is the goal of the book before you: to struggle against the problem of excarnation and to struggle for a rediscovery of the beauty of the incarnation of God.

15. Taylor, *Secular Age*, 771, 753.

I

The Body Prepared for Jesus

FLEMING RUTLEDGE

The subject of the 2019 Wheaton College Theological Conference is the material life of Jesus—his humanity, if you will. In this presentation I propose to focus on his humanity considered specifically as his *body*.

But I'm a preacher, not a lecturer. I require a biblical text. I have several, as we shall see. To begin with, here are the well-known words from the salutation at the beginning of the First Epistle of John:

> That which was from the beginning, which we have heard, which we have seen with our eyes, which we have looked upon and touched with our hands, concerning the word of life—the life was made manifest, and the eternal life which was with the Father and was made manifest to us—that which we have seen and heard we proclaim also to you, so that you may have fellowship with us; and our fellowship is with the Father and with his Son Jesus Christ. And we are writing this that our joy may be complete (1 John 1:1–4).

It is generally recognized that this is the Johannine author's deliberate reframing and expansion, not only of Genesis 1, but especially of the prologue of the Gospel according to John: "In the beginning was the Word . . . and the Word became flesh and dwelt among us, full of grace and truth."[1]

I can't speak for you, but that passage in First John has always struck me as extraordinary. In this introductory passage, the author gives powerful testimony to the *material, fleshly* life of Jesus in emphatic, insistent, artfully repeated phrases:

- The word of life was from the beginning
- We have heard it
- We have seen it *with our eyes*
- We have touched it *with our hands*

. . . and it is this *enfleshed presence* that motivates and confirms John as he declares, "that which we have seen and heard we proclaim also to you."

This is great writing. John says essentially the same thing twice in very similar words, and yet it does not sound annoyingly repetitive. Calvin writes that "the Apostle heaps together . . . many things in confirmation of the gospel" but there is "no redundancy, but a fuller expression for the sake of amplification."[2] When it comes to heaping up words for the sake of amplification, no one can touch Paul in Romans 5, where he says the same thing five to seven times in one paragraph, depending on how you count. We'll get back to Romans 5 at the end.

It's the part about "we have touched *it* with our hands" that strikes me in the context of our theme. Isn't it interesting that John refers to "it" instead of "him"? The Fourth Gospel doesn't do that, but says, more as we would expect, "*He* was in the beginning with God." Why then does the author of the Epistle say "it"? We have touched "it" with our hands. It seems to me to be because John wants to speak here very particularly of Jesus not only as the enfleshed only-begotten One, but as "the Word of life." He is the Word, and the Word is the incarnate Son, the living Word of God "which was from the beginning." John has a particular investment in the Word

---

1. I don't propose to get into the discussion here about who actually wrote the Johannine literature. After spending more than a decade studying the authorship question in depth, I decided to embrace the canonical approach. I thereby saved myself, as a preacher, from a great deal of *angst*. I doubt that "John," whoever he was, wrote all of the Johannines, but I no longer care very much, except for lingering historical curiosity. The "beloved disciple" is the underlying witness, and it is the power and authenticity of the Johannine witness that counts.

2. Calvin, *Commentaries on the Catholic Epistles*, 157–58.

of proclamation. He is an apostle—a divinely appointed messenger of the greatest news the world has ever heard.

And we are an apostolic church. Back in the seventies, when I was new to preaching and pastoring, I was somewhat intimidated by older clergy who were trained in the historical-critical method and had no particular commitment to a theology of the word of God. I was rescued from this by reading Amos Wilder's book *Early Christian Rhetoric*. To this day I can feel the thunderclap. The preaching of the apostles, he wrote, was a new dynamic in human speech, something that had never been heard before. The proclamation of the gospel was "the power of God effecting what was impossible with [human beings]." The apostles "announced the overthrow of Satan's whole reign and the transformation of the world." The particular stories of Jesus's healings and exorcisms in the Gospels "exhibit the ultimate omnipotence of [the] grace [of God]."[3] All of this is present in the Son of God; all of it is present in the Word of power that he gives all who are called to apostolic ministry.

We do not deepen our knowledge of Christ by developing our own "spiritual" capacities, but by receiving the incarnate and written Word in faith. Christ Jesus is himself the living and embodied Word, the second Person of the Trinity. God is uniquely the One who communicates himself: *first* in the spoken Word to the prophets, and *then* conclusively in the incarnate person of the Son as we come to know him—or rather as he is pleased to reveal himself to us—and *finally* in his gift of himself in the Word written. As the Epistle to the Hebrews puts it, "In many and various ways God spoke of old to our fathers by the prophets; but in these last days he has spoken to us by a Son" (Heb 1:1–2). It is the speaking of God to us through Jesus that defines the speaking of the prophets and the apostles, and in their line of succession, the apostolic church—that is to say, you and me. It is that speaking which is replenished and renewed by the expository preaching of the Word.

This unique feature of Christian faith, the doctrine of the living Word of God, may be obvious to those attending this conference who were raised in, or converted to, a tradition in which the theology of the Word of God is held in the highest place; but I can assure you it is scarcely known at all in many Protestant circles today. Few are seeking to drink deeply from Scripture; rather, they are looking for what is being called "spirituality." The Dalai Lama once protested that he should not be compared to Jesus, who

3. Wilder, *Early Christian Rhetoric*, 9, 29, 64.

was "a great master." The Dalai Lama certainly meant well, but with all due respect, Jesus was not and *is* not a "spiritual master," not even one greater than others. He is not a spiritual master at all, but the Word become flesh. We should be careful with the word "spiritual." The apostle Paul uses the word "spiritual" often, but he intends something very different from the way it is generally used today. He means the sphere of the work of the Holy Spirit, the third Person, which can more often be located in gritty physical reality—in prisons, in homeless shelters, in hospitals, in refugee camps, at our southern border—than in walking around labyrinths. It is remarkable how little Paul writes about so-called spiritual practices. He wrote, "Pray without ceasing," but we are on firmer ground to think of him in constant, urgent appeal to God for the stamina he would require for his journeys and for the life of his churches rather than pausing for "spiritual practices," which he never mentions. Rather, he writes like this:

> I decided to know nothing among you except Jesus Christ and him crucified. And I was with you in weakness and in much fear and trembling; and my speech and my message were not in plausible words of wisdom, but in demonstration of the Spirit and of power, that your faith might not rest in the wisdom of men but in the power of God (1 Cor 2:2–5).

He was writing to the Corinthians, who were caught up into a spirituality of signs and wonders—experiences of the divine, you might say. They were, essentially, gnostics. Bodily life was something they thought should be shucked off. That's why Paul wrote sternly to them about the physical demands of his apostleship:

> I think that God has exhibited us apostles as last of all, like men sentenced to death; because we have become a spectacle to the world. . . . . We are fools for Christ's sake, but you [Corinthians] are 'wise' in Christ. We are weak, but you are 'strong' . . . To the present hour we hunger and thirst, we are ill-clad and buffeted and homeless . . . we have become, and are now, as the refuse of the world, the offscouring of all things (1 Cor 4:9–13).

That just doesn't sound like a man who is constantly thinking about the spiritual dimensions of life. The Corinthian correspondence is a strong corrective against the gnostic tendencies of the Corinthian church. They were the original "spiritual" congregation.[4] They thought they had left their

---

4. When Paul writes that the Corinthians are "of the flesh" (3:3) he doesn't mean literal flesh. He uses the terms "flesh (*sarx*)" and "spirit (*pnuema*)" to denote the

bodies behind as of no importance when they were converted. Curiously, the Corinthians seem to have carried their gnostic disdain for the body in two opposite ways: either they withdrew from sexual relations, even in marriage, altogether (7:1–7) or they played fast and loose with sexuality—to which Paul said, "the body is not made for immorality, but for the Lord"(6:13).[5] To these two opposing errors in the Corinthian congregation, Paul directs his teaching about the body that is truly distinguishing: "Do you not know that your bodies are members of Christ? . . . [so] glorify God in your body" (1 Cor 6:20).

The true glory of the human body derives from the human body of Jesus Christ himself, and his identification with us. Here is the heart of the matter. Just as in the Old Testament the various post-Edenic characters are often famously lusty, pugilistic, intemperate, and violent, yet for all that they are recognizable human beings living actual bodily—not mythical— lives, all in the sight of an unsurprised God who continues to dignify them by his address to them. His Word to them is usually unsuspected, destabilizing, unnerving, but ever-restorative and revelation-creating—and very much addressed to them bodily: "Gird up your loins like a man," God says to Job: "I will question you, and you will declare to me" (Job 38:3). This is the unique voice of God in our Scriptures.

So the material existence of the Son is also the living presence of the Word of God in all of its freshness every day. There is a lovely moment in Marilynne Robinson's *Gilead* when the preacher and his son are on their quest to find the grave of the grandfather. They stop at a house along the way to ask for help—"We offered to do some chores in exchange for goods," the old preacher writes. But the householder does not ask for any chores to be done. He asks the preacher if he "would just open a bit of Scripture." How surpassingly wonderful that is! Nowadays, in the church circles I frequent, no one ever says anything like that. In the beleaguered mainline churches, what I hear nowadays is all about developing our spirituality, but very little about the living Word. I would be deeply thankful if I could "open a bit of Scripture" today. This is the vocation of the apostolic messenger in every age of the world in which we labor, and there is a promise attached to it: "'My word shall never return to me empty,' says the Lord; 'it shall

---

world-order of the flesh and the world-order of the Spirit. Hence, "your *body* is a temple of the Holy Spirit" (6:19).

5. Paul is uniquely important to the church, but it must be admitted that his teaching on marriage is singularly lukewarm! The Song of Songs has its place in the Scripture.

accomplish that which I purpose, and prosper in the thing for which I sent it'" (Isa 55:11).

So let us now turn to the gospel declaration concerning the human body of Jesus Christ, as we read it in the first chapter of the Epistle to the Hebrews. Speaking of the temple sacrifices, the author writes,

> But in these sacrifices there is a reminder of sin year after year. For it is impossible that the blood of bulls and goats should take away sins.
>
> Consequently, when Christ came into the world, he said [quoting from Psalm 40],
> "Sacrifices and offerings thou hast not desired,
> but *a body* hast thou prepared for me;[6]
> in burnt offerings and sin offerings thou hast taken no pleasure.
> Then I said, "'Lo, I have come to do thy will, O God,' as it is written of me in the roll of the book" . . .
> And by that will we have been sanctified through the offering of the *body* of Jesus Christ once for all (Heb 10:3–7, 10; emphasis added).

What a remarkable imagination our author has![7] In our passage, Jesus is depicted saying the words of the Psalmist as though they were his own—and indeed, this is one way of understanding the Psalms—as Jesus's own voice, Jesus's own prayers. In any case, it's the emphasis on the *body* of Jesus—his material human flesh—that strikes us here. Jesus is depicted as joined in one will with the Father who has prepared a body for him. Behold, he says, I am here to do your will, as is already written of me. Jesus's greatest desire is to do the will of the Father. There is no seam between them. The will of the Father and the Son are one will. Should there be any doubt, the author writes, "And by that will we have been sanctified through the offering of the *body* of Jesus Christ once for all" (Heb 10:10).

---

6. It was well-known by Calvin's time that "body" was a misreading of the LXX by the author of Hebrews. Calvin passes over this mistake because it seems inspired, and does no violence to the overall theological message either of the Psalm or of Hebrews.

7. Hebrews is much neglected in my mainline Episcopal church, probably because of its emphasis on the unpopular theme of sacrifice and its misuse in nineteenth-century Protestant scholasticism as a proof-text for penal substitutionary atonement. This sidelining of Hebrews has been unfortunate, for Hebrews is a wonderful book which fully, if not exhaustively, incorporates the Christus Victor theme that is so prominent in Paul's letters (e.g., Heb 2:14–15).

And what happens to that body? After serving a healthy young man for 33 years, walking many miles a day over challenging terrain, often sleeping rough and in need of food and water, that body is publicly condemned, reviled, spat upon, scourged, tormented, publicly exhibited, nailed, mocked, and made to die at excruciating length upon a wooden instrument of torture in full view of the whole populace. That is what happened to the *material flesh* of Jesus, to the *body prepared* by the will of the three-personed God.

In his commanding work, *The Cross and the Lynching Tree,* James H. Cone makes the connection between crucifixion as a method of dehumanizing and killing a person and the practice of lynching Black Americans. I am profoundly regretful that I did not know of this book during the twenty years I spent writing my own book *The Crucifixion.*[8] Cone's work is crucial to understanding "the dialectic of despair and hope," "of doubt and faith" so characteristic of the African-American church. A significant number of white Christians, including myself, have spoken publicly about the miracle of the Black church.[9] How else could Black Americans tolerate their former slave masters, let alone forgive us, except for the depth of the identification of the Black church with Jesus Christ? "The cross was the foundation on which their faith was built."[10] And make no mistake, it was the suffering of Jesus *in his body* that made the difference to Black Christians. The complete, total, unreserved giving of God's self in the human body of Jesus was sufficient to encompass the world of humiliation that Black people must endure and overcome on a daily basis.

Cone writes, "the spirituals were the soul of the [civil rights movement] and the church was its anchor."[11] He quotes many of the African-American spirituals:

> Poor little Jesus boy, made him to be born in a manger,
> World treated him so mean,

8. Cone's book was published as I was winding down my own book and to my great regret, I did not learn of it in time. See Cone, *Cross and the Lynching Tree*; Rutledge, *Crucifixion.*

9. W. E. B. DuBois was not a conventional churchgoing Christian, but he strongly identified the Black church with the faith of former slaves: "[Jesus Christ] was persecuted and crucified; and we were mobbed and lynched." I personally enjoyed DuBois's swipe at the Episcopal Church: "He [Jesus] would seldom see the interior of St. John the Divine" (quoted in Cone, *Cross and Lynching Tree*, 103).

10. Cone, *Cross and Lynching Tree*, 21.

11. Cone, *Cross and Lynching Tree*, 28.

Treats me mean too . . .
Dey whupped him up and dey whupped him down,
Dey whupped dat man all over town.
Look how dey done my Lawd.[12]

Physical suffering is not all that Jesus endured. Whole chapters have been written about the suffering of shame, humiliation, and abandonment that were deliberately designed to be part of the whole ritual of crucifixion. This, too, resonates with all who are outcast or derelict in some way. Hebrews, again, is the book that points out the role of *shame* in the story of Jesus's offering of his body. Note that the shame he endured is the source of strength for us as we face painful experiences in our own lives:

> Let us run with perseverance the race that is set before us, looking to Jesus the pioneer and perfecter of our faith, who for the joy that was set before him endured the cross, despising the shame (Heb 12:1–2).

In mentioning "painful experiences," I thought of what I've been reading about "experiences." I read that people today don't spend as much money on clothes and furniture as they used to. Instead, they spend it on restaurants and travel. They want "experiences." There's nothing intrinsically wrong with that; I'm all for good experiences myself. But most people in this world don't have the luxury of "experiences." They are fortunate if they have something to eat at home, a chair to sit on, and a table to put their plate on—if they have a plate, or indeed if they have a home. I read about the Central American children on the border, sleeping night after night on the bare dirt under an overpass in a Texas town. Think of how shameful that is, to have nothing, and to have other people stare at you. Jesus shared that shame in his own body.

While I was writing this I became even more interested than before in the suffering that people endure in their bodies. We learn much more about this by reading written reports than we do from television news. People are having "experiences," indeed, but not the kind that we see in the commercials. Here are two illustrations from the recent news about people suffering in their bodies. A woman named Tricia Newbold is a whistle-blower in the US government. She is a skilled security professional who has worked at the White House for 18 years. She went to the Congressional Oversight Committee to tell them what she knew about security clearances that should

---

12. Cone, *Cross and Lynching Tree*, 22.

not have been given. Her boss became suspicious and began to humiliate her in various ways. For one thing, she was removed from her supervisory role. More to the point, however, Ms. Newbold has dwarfism; she is exceedingly short of stature. Her boss maliciously sought to shame her by having file boxes that she needed for her work moved to high shelves so that she couldn't reach them. "It's humiliating," she said to the committee. She was being attacked, so to speak, *in her body*.[13]

A second illustration is an obituary for a remarkable woman. Her name is Tejshree Thapa, and she died of an illness at only 52 years of age. She was born in Nepal to Nepalese parents, both of them prominent public servants. When she was a teenager, her father was named ambassador to the US, and the family moved to Washington, DC (she graduated from the National Cathedral School). She went on to Wellesley and the Cornell Law School. Instead of following the usual pedigreed track, Tej (as she was called) went to work on human rights and violence against women. Her entire career was devoted to exposing and prosecuting mass rape and sexual enslavement. There was not much established legal doctrine in these areas, said an advocacy director for Human Rights Watch; he explained that Tej's work helped to win several cases involving mass rape and enslavement of Muslim women during the Balkan wars in the 1990s. "It was her work with victims . . . that helped make this happen." Now we're getting close to the point. For many years in the field, she interviewed hundreds of women who had been bodily assaulted in the most dreadful way, and families whose members had been tortured and "disappeared." She earned their trust, recorded their testimony in detail, and stood by them in court. And here is the point: in the case of these women, these families of people who had suffered extreme torment *in their bodies*, she stayed in touch with many of them long after she had finished her work for them in court. Here is what the South Asia director for Human Rights Watch said: "She handled [the survivors and families] with so much empathy. At some point, most people in her position walk away. She never walked away."[14]

Both of these women suffered in a particular way. Ms. Newbold was treated cruelly by her boss, partly because of her gender no doubt, but principally because of her body—her dwarfism. She soldiered on in that small body, returning to work, and saying to the House Committee, "As little as

13. She also said, "As little as I am."
14. Seelye, "Tejshree Thapa."

I am, I'm willing to fight and stand up for what I know is right."[15] And Tej Thapa suffered alongside countless victims of bodily harm that you and I can scarcely imagine. I think most of us would not be able to hear many testimonies like the hundreds that she heard. People who have heard such accounts say that they feel damaged afterward. But Tej kept their phone numbers and did not walk away.

These are just two recent examples. We could give hundreds more. PTSD, for instance, is not precisely a bodily ailment, but it has physical effects, and the soldier who suffers from it feels shame, feels humiliation. The Methodist pastor Jason Micheli, who lives with the specter of incurable cancer, has written a book called *Cancer is Funny*, which is the kind of laugh-to-hide-your-breaking-heart book that only a man who is undergoing the most drastic kind of chemotherapy can write.[16] He is merciless in describing the bodily shame that is an inevitable result of the treatment.

The recent film *Hotel Mumbai* made an impression on me along these lines. In many ways it's just another suspense thriller, but there is a scene in it that makes a point I want to emphasize. It tells the true story of the three-day siege of the famous Taj hotel in Mumbai, India, by a group of young Muslim terrorists. As the terrified people staying at the hotel cluster together in a safe room, a rich, older white woman displays destabilizing fear of a young hotel staff member who wears a turban. She thinks he is one of the terrorists. This fear begins to spread to the others, putting them all in peril. The young man goes to her and shows her the photos on his cell phone, photos of his little son and pregnant wife. The white woman begins to calm down. Then he explains to her, softly and patiently, that he is a Sikh, that the turban is sacred to a Sikh, and that he never takes it off except in private. It would be *shameful* to take it off, he says, but if you want me to, I will take it off. She backs down, abashed, and he keeps the turban on. Later, however, as the group attempts to escape, more and more people are shot and killed, and in the midst of the carnage we see the young Sikh, wordlessly and without display, taking off the turban so he can use the fabric to make a bandage. He did not "despise the shame."

I read an interview with the young actor Dev Patel who plays the part of the Sikh. In the original script his role is not that of a Sikh. He persuaded the filmmakers to change it. He wanted to play a Sikh particularly, he said, because after 9/11, he said, many Sikhs were personally attacked and their

15. Rogers, "Whistle-Blower Did the Unexpected."
16. Micheli, *Cancer is Funny*.

turbans snatched because people thought they were terrorists, and he wanted to seize the opportunity to give them support, to take their part. Not an artistic decision, perhaps, but a profoundly humane one, seeking to identify with those who are shamed.

At this point, I stop—to summarize and to bear witness. I said earlier that the original apostles, including especially John, Paul, and the author of Hebrews, made a point of Jesus's bodily existence and the really quite extraordinary doctrine of the incarnation of the Word of God. These affirmations are unique to Christianity. As much as we want to be respectful of other faiths and defend them when they are persecuted, at the same time we cannot betray our own faith. There is no story like that of the Bible, the story of God who takes on the burden of the whole of humanity in his own material flesh, sharing in our bodily condition at the point of its greatest vulnerability.

I affirmed earlier, with the historic Creeds, that the church is an *apostolic* church. As I look out at you, knowing something of the composition of this audience, I beseech you always to remember your commission, given to you by the Lord of the church. There is a most unfortunate saying attributed to St. Francis of Assisi: "Preach the gospel—if necessary, use words." Francis never actually said that, but I hear it quoted constantly. It reinforces the ignorance of the church when it does not believe in the doctrine of the word of God. It robs us of the inexhaustible riches of the Scriptures. It throws us back on our own resources. Again: It is the speaking of God to us in an embodied second Person that defines the speaking of the prophets and the apostles, and in their line of succession, the apostolic church. It is that speaking of the prophets and apostles that we find in Holy Scripture. It is the vocation of every Christian to love that Word and to believe in its power to create something *ex nihilo*, out of nothing. For as Paul wrote concerning Abraham, the father of faith: he never ceased to trust in "the God who raises the dead and calls into being the things that do not exist" (Rom 4:17). It is that God, the God who gave up his very self to endure every gruesome bodily detail of suffering, shameful human existence, who gives us our apostolic vocation. "So glorify God in your body." There is only one true way to perform this, and that is by "looking to Jesus, the pioneer and perfecter of our faith," the only Son of God, who said,

> Sacrifices and offerings thou hast not desired,
> but *a body* hast thou prepared for me . . .
> Lo, I have come to do thy will, O God.,

And the apostolic author concludes, as do I:

And by that will we have been sanctified through the offering of the *body* of Jesus Christ once for all. (Heb 10:5, 7, 10).

That Which Was Revealed

Scripture and the Humanity of Jesus

2

"Could This Be the Christ?"

The Samaritan Woman's Testimony and Jesus's Identity

LYNN H. COHICK

Denver Seminary

I have been fascinated by the story of Jesus's encounter with the Samaritan woman for decades. In my 2009 book, *Women in the World of the Earliest Christians*, I explore how the details of John's narrative of her life (John 4:1–42) might connect with the reality on the ground in first-century Samaria.[1] I would like to explore this same area, but now with an eye to the theological impact of the encounter.[2] I will then articulate how the theology expressed in the discussion further reveals who Jesus is. The Samaritan woman explained to her local community the answer to Jesus's question, "Who do you say that I am?" (Matt 16:15).

The Samaritan woman's testimony that Jesus is a prophet, and is probably the messiah, follows Jesus's claims that he brings living water and his revelation that he knows her marital history and situation. Acknowledging that he is a prophet, she proceeds to question him about the relative worth

---

1. Cohick, *Women in the World of the Earliest Christians*.

2. I beg your indulgence to view the Samaritan woman as a historical figure, for the sake of this essay. I realize that scholars debate the historicity of the story. My contention is that her exchange with Jesus is historically plausible, for reasons I expound upon below.

of Jerusalem and the Samaritan holy place, Mt. Gerizim. The apparent change of subject has led some to suggest that she dodges Jesus's challenge to her sinful lifestyle, for she is not married to the man she is with currently. I argue, however, that this unnamed woman acts in typical ways that reveal Jesus's atypical qualities, and that demonstrate to her and her town that he is the Savior of the world.

To defend my argument, I will look at three typical features of the Samaritan woman's life, and then follow with three atypical characteristics of her life that spotlight Jesus's remarkable mission and person. The typical features include (1) that she identifies herself based on her marital status; (2) that she engages in religious conversation with Jesus; and (3) that she speaks to the town about her discovery. As will become apparent, these "typical" features have been improperly presented as atypical for a first-century woman, and I think when that happens, the entire encounter is misunderstood. As such, the presentation of these features as typical corrects these misreadings. Additionally, there are some genuinely atypical characteristics of this narrative, including (1) that she has had five husbands; (2) that she would meet a Jew, especially one who asked for a drink from her bucket (4:11); and (3) that the encounter would lead to the town's confession that Jesus is the Savior of the world.

I. FEATURES OF TYPICAL BEHAVIOR/ATTITUDES

A. That She Identifies Herself Based on Her Marital Status

The Samaritan woman asks Jesus to give her water that will quench her thirst forever. Jesus asks in response that she find her husband and return with him to the well. Jesus assumes that she is married, a pretty safe bet, as most people were married or widowed.[3] Her response is simple and direct: "I have no husband."[4] Jesus agrees with this statement and then adds that

3. Hanson, "Widow Babatha and the Poor Orphan Boy," 86–87. Most women first married in their mid-teens and were still married (although not necessarily to their first husband) when they were 30 years old. After this, the rate of married women declines, while for men, most are still married in their forties. The average age gap between husband and wife is about seven years for their first marriage, and about seventeen years as they grow older.

4. Wallace, *Greek Grammar Beyond the Basics*, 455, argues the Greek order of words that places "husband" first suggests "great rhetorical power." However, Abbott, *Johannine Grammar*, 401, notes that John often has repetition, with a bit of variation on word order. Often the variation is to put the last word of a saying first in the repetition of that saying

she has had five husbands, and is currently with a man who is not her husband. He concludes, "what you have said is true." This answer leads her to conclude, "Sir, I can see that you are a prophet," after which she asks questions related to proper worship of God. This exchange has puzzled scholars, leading some to presume that she is immoral and crafty: immoral because she is not married to the man she is living with, and crafty because she changes the subject when Jesus touches on her allegedly sinful life.

But is she immoral? To help answer this question, I would like to look at what we know about marriage at this time, and do so primarily through the lens of the Babatha and Salome Komaïse archives. These second-century Jewish women saved a collection of personal documents, including marriage and dowry documents. I hope to show the complex alternatives available for couples at this time, as well as describe what legal options might have been available to sort out family problems. These complexities include polygyny, "unwritten marriage" (*agrapha gamos*), and concubinage. Added to the considerations are the facts that many women could not read (true of many men as well) and that women required a guardian in any court proceedings. The legal claims on property and inheritance play an important role in marriage matters. Moreover, women were required to have guardians for executing legal documents, including dowry certificates or loans or property disputes. Sometimes husbands served as guardians, but not always.[5]

Before discussing the complexities, I would like to outline the typical marriage expectations. Women often brought a dowry into marriage, and its content was spelled out in detail in a legal document. The husband had full use of the (dowry) money, and kept any interest or profit gained. The dowry principle, however, belonged to the wife, who could ask for its return if the marriage ended, or if she became a widow. She was then free to use the money as she wished. However, a husband's family might require that when they returned the dowry money to the widow, neither the widow nor any children of the union could make a further claim on the husband's estate.[6]

(see 1:26–33; 4:31, 49).

5. Babatha's literacy is an open question. In *P. Yadin* 15, she identifies herself as illiterate; however this might refer only to Greek, for she signs the Aramaic document, *P. Yadin* 10. See Czajkowski, *Living Under Different Laws*, 65.

6. Hanson, "Widow Babatha and the Poor Orphan Boy," 96–97.

Jewish women could receive property from their parents or husband through the provision of a document called a "deed of gift." In this way, daughters could inherit, if you will, from their parents' estate.[7] Implied in this practice is the custom that without such a legal decision, wives and daughters who had brothers did not inherit, but all assets went to the sons or the father's brothers and his heirs.

a. The Archives

We now turn to Babatha's documents, part of the Yadin Papyri discovered in the Cave of Letters, Nahal Hever, in 1960–1961. Babatha's archives consists of thirty-five documents written in Nabataean Aramaic, Judean Aramaic, and Greek. She kept them in a leather purse that was placed in a waterskin along with balls of flax thread.[8] Additionally, she individually wrapped her own marriage document, her mother's deed of gift from her father, and her second husband's daughter's marriage contract.[9] Overall, her documents reveal a woman of means, whose parents had property and money.

Babatha was born about 100 CE at the southern tip of the Dead Sea in the town of Mahoza, and lived around the sea for her whole life. From her legal documents, we can trace Babatha's timeline.[10] In 120, Babatha married a man named Jesus, and they had a son, also named Jesus. In this same year, Babatha's father gives a deed of gift of four date groves to her mother, Miriam (*P.Yadin* 7). In this document, Shimeon stipulates that if Babatha becomes a widow, she is entitled to live in a "hut" in the courtyard. She forfeits this if she remarries. It is also likely that in 120, Babatha receives a deed of gift of the property her father bought in 99 (see *P.Yadin* 15).[11] Within the

---

7. Similarly, Num 27:1–11 speaks of Zelophehad's daughters who inherit their father's property because he has no son.

8. Hanson, "Widow Babatha and the Poor Orphan Boy," 93, claims that she used the colored strings as markers to identify the documents, for she could not read them.

9. Hanson, "Widow Babatha and the Poor Orphan Boy," 93.

10. Esler, *Babatha's Orchard*, 94–99 examines *P. Yadin* 1, 2, 3 4, that describe Babatha's father's property that he gifted to her. These four documents relate to her father's purchase of an orchard from a Nabataean woman. This woman's situation mirrors Babatha's current predicament. Amat-'Isi loaned her husband, Muqimu, a sizable amount of money, 600 denarii, from her dowry to rent property for two years. The hope was that the harvest would cover the amount of the loan and more. Instead, his venture fails, and Babatha's father is able to purchase the land.

11. Esler, *Babatha's Orchard*, xvii; Cotton and Greenfield, "Babatha's Property," 217.

next four years, her husband Jesus dies, leaving Babatha a widow with a son, who is legally an orphan. It may be that Babatha and her toddler live with her mother in the "hut" in the latter's courtyard.[12]

Between 125–128 CE, Babatha remarries a man named Judah. She is now about 30 years old.[13] We have this marriage contract, written in Aramaic by her husband, that indicates Babatha brings a dowry of 400 *denarii* (*P. Yadin* 10). This document includes the stipulation that if he dies, she can live in his house and be cared for until his heirs return her dowry (*ketubba*). Most scholars believe that Babatha's second husband, Judah, was also concurrently married to a woman named Miriam.[14] That is, Judah had not divorced Miriam before marrying Babatha. Josephus, the Jewish historian in the late first century, addresses this Jewish custom of bigamy with approval (*Ant.* 17.14). Ben Sira, a Hellenistic-Jew (fl. second-century BC) and the author of *Sirach,* assumes the practice as he decries the jealousy between wives that the system created (Sir 26.5–6; 28:15; 37:11). Bigamy, however, was not recognized by the Romans. We can only speculate on why Babatha entered this bigamous relationship.[15]

In February, 128 CE, Babatha provided her second husband, Judah, a loan of three hundred denarii (*P. Yadin* 17). In April, 128 CE, Judah's daughter and Babatha's stepdaughter, Shelamzion, married Judah Cimber. Shelamzion's father contributed two hundred denarii to his daughter's dowry, likely using part of the money borrowed earlier from Babatha. Judah Cimber promised three hundred denarii more (*P. Yadin* 18). Shelamzion also received a deed of gift from her father in 128 CE, eleven days after her wedding (*P. Yadin* 19). The father's gift includes half a courtyard and rooms

---

12. Hanson, "Widow Babatha and the Poor Orphan Boy," 96. Babatha becomes frustrated with her son's guardians, who are not distributing funds with the generosity that Babatha wants. She asks to manage his funds and increase them threefold by contributing from her own resources. It does not appear that she is successful, even after several attempts over eight years. The documents do not indicate why her requests were unheeded (*P. Yadin* 13–15).

13. Hanson, "Widow Babatha and the Poor Orphan Boy," 88.

14. Kraemer, "Jewish Women and Women's Judaism(s)," 55.

15. Perhaps Babatha married for love, see Dixon, "Sex and the Married Woman in Ancient Rome," 127–28: "So strong indeed was the cultural presumption that Roman men did expect sexual pleasure in marriage, particularly in the early years, that husbands were conventionally cautioned against sexual infatuation with their wives." Interestingly, Judah acts as Babatha's guardian in her legal battle with her son's guardians, as reflected in her archive (*P. Yadin* 14, 15, 16). Did she grow to trust him as he functioned on her behalf?

for use at that time, and she would receive the other half of the courtyard upon his death. Within five years, Judah dies (*P. Yadin* 19, 20) without having repaid the loan, and Babatha takes his property as payment (*P. Yadin* 21–26).[16]

A second, smaller archive contains similar documents from a woman who lived in the same region as Babatha. Salome Komaïse saved six documents written between January, 125 and August, 131 CE. In 129 CE, Komaïse received a deed of gift from her mother that includes a date orchard, and half a courtyard with several rooms. The gift was activated at the time the deed was signed, and not when her mother dies (*P. XHev/Se gr* 64). Her mother had just remarried, and it may be that she deeded the property to her daughter to preserve the family's wealth, lest Grapte bear a son to her new husband, who would then inherit her wealth.

At this point, Salome Komaïse had been married and divorced to a man named Sammouos, and was living with her future husband, named Jesus. There are no documents preserved about her first marriage. In 131 CE, Komaïse and Jesus drew up a marriage document that includes a dowry of jewelry and clothing valued at 96 denarii of silver (*P. Yadin* 37; *P. XHev/Se gr* 65). The text includes the phrase "[that they continue] life together . . . as also before this time."[17] The question is whether the couple, their neighbors and family, and the religious leaders would have agreed that before this document was written, the two were married. That is, did the document create a marriage from two who were cohabitating, or were they already married and the document merely reinforced that reality with stipulations about their finances?[18] Did the new document spring from the happy possibility that Salome and Jesus had a child, and wanted to care for his or her inheritance?[19]

b. Samaritan Woman's Situation

The legal archives of Babatha and Salome Komaïse, including the stories of their husbands, daughters, sons, and various relatives, create a sketch of

16. Oudshoorn, *Relationship between Roman and Local Law*, 235, writes, "she had distrained the produce of the orchards in lieu of her dowry and debts owed her."

17. Kraemer and D'Angelo, *Women's Religions in the Greco-Roman World*, 154.

18. Ilan, "Premarital Cohabitation in Ancient Judea," 247–64. Republished in her book, *Integrating Women into Second Temple History*.

19. Satlow, *Jewish Marriage in Antiquity*, 99–100.

real lives engaged in typical human interactions and struggles. How might their stories help us better understand the Samaritan woman? On the one hand, the archives demonstrate how frequently women were widowed and remarried. On the other hand, we do not have any evidence that a woman might be married five times, as was our Samaritan woman—which I will discuss below. Both Jesus and the woman agree that "the man she is with is not her husband." What might her current situation be referring to?

We know that the Samaritan woman's current situation was not the same as her previous five relationships, which were identified as marriages. Did she receive a divorce from her fifth husband that was based on, from her perspective, non-valid reasons? Did that render her unable to describe her current situation as a marriage? Komaïse's documents indicate that she was divorced prior to her marriage with Jesus, son of Menahem. So women could separate from their husbands, but they required a male guardian to affect the process in court. Few women sought divorce, and history tends to preserve the accounts of the wealthy and politically powerful. Valeria Paulla divorced her husband, Decimus Brutus, the lead conspirator behind the assassination of Julius Caesar. Queen Berenice, known from Acts 26, divorced her third husband. But we have no record of a woman filing for divorce more than once. It is quite plausible, therefore, that the Samaritan woman was divorced by one or two of her husbands, or initiated one divorce through her guardian. It is highly improbable, however, that she divorced (or was divorced by) five husbands.

Did the Samaritan woman lack dowry documents? Would she and Jesus both have assumed that a document was necessary to make the marriage valid? I am inclined to think that most people in Jesus's day would not have disapproved of an unwritten marriage, as documents were expensive to produce, and were useful primarily to protect property and valuables. If one had little to protect, then there was little felt need to create a document defending it. We have no idea whether the Samaritan woman had wealth, but John's silence probably indicates that she was unremarkable in that category. Therefore, it is unlikely that the possible non-documented nature of her relationship with this last man distinguishes it from her previous five "marriages."

Was the Samaritan woman in a polygynous situation? If so, Jesus might have discounted it as an invalid marriage, given his other words in the Gospels about a marriage representing the "two" becoming one flesh. This quotation from the LXX modifies the Hebrew of Gen 2:24, "they shall become one flesh." It was likely the part of Judaism that Jesus inherited from his Greco-Roman *milieu*. But would the Samaritan woman have shared his position? We would have to postulate that she did, if we follow John's text.[20] Relatedly, could it be that her fifth husband died, but his brother refuses to marry her? As such, she is unable to enter into a valid marriage with another man. The assumption here is that the Samaritans followed the levirate marriage patterns as outlined in Deut 25:5–10.[21] What if her answer, "I have no husband," refers to the fact that she is living with a kinsman? What if she has no sexual relations with the man she is with?[22] Census data from this time shows that widows, if they did not remarry, would likely live with a kinsman, be that her father, brother, or uncle, or with her children or her mother or sister.[23]

Given the evidence about the various marriage practices at this time, and the number of women who remained widows, we cannot say that the Samaritan woman's situation was viewed by her neighbors as immoral. The townsmen and women believed her without qualification, a posture they are unlikely to take if she were a prostitute. Unless, of course, the Samaritan men typically believed women of ill repute—I have yet to see this argument made about men, Samaritan or otherwise!

So why did Jesus even mention her marital status? Part of the answer, as I will note below, is that the number of husbands is remarkable. But an additional reason is that most women were identified by their marital status, whether they were yet to be married, married, or widowed. This is evident from literature, documents, and inscriptions. Jacobine Oudshoorn in her book on Roman and local law represented in the archives, observes, "That women's archives yield more personal information than men's is due to the simple fact that documents on personal matters like marriage, gift within a family and so on, were usually drawn up in favor of women and were therefore kept in their archives." She continues, "marriage contracts, deeds of gift and comparable documents ensured the women of rights they might have to claim many years after the event."[24] Interestingly, when we compare this with archives of men in Nahal Hever, we find that men preserved

20. McGrath, *Woman at the Well*.

21. O'Day and Hylen, *John*, 53.

22. Day, *Woman at the Well*, argues a similar point. I discovered her work after wondering about this possibility.

23. Hanson, "Widow Babatha and the Poor Orphan Boy," 98.

24. Oudshoorn, *Relationship between Roman and Local Law*, 18.

business, military, and administration correspondence. This matches what we know about women's public personas, that they rarely identified themselves or were identified by their occupations.[25] Instead, they were identified on gravestones and inscriptions in relation to their male family members. Additionally, their legal claims for their children's inheritance and their dowry rested on proving their marriages and gift and property deeds, as seen in Babatha's careful preservation of her deeds.

B. That She Engages in Religious Conversation with Jesus

Unfortunately, our legal documents do not shed light on the religious affections or temperament of Babatha or Salome Komaïse. They do show that women were present in court, as well as in the buying and selling of their produce, and in the business of loaning money. I cannot imagine that Babatha engaged in all the commerce and family business without speaking in public on numerous occasions. Thus, the mere fact that the Samaritan woman spoke with Jesus should not give rise to concern.

Some commentators argue that the woman was immoral, in part based on the fact that she was at the well at noon.[26] The evidence includes a comment in Gen 24:11, that indicates women came to draw water in the evenings. Yet this story is from the time of the Patriarchs, and reflects nomadic culture, not first-century Roman Palestine. Moreover, the mention of the time of day serves the wider point that Abraham's servant seeks a wife for Isaac among the young women of Nahor. We have a similar story in Gen 29:1–12. Rachel brings her sheep to the well at noon, but she is not condemned as immoral. Jacob helps her give water to her sheep, and this event leads him to meet Laban, his future father-in-law.[27] We have no evidence that, in itself, drawing water at noon was problematic. In our story, John notes the hour to explain why Jesus is thirsty.

Why would the Samaritan woman talk about religion with Jesus? In fact, one could say that it would have been quite odd if she had not raised the

25. Cohick, *Women in the World of the Earliest Christians*, 226.

26. Carson, *Gospel According to John*, 217.

27. Kruse, *Gospel According to John*, 128, suggests that it is "strange" that the Samaritan woman was alone, and attributes this to her "sense of shame." I point out that Rachel was alone in tending her flock, and Rebekah seems to be without companions when she meets Abraham's servant. If the Gospel of John was drawing on Old Testament exemplars of men meeting women at a well, we could point to Moses meeting Jethro's daughters (Exod 2:15).

question about Mt. Gerizim and Jerusalem when she encounters a prophet, for this seems to have been the burning question of her day. We pick up a bit of religious conversation among the Samaritans from inscriptions. For example, from Delos, we have a second-century BCE inscription that reads, "The Israelites in Delos, who send the temple tax to holy Ar-garizein" which we call Mt. Gerizim.[28] This inscription highlights a diaspora Samaritan community who self-identified with the ancient Israelite faith, and saw its holy place as Mt. Gerizim.[29] This holy place was destroyed in ca. 110–107 BCE by the Hasmonean king John Hyrcanus, thus the wounds are still fresh in Jesus's day, about 150 years later.

Additionally, the Scriptures used by Samaritans emphasized Mt. Gerizim. The sectarian nature of the Samaritan Pentateuch (SP) is on display in its insistence that Mt. Gerizim is the holy site for God's temple.[30] The SP harmonizes in places, and makes linguistic corrections to unusual forms of words. We find similar corrections in the Dead Sea Scroll 4QpaleoExm, without the sectarian additions found in the later SP.[31] The proto-SP text type circulated among the Qumran community. This indicates that Jews and Samaritans used similar biblical material during Jesus's time. My point is that the Samaritan woman's question was hardly an idle one designed to switch topics. Instead, it represents long engrained practices between her people and Jews, based on shared biblical texts interpreted in significantly different ways at key points.

The importance of this theological conversation between the Samaritan woman and Jesus in John's Gospel can be highlighted by a few points. First, John expresses his theology often through dialogue; the conversation between Jesus and the Samaritan woman is one of the longest in John's Gospel.[32] John also highlights Jesus's preternatural knowledge at several points

28. Kartveit, *Origin of the Samaritans*, 216, inscriptions from Delos. See also Pummer, *Samaritans*.

29. Josephus, *Ant* 14.10, indicates a Samaritan synagogue at Delos.

30. This view is promoted by adding another commandment, and revising the first commandment to be a preface to the list of ten. The new "10th commandment" in the Decalogue is inserted after Exod 20:14 and Deut 5:18. The commandment strings together language from Deut 11:29a; 27:2b, 3a, 4–7; 11:30.

31. Tov, "Proto-Samaritan Texts and the Samaritan Pentateuch," 406, mentions 4Q15815; 4QNumb; 4Q175 (Test), "They share with the Samaritan Pentateuch its linguistic simplifications, harmonizations in small matters, as well as non-characteristic readings, yet differ in many details in these areas."

32. Davidson, "Well Women of Scripture Revisited," 220.

(1:42, 48; 2:43–32); this aspect of Jesus's person is spotlighted in our story, too. Finally, Jesus's conversation with a woman is not entirely out of the ordinary. My Wheaton College colleague, Michael Graves, pointed out the story of Beruriah, wife of R. Meir, likewise talks to men about religion.[33] We have other places in the rabbinic texts where rabbis speak about religious matters with a wealthy Roman woman. While it is difficult to establish the historical veracity of each story, overall the picture painted is that in certain circumstances, it is neither immoral nor incongruous for men and women to speak together about religious matters.

C. That She Speaks to the Townspeople About Her Discovery

I have talked about the Samaritan woman's marital status and her religious conversation with Jesus. Left to be examined is her testimony to her town. It is commonly held that women had no authority in their communities, that men lived in the public realm and women stayed in the private sphere. However, ancient evidence to the contrary greatly weakens this supposition. Women could make vows, execute loans, and buy and sell goods and real estate. Admittedly, women were potentially handicapped in needing a male guardian to execute legal documents, but sons were also under their father's *potestas* during the latter's lifetime.

Guardians were male, apparently without exception. They could be relatives or husbands. Yet the lack of unmediated access to courts need not imply that women had no public voice. The archives we have examined indicate active engagement in making loans and understanding finances. Babatha vigorously seeks the welfare of her son through the courts, aided by her guardian. The system was prejudiced against women, but did not silence them.

The charges that Jewish women's voices were discounted and that Jewish men held Samaritan women in contempt often draw on a few rabbinic texts that were codified at least one hundred years after Jesus.[34] The rabbinic

---

33. Hoshen, *Beruria the Tannait.*

34. De Boer, *Gospel of Mary,* 164, describes the encounter, "Jesus addresses her briefly which according to Rabbinic texts befits a man talking to a strange woman." For example, *Pirke Avot* 1.5 reads, "Yossei the son of Yochanan of Jerusalem would say: Let your home be wide open, and let the poor be members of your household. And do not engage in excessive conversation with a woman." The Gemara (*Bava Metzia* 87a) says that women do not have a good attitude towards guests. The main point is that the husband should invite guests, and not listen to his wife's complaint of extra work, but roll up his sleeves

material can be misused by scholars. The historical evidence is much more complex, and includes both positive and negative evaluations about women from both gentile and Jewish authors, both before and after Jesus's life. The later rabbis did not "invent" a negative view of women, nor does their corpus solely reflect negative attitudes towards women.

Moreover, Jewish women made religious vows and worshiped with men in the temple. We tend to think that the "court of the women" was like the ladies' room. In fact, all Jews gathered there, but only men were permitted to go up the curving flight of steps to the court where sacrifices were made.

Therefore, there is no *a priori* reason to assume that the Samaritan woman's voice would be tuned out by her male neighbors. They would be aware of Jesus's presence because his disciples were in town buying supplies. According to John, the disciples do not invite the townspeople to meet Jesus. When the Samaritan woman reports her conversation and conclusions, she reveals the expansive truth brought by Jesus, a message not fully appreciated or owned by his (Jewish) disciples.

Within the narrative itself, Jesus insists that what she has said is "true" (*alēthēs*). The term is used by John in a positive way throughout the Gospel, so Jesus's appraisal here should be heard as positive, or at the very least value neutral. Again, her testimony to Jesus's miraculous knowledge is similar to Nathanael's amazement at Jesus's preternatural perception of his person and his immediate past (John 1:45–51).[35] Her conversation parallels Nicodemus's in that both misunderstand Jesus's claims, but she testifies to her people that "he told me everything I'd ever done." Nicodemus questions Jesus twice, and then fades from the narrative.

To summarize my argument thus far: the typical aspects of the narrative include that Jesus would identify the woman based on her marital history, that the two would have a conversation about the religious significance of Mt. Gerizim and Jerusalem, and that men would listen to a woman's comments, all things being equal. I have argued that, rather than

and help her. Maccini, "Reassessment of the Woman at the Well in John 4," 39, quotes from *m. Nid* 4.1, "The daughters of the Samaritans are [deemed unclean as] menstruants from the cradle." The rabbis, and their predecessors, acknowledged that Jewish women had expertise in certain areas, including those that focused on female purity codes. There is no evidence that Jews needed to enter a *miqveh* (ritual immersion bath) before entering their local synagogue.

35. Maccini, *Her Testimony Is True*, 130–31, evaluates the evidence. See also 118–19, which draws comparisons with the wedding at Cana (John 2:1–10).

evidence of immorality and craftiness, these behaviors are typical for a Samaritan woman of her time. There are, however, atypical features within the narrative that further clarify Jesus's remarkable mission.

II. FEATURES OF ATYPICAL BEHAVIOR/ATTITUDES

A. That She Had Five Husbands

We have no evidence that a man or woman had five consecutive spouses, and was living with a sixth. Two figures, however, come very close. Agrippa, close friend of Augustus, was married to his fifth wife when he died. And Queen Berenice, the granddaughter of Herod the Great, was married three times, widowed twice by age 22, and divorced once. Josephus alleges that before her third marriage, she conducted an incestuous relationship with her brother, Herod Agrippa II. In her forties, Berenice had a tumultuous love affair with Titus, the heir apparent to Vespasian and several years her junior. However, our Samaritan woman is clearly not at the level of Queen Berenice.

There is a tradition of interpreting the five husbands symbolically here (4:18), which would certainly then relieve the woman of the shame label that so many have placed on her.[36] And we can also find examples where a number is used for rhetorical effect. For example, from the book of Tobit we read the sad story of Sarah whose seven husbands die on their wedding night (7:11). Fortunately for Tobit's son, Tobias, he survives his wedding night with Sarah, thanks to angelic intervention. From the New Testament, the Sadducees try to trick Jesus with a hypothetical case of seven brothers who marry the same woman consecutively and, in short order, die (Matt 22:23–33). The hyperbole in both stories serves to heighten the drama, because such possibilities are impossibly far-fetched. But in our story, the Samaritan woman agrees with Jesus that she has been married five times. This number is remarkably high, but not absurd. The takeaway here is

---

36. Augustine, "Lectures or Tractates on the Gospel According to St. John," NPNF1 7:104, suggests that the five husbands represent the five senses of the body. Hoskyns, *Fourth Gospel*, 242, suggests the five husbands reflect five foreign deities brought into Samaria during the time of the ancient Israelites, based on 2 Kgs 17:24–30. However, the biblical text speaks of seven deities. See also Cahill, "Narrative Art in John IV," 44. Moore, *Poststructuralism and the New Testament*, 43–64, points to the hypocrisy of those who chastise the Samaritan woman for understanding Jesus's words about water literally, but then insist that the woman's marital history is a literal one.

that Jesus's statement that she had five husbands highlighted a remarkable reality.

B. That She Would Meet a Jew, Especially One Who Asked for a Drink, for Most Chose to Circumvent Samaria as They Traveled Between Galilee and Judea

The Samaritan woman was surprised to receive Jesus's request for a drink. John tells us of the antagonism between the two groups—Jews and Samaritans. Often readers today assume the feud extended into the distant past, as told in 2 Kings 17. However, some wounds were much fresher. John Hyrcanus, one of the Hasmonean kings, destroyed a temple on Mt. Gerizim somewhere between 117 and 110 BCE. With this social background, Jesus's request (as a Jew) for water from a Samaritan is surprising. The earthiness of this story—Jesus sitting down at a well, tired and thirsty—will contrast sharply with the conclusion drawn by the Samaritans at the end of the story. This tired and thirsty man is also the Savior of the World.

C. That the Encounter Would Lead to the Town's Confession That Jesus Is the Savior of the World

The townsmen heed the Samaritan woman's witness, and believe. They subsequently speak with Jesus and their faith is reinforced. They pronounce him the Savior of the world—an exalted title that he is worthy to accept (4:42). It reflects his own pronouncement "I AM" (4:26), to her statement that the messiah is coming. Because Jesus is no ordinary human, this encounter has an extraordinary conclusion. What is further, Jesus is the atypical savior because he comes not to save his people to the exclusion of their rivalrous neighbors, but that he comes to be the savior of the world.

CONCLUSION

This encounter with Jesus is both typical and atypical, revealing to the Samaritan woman, and the reader today, the atypical human that we meet in Jesus. Jesus engages this typical woman in a typical way, modeling right relationships for us today. He dignifies her as a person by engaging her and dialoging about the core religious issues of his day. Jesus evidences that these kinds of discussions with women and among women ought not to be surprising nor exceptional, but expected and ordinary. Jesus shows us that these conversations and relationships are a part of the regular rhythms of the church. Likewise, Jesus accepts the testimony of the Samaritan woman as true and does not cast suspicion on her.

Jesus manifests his atypical nature as the savior of the world in the atypical features of this encounter. Jesus is a Jewish man who not only dignifies the Samaritans by intentionally journeying through the area, but by engaging the Samaritan women, Jesus comes as the fulfillment of the promises to Abraham and to institute a salvation that includes all people who "worship the Father in spirit and truth" (4:23). Jesus knows her marital situation, and offers her an identity that no marriage relationship or social convention could bestow. Additionally, these atypical features are not merely atypical because they are rare among sinful humans, but ultimately atypical because no other human can offer "a spring of water welling up to eternal life" (4:14). Only Jesus, who is God incarnate, can offer drink to all people, Jew and Samaritan, men and women, such that they will never be thirsty again.

Ultimately, what is at stake in my reading of the Samaritan woman? I think it challenges the status-quo assumptions about women's basic worth and their capacity for religious thought. The Samaritan woman is not a trope, a symbol, or a metaphor. Within the narrative of John's Gospel, she is a flesh and blood woman who speaks with a flesh and blood man. The man is tired and thirsty, the woman is needy and curious. This is the stuff of everyday life. This story is an example of "the Word became Flesh and dwelt among us." Jesus explains to the Samaritan woman that a day will come when all people will worship God the Father in the Spirit and truth (4:23–24). He does not say that humans will become merely spiritual beings. Jesus points to creaturely, embodied worship of the true God that is based on revealed knowledge that he brings. Jesus's incarnation was not mere clothing for a disembodied soul, for Jesus now exists in his post-resurrection, immortal body. John tells us at the end of his Gospel that Jesus invited Thomas to touch this raised, glorified body, this body which displays the wounds of the cross.

As we consider the mosaic located outside the Barrows auditorium on the Wheaton College campus, we notice that it draws similar points of emphasis from the Samaritan woman's encounter with Jesus.[37] The woman's

---

37. The image on the cover of the book is a picture of this mosaic.

face is on the same plane as Jesus's face. They are presented as the same size, and I see in that a visual affirmation of the text's presentation of the Samaritan woman. She is every bit the human that Jesus is. In the mosaic, she focuses her gaze on Jesus, thereby accurately representing her testimony to her people. And Jesus looks directly at us, bids us to listen to her testimony, and so believe.

3

Suffering, Solidarity, and Salvation

The Humanity of the Son in Hebrews 2, 4, and 5

Dana M. Harris
Trinity Evangelical Divinity School

I. INTRODUCTION

The more I study the Epistle to the Hebrews, the more I am struck by how remarkable it is. It is a veritable textbook on the use of the Old Testament in the New, and on Old Testament exegesis itself in many ways. It obviously offers significant christological contributions, and yet it has surprising insights into the role of the Spirit and of the Father. As I often say to my students, all biblical roads eventually lead to Hebrews! And this is particularly true when discussing Jesus's humanity. There are many ways to consider Hebrews's contribution in this regard, but I suggest that three themes concerning Jesus's humanity emerge organically from the text of Hebrews.[1]

We can begin with the *solidarity* of the Son, who shares the same flesh and blood as the sons and daughters. We move to the *suffering* that was

---

1. I have indicated where I have discussed key issues in other published writings or my unpublished dissertation. The discussion here is, therefore, not intended to be exhaustive in any way.

43

necessary to perfect the Son in his role as the great high priest, so that he could bring these sons and daughters into the very presence of God. And we conclude with the *salvation* that the Son effected because of his solidarity and suffering.[2]

II. SURVEY OF RELEVANT PASSAGES IN HEBREWS

In this essay, I want to trace the themes of solidarity, suffering, and salvation as they emerge from the letter to the Hebrews, focusing especially on Hebrews 2, the end of Hebrews 4, and the beginning of Hebrews 5. Then I will draw out some conclusions and specific implications that emerge from these three themes.

Hebrews 1: The Exalted, Eternal Son

Any discussion of Jesus's humanity in Hebrews, however, must be set within the context of his exaltation, which is how the epistle starts and is a major focus of much of it. So a brief overview of the exalted Son in Hebrews 1 is a necessary starting point.

The opening verses of Hebrews (1:1–4), the exordium, present seven statements about the Son, beginning in verse 2. The first two statements set his person and work in an eternal perspective: (1) he is the eschatological heir of all things; and (2) he is the protological agent of creation, through whom the universe was made. The next three present his ontological, divine status: (3) he is the exact radiance of God's glory; (4) he is the very image of God's essence; and (5) he is the one who upholds all things by his powerful word. The final two statements offer a succinct summary of his work: (6) he is the source of atonement, the one who made purification for sins; and (7) he now sits at the right hand of Majesty on high. He alone spans the creation of the universe and the redemption of all things. These seven statements about the Son lay the foundation for the rest of Hebrews. Of course, the number seven is significant and here associates the Son with perfection: this is the Perfect Son who perfectly accomplishes all of God's purposes.[3]

---

2. For the sake of clarity, these three themes are italicized throughout this essay.

3. For a fuller discussion of these points, see Harris, *Hebrews*, 12–17.

By starting out these seven statements with the Son as the heir of all things, the author suggests that the Son's status *as* heir is the key to understanding all the other declarations. By ending these statements with the Son seated in glory, the author anticipates the final destination to which believers are headed, namely, the same glory associated with the person of the Son. Furthermore, the author indicates how that destination will be reached, namely through the purification for sins accomplished by the Son. The fact that the Son is seated underscores the finality of his priestly work and the fact that he is seated in glory assures the audience that the Son is already present in this final destination to which he is leading them. These verses anticipate key themes throughout the epistle.

These opening statements are followed by seven key Old Testament citations, although there is not a one-to-one correlation between the opening statements and each citation. Since the designation Old Testament is anachronistic from the point of view of the author of Hebrews, the term *Scripture* is preferred and will be used from here forward to refer to the canonical Old Testament.[4] Regarding this catena of citations, once again, the number seven is significant and indicates completeness or perfection. This is one of the highest concentrations of Scripture citations in Hebrews—an epistle filled with Scripture citations! These citations highlight the essential role that the Scripture plays for the author of Hebrews in making his christological claims. These citations can only be briefly summarized here.[5]

The first pair of quotations (v. 5) shows that the Son is superior because of his unique relationship to the Father and draws upon the messianic and eschatological assertions in Ps 2:7 and 2 Sam 7:14. The second pair (vv. 6–7) quotes Deut 32:43 or Ps 97:7[6] and Ps 104:4. These citations refer to the positive but inferior ministry of angels, when compared with the Son. The final pair of Scripture citations (vv. 8–12, quoting Ps 45:6–7 and 102:25–28) focus on the Son's eternal, unchanging nature. Although the created order will pass away, the Son remains forever, another key theme in Hebrews (7:3, 24; 12:25–27; 13:14).[7] The catena of citations also demonstrates "visually" the author's rhetorical skill—each pair of citations is increasingly longer

4. See discussion in Harris, "Typological Trajectories," 282n7.

5. For a fuller discussion of these citations and the relevant literature, see Harris, *Hebrews*, 21–37.

6. LXX Ps 96:7; the exact source of this citation is debated. See Cockerill, "Hebrews 1:6," 51–64; Guthrie, "Hebrews," 932–33.

7. Harris, "Eternal Inheritance," 268n40; *Hebrews*, 160, 397.

thereby amplifying the overall effect. The final citation (Heb 1:13) functions as a summary and the climax of the previous six citations. The allusion to Ps 110:1 in verse 3 is now made clear with the explicit citation of this verse in Heb 1:13. Verse 14 closes off this section with a reference to inheritance, which brackets the similar references to inheritance in earlier verses (1:2, 4). More importantly for our purposes, this verse introduces the concept of *salvation*. As we will see, the author of Hebrews frequently introduces a key theme or concept very briefly and subsequently develops it more fully at a later point in the epistle. This is similar to a symphonic piece or a film score in which a theme is briefly introduced to train the audience's ear and then the same theme is repeated several times before it is fully explored and developed. Thus this opening chapter is essential for any discussion of the Son in Hebrews.

Hebrews 2: The Suffering, Incarnate Jesus

Hebrews 2 shifts from the emphasis on the divine Son in Hebrews 1 to focus on Jesus's humanity. It is, of course, a false dichotomy to suggest the Son's divinity and humanity are completely separated. Richard Bauckham rightly notes that "sonship in Hebrews is both a divinely exclusive category (Jesus' unique relationship with the Father) and a humanly inclusive category (a form of relationship to the Father that Jesus shares with those he redeems)."[8] The significance of this is developed further at the end of this essay. Following the so-called warning passage in Heb 2:1–4, the rest of Hebrews 2 divides into four sections, or movements: (a) Heb 2:5–9; (b) Heb 2:10–13; (c) Heb 2:14–16; and (d) Heb 2:17–18.

Hebrews 2:5–9

In Heb 2:5, the author makes clear that the Son's inheritance includes not only the entire present cosmos but also the world to come.[9] The author also wants to make it very clear that the final subjugation of all things applies to the Son, not angels ("for not to angels did he not subject the world to

---

8. Bauckham, "Divinity of Jesus Christ," 19.

9. In Heb 1:6, the referent of οἰκουμένη could be understood to be the present world; the addition of τὴν μέλλουσαν in 2:5, however, indicates that the "world to come" is intended. See Harris, "Typological Trajectories," 289–90.

come").[10] This subjugation has already been indicated in the citation of Ps 110:1 in Heb 1:13, but its reintroduction in Heb 2:5 prepares for the very important point that the author wants to make from Psalm 8.

In Heb 2:6–8, the author quotes Ps 8:5–7. The ambiguous way in which he introduces the citation—"there is a place where someone has testified"—continues an emphasis in Hebrews on God *speaking*. The downplaying of the human author has the effect of stressing that God is *still* speaking through the psalm.[11]

In its original context, Psalm 8 presents David marveling over the glory and majesty of God's creation and the staggering truth that God is mindful of human beings at all—creatures who are seemingly insignificant when compared to the glory of creation. Even more remarkably, God entrusted the dominion over his creation to mere created human beings, which shows the tremendous dignity that God has bestowed on humanity. Moreover, this psalm represents David's later theological reflection on the original intention for humanity as presented in Gen 1:26–28. The author's use of the psalm establishes a "typological trajectory," a repeated pattern of appropriating Scripture in Hebrews whereby the author cites a later theological reflection (usually from the Psalter) back on an earlier historical event (recorded in the Pentateuch) so as to establish a trajectory within Scripture that ultimately points beyond these scriptural passages to the Son.[12]

As the author of Hebrews considers Psalm 8, he poignantly acknowledges that the intended dominion for humanity is not seen at present. As noted, the author saw a connection between the subjection of enemies under the Davidic king's feet in Ps 110:1 (cited in Heb 1:13), and the subjection of all things under humanity's feet in Ps 8:6, cited in Heb 2:8. Understanding Ps 110:1 in terms of the subjection of all things to Christ naturally raises the question why this subjection is not visible at the present time. So the author uses Psalm 8 to indicate the means by which Psalm 110 is also fulfilled.

10. Unless otherwise noted, translations are my own.

11. For a fuller discussion of these points, see Harris, "'Today if You Hear My Voice,'" 112–14; Harris, *Hebrews*, 3, 46. Even though the psalm is ascribed to David in both the MT and LXX, the author does not indicate this. In the citation from Psalm 95 in Hebrews 3–4, however, the author indicates Davidic authorship of that psalm to establish an important temporal framework (see Harris, "Typological Trajectories," 284–88). See also the discussion of the introduction to the citation of Psalm 8 in Pierce, "Divine Discourse in the Epistle to the Hebrews," 116–18.

12. See Harris, "Typological Trajectories," 280–92.

There is debate about how the reference to "son of man" in Psalm 8 is understood in Hebrews. It is doubtful that the author understood "son of man" as a messianic title.[13] Instead, it is more likely that he understood the psalm christologically in the sense that the incarnate Jesus is the perfect human being who now fulfills God's intended purposes for humanity.

In the citation of Ps 8:6 in Hebrews, the status of humanity is described as qualitatively lower than angels, but in the author's subsequent exposition of the psalm in Heb 2:9, he understands "a little lower" temporally in terms of Jesus's incarnation and death.[14] The psalm refers to the glory and honor with which humanity has been crowned, which is stated in Ps 8:6 and quoted in Heb 2:7. The author of Hebrews then understands this crowning in terms of *Jesus's* exaltation in Heb 2:9, further indicating that the author views "son of man" in terms of Jesus's humanity.

As noted, Psalm 8 indicates both the dominion and the glory intended for humanity, but this original intention for humanity contrasts sharply with present reality. The answer to this apparent contradiction is therefore to be found in the life and death of Jesus. Indeed, the author makes this clear by stressing that we *do* see Jesus. But we see Jesus who suffered death—not just for himself but for all human beings. Heb 2:9 indicates that Jesus's suffering death is the pivot, or turning point, between his humiliation and his exaltation.

As is common in Hebrews, the author introduces Jesus's suffering but does not develop it at this point. Significantly, this is the first reference to the name "Jesus" in Hebrews, which is used mainly in association with his humanity. And this is also the first mention of his death. Thus, the author indicates that Jesus's suffering, death, and eventual exaltation are the means by which the original intent for humanity is restored. The author's wording in verse 9 emphasizes the experience of *suffering* that Jesus underwent in his death.[15]

13. As, for example, in Mark 10:45: "For even the Son of Man did not come to be served, but to serve, and to give his life as a ransom for many." Although articularity in Koine Greek does not indicate definiteness, the fact the article is not present in this citation suggests that the author did not view "son of man" in Psalm 8 as a messianic title (see Harris, *Hebrews*, 47).

14. Cf. Bauckham, "Divinity of Jesus Christ," 23. He suggests that angels function as an ontological marker, such that above angels is God and below them are humans. He discusses this in terms of Jesus's divine and human identity.

15. Amy Peeler makes a similar observation in "With Tears and Joy," 14.

To summarize this first movement in Hebrews 2: Jesus is the perfect human being, who now fulfills God's original intentions for humanity as meditated upon in Psalm 8. Moreover, the overlap between Ps 110:1 and Ps 8 indicates that Jesus's incarnation, suffering, and exaltation are the means by which Psalm 110 is also fulfilled, namely the subjugation of all things under the promised Messiah's feet. This movement introduces the themes of *solidarity* and *suffering* in conjunction with Jesus's humanity, but this also hints at the theme of *salvation*.

Hebrews 2:10–13

The next movement occurs in Heb 2:10–13. In verse 10, the author draws together the Son's suffering and the glory intended for humanity that came out of his appropriation of Psalm 8 and links it the solidarity that the Son has with the sons and daughters. The claim is remarkable: it was fitting, or appropriate, for God to bring his people to glory through the suffering of his Son, Jesus. This verse anticipates the subsequent development of this astonishing truth in Hebrews 5.[16] In the overall context of Hebrews 2, verse 10 both concludes the discussion in Heb 2:5–9 and anticipates the final movement of Heb 2:17–18 (which explains the necessity and appropriateness of Jesus's suffering to qualify him as our high priest).

Verse 10 also draws in the theme of *salvation*, and introduces the very important christological image of the Son as the ἀρχηγός, which is best understood as pioneer—one who has gone before. Here the Son is leading the sons and daughters to the place where he is already, namely, seated at the right hand of God. The imagery here recalls the exodus. Just as God led the people out of Egypt to the promised land, so too the Son is leading the sons and daughters out of bondage to glory. Thus, entering glory parallels entering the promised rest and recalls the reference to inheriting salvation in Heb 1:14. All of these images converge into the idea of the eternal inheritance in Hebrews, which includes the city to come (Hebrews 11, 13) and the heavenly Zion (Hebrews 12).[17] So even as the author prepares to develop the theme of *solidarity* in 2:11–13, he creatively weaves in *suffering* and *salvation*. This same overlap of solidarity, suffering, and salvation also

16. For a fuller discussion of these points, see Harris, *Hebrews*, 53–55.

17. For the merging and development of this understanding of the eternal inheritance, see Harris, "Eternal Inheritance."

occurs in Hebrews 12, where Jesus is again described as the ἀρχηγός.[18] The concept of perfection introduced in this verse will be discussed in conjunction with Hebrews 5.

Heb 2:11 continues the theme of *solidarity*, drawing upon the familial imagery introduced in verse 10. The Son is the one who sanctifies, and the sons and daughters are the ones who are sanctified. Remarkably, both are of the same family and share the same human nature. But unlike the sons and daughters, Jesus is not merely human, but is the fully divine Son. Perhaps even more remarkable is the fact that Jesus is not ashamed to call those whom he has made holy his brothers and sisters.

In Heb 2:12–13 there are three Scripture citations that further the theme of Jesus's solidarity with those whom he has made holy. The first citation is from Ps 22:22 (LXX 21:23), where the psalmist transitions from lament and supplication to praise and thanksgiving for God's vindication following his suffering and affliction. The psalmist declares that he will sing God's praises to his brothers and sisters. The author of Hebrews put these words on the lips of Jesus to underscore Jesus's own humanity and his solidarity with the sons and daughters as well as his suffering. The second citation (2:13) likely comes from Isa 8:17. In the original context, Isaiah expresses his confidence in God despite opposition and impending judgment. Like Jesus, Isaiah suffered and was rejected by the people, but his faith in God never wavered. Again, the author of Hebrews takes the words of Isaiah and puts them on the lips of Jesus. The third and final Scripture citation comes from Isa 8:18, which refers to Isaiah's own children and indicates the prophet's hope that these children would be signs to Israel of God's faithfulness. This is the only place where believers are called Christ's children in the Bible. The focus in these verses is clearly on *solidarity*.[19]

Hebrews 2:14–16

The third movement in Hebrews 2 picks up the theme of *salvation*. Verses 14–16 give one of the reasons why Jesus became incarnate—to deliver the sons and daughters. This movement restates the theme of *solidarity*—the Son shares the flesh and blood of the children (v. 14)—as the means of this deliverance. The key point of these verses is that because Jesus shares in

18. See Rhee, "Chiasm and the Concept of Faith in Hebrews 12:1–29," 273.

19. This discussion summarizes Harris, *Hebrews*, 53–63. See also the extended discussion in Pierce, "Divine Discourse," 120–38.

the children's flesh and blood, he is able to render powerless the one who has enslaved the children through the fear of death (vv. 14–15). As Psalm 8 reminded the audience, humans were created to have dominion over God's creation, but instead they became fearful slaves to sin. These verses continue the exodus typology, which is now understood as release from the fear of death, and introduce the Christus Victor motif that draws upon the biblical theme of the divine warrior.

Verse 16 offers a final comment about the familial status of believers. The Son is now depicted as helping the descendants of Abraham, anticipating the help available from Jesus, the high priest, in the final movement of Hebrews 2. Verse 16 also indicates that Abraham's descendants, understood as redeemed humanity, not angels, are the objects of Jesus's deliverance. The reference to Abraham also puts Jesus's work of rescuing and delivering within the context of the Abrahamic promises and is another way that Hebrews indicates that Jesus fulfills all of God's purposes. Thus, a parallel is suggested between Jesus and the sons and daughters, and God and Israel. Just as God led his people from Egypt, so also Jesus leads his brothers and sisters to freedom. In this way those whom Christ leads are the true heirs of Abraham.

Hebrews 2:17–18

The final movement in Hebrews 2 (vv. 17–18) offers another outcome of Jesus's incarnation—namely, that he has become the merciful and faithful high priest. Notice again the theme of *solidarity*: Jesus had to be made like the sons and daughters, "fully human in every way" (v. 17). The introduction of Jesus as a high priest may feel abrupt, but it was foreshadowed in Heb 1:3—"having provided purification for sins"—and it anticipates the main focus of Hebrews 5–10. The theme of *suffering* returns, namely the suffering that Jesus experienced when he was tempted, which is why he is able to help those who are also tempted. Interwoven within this theme is theme of *salvation*, understood in terms of making atonement.

The link between Jesus as the merciful and faithful high priest and his suffering is a significant part of Hebrews 5 (discussed below). The author of Hebrews develops what it means to be faithful with the positive example of Moses in Heb 3:1–6 and the negative example of the wilderness generation in Heb 3:7–19. The promise of mercy is further developed and linked with atonement in Heb 4:14–16.

Hebrews 4:14–16: Jesus, the Son, the Great High Priest

Hebrews 4:14–16 concludes the second warning passage in Hebrews (3:7—4:13), which focuses on the wilderness generation.[20] This passage also furthers the description of Jesus as the high priest who has gone through the heavens that was introduced in Heb 2:17–18. This passage in turn points forward to the next major section in Hebrews, namely 5:1—10:18, which focuses on two main themes: the high priestly work of the Son (5:1—7:28), and his fully efficacious offering (8:3—10:18).

The distinctive use of "great" (μέγας) with high priest (ἀρχιερεύς) in Heb 4:14 emphasizes the uniqueness of Jesus's high priesthood, as compared with the Levitical one. Later, the author develops this priesthood in terms of Jesus's sinlessness (Heb 5:1–3; 7:26–28), his appointment by divine oath (Heb 5:4–10; 6:17–20; 7:15–22), and the eternality of his priesthood (Heb 7:16–25). Moreover, his once-for-all-time offering (Heb 10:1–18) of superior blood (Heb 9:1–28) is associated with a superior covenant (Heb 8:7–13) and is presented in the heavenly tabernacle (Heb 8:2; 9:1–28). The image of Jesus passing through the heavens recalls the earthly high priest passing through the earthly tabernacle, but then only once a year (see also Heb 6:19–20; 8:1–2; 9:11, 24; 10:20), whereas Jesus has entered the heavenly tabernacle once for all time. Yet, even though Jesus is the great high priest, far superior to any earthly high priest, he is able to sympathize with human weaknesses because he knows what it is to be human, developing further the theme of *solidarity*.

This passage indicates that, although tempted in every way as other humans were, Jesus did not sin. Accordingly, the question arises: *could* Jesus have sinned? The logic of Hebrews necessitates this very possibility. It is hard to understand how Jesus could have been tempted in every way and thus be able to empathize with human weakness if it was actually impossible for him to sin. On this view, the sinlessness of Jesus is even more remarkable.[21]

Hebrews 4:16 shows the tremendous outcome of Jesus's high priesthood—worshipers are now able to approach the throne of grace with confidence. The throne of God, depicted as the seat of God's glory, power, and authority (Ps 47:8; 97:2; Isa 6:1), corresponded to the mercy seat of the ark

---

20. The designation and boundaries of these passages are debated. For the present essay, different boundaries would not change the overall argument.

21. See the discussion in Cockerill, *Epistle to the Hebrews*, 226–28.

in the tabernacle, which could only be accessed by the earthly high priest and on the Day of Atonement.[22] Yet now because of Jesus's *solidarity, suffering*, and *salvation* worshipers have the right to approach this throne, and with boldness.

Hebrews 5:1–10: The Son, His Suffering, and His Priesthood

Hebrews 5:1–10 also weaves together the themes of *solidarity, suffering*, and *salvation*. In the first part of Hebrews 5, we learn that like the Levitical high priests (Exod 28:1; cf. Lev 8:1–2; Num 3:10; 18:1), Jesus was also selected from among the people (v. 1). Unlike them, however, he was appointed high priest on the basis of the same oath associated with his Sonship, namely Ps 2:7. Also, unlike the Levitical priests, Jesus did not have to make offerings on behalf of his own sin.

Our focus here, however, is Heb 5:5–10. The citation from Ps 2:7 in v. 5 indicates that Jesus's appointment to be high priest is based on his "appointment" to be the Son.[23] This citation is followed by one from Ps 110:4 in verse 6. By aligning these two citations, the author shows that the Melchizedekian priest of Ps 110:4 is none other than the messianic Son of Ps 2:7.[24] This could also be inferred by the application of both Ps 110:1—the subjugation of all things under the Messiah's feet—and Ps 110:4 to Jesus, as the author does throughout the epistle.

Hebrews is unique in citing Ps 110:4 and discussing the christological connection with Melchizedek. The author throws out this reference to Melchizedek seemingly from nowhere (Heb 5:6), but as is common in Hebrews, he picks up the reference again in Heb 6:20, and develops it in Hebrews 7. In this chapter he also draws upon Gen 14:17–20 employing once again a later theological reflection on Ps 110:4 (Heb 7:17, 21), thereby presenting another typological trajectory. We can only touch briefly on this enigmatic individual.

Melchizedek is the only person in Scripture referred to as both a king and a priest of the God Most High. Although the word "order" could suggest the idea of succession, there is no such succession in the line of

22. See discussion in Attridge, *Epistle to the Hebrews*, 141–42.

23. Cockerill, *Hebrews*, 238 notes the "three key oracles of God directed to Christ" in Hebrews: Ps 2:7 (Sonship), Ps 110:1 (exaltation), and Ps 110:4 (priesthood).

24. "The association of Ps 110:4 with Ps 2:7 and Ps 110:1 suggests that God proclaimed him High Priest at his exaltation" (Cockerill, *Hebrews*, 239).

Melchizedek, so something like "type" or "kind" is in view. In other words, Jesus's priesthood is of the same type or kind as Melchizedek's, which the author will develop in terms of a priesthood that is not dependent upon genealogy and is eternal. If we were to continue through the epistle, we would see that the superiority of this priesthood is affirmed in numerous ways: the great high priest is also the mediator of the new covenant (Heb 7:22; 8:1–6), which follows the startling revelation that this change in priesthood also necessitated a change in the law (Heb 7:12). Additionally, this priesthood is superior because it is carried out in the heavenly sanctuary (Hebrews 9).

For our discussion, however, the key is Heb 5:7. Even though Jesus is the Son and his appointment as high priest exceeded the appointment of the Levitical priests, his priesthood involved tremendous obedience and suffering. The prayers and petitions described in this verse could refer to Jesus's time in Gethsemane (Matt 26:36–46 and par.), where Jesus prayed to be delivered from death but then yielded to God's will. Yet the images in 5:7 do not fully align with the Gethsemane accounts. The author may well have the "prayers of the righteous sufferer" in view, such as are found in Psalm 116 (LXX 114), or possibly Psalm 22 (LXX 21), which he cited earlier.[25] Additionally, the loud cries referenced here could also refer to the cross (Matt 27:46–50). Regardless of referent, the point is that Jesus faced this suffering with prayer and faith, and that his "appointment" to the high priesthood involved tremendous suffering (see Heb 2:10, 18).

Perhaps even more remarkable is the statement that Jesus, the Son(!), learned obedience from what he suffered (Heb 5:8–10). The word play here in the Greek can be roughly translated as "no pain, no gain," or perhaps less flippantly, "learning comes by suffering."[26] Yet clearly what Jesus learned was not the result of learning from his sin or mistakes, but rather he learned obedience through his suffering before and on the cross, all of which involved his submission to the Father's will. Thus the Son learned obedience by perfectly conforming to God's will.

This recalls the reference to Jesus and his perfection in Heb 2:10. Perfection is one of the key concepts in Hebrews. Although it is common to think of "perfection" in terms of moral perfection, that is not the point

---

25. See Harris, *Hebrews*, 11–22; see esp. Guthrie, "Hebrews," 962.

26. καίπερ ὤν υἱὸς ἔμαθεν ἀφ' ὤν ἔπαθεν τὴν ὑπακοήν; this wordplay between ἔμαθεν and ἔπαθεν was "very widespread, and probably originates in popular speech" (Ellingworth, *Epistle to the Hebrews*, 291).

here. In Hebrews "perfection" is vocational or teleological.[27] It has to do with perfectly accomplishing God's intended purpose. Applied to Jesus's high priesthood, this means that in order for Jesus to be the perfect high priest, he needed to be perfected through suffering. If Jesus is to be the perfect high priest (*salvation*), who can perfectly represent humans before God, then his participation in humanity (*solidarity*) was necessary and this participation necessarily involved *suffering*.

But the perfection associated with Jesus becoming the perfect high priest cannot be separated from the perfection that Jesus has achieved for believers, which is linked to Jesus as the source of "eternal salvation" (Heb 5:9; cf. 1:14). This eternal salvation will be linked later with the eternal inheritance (9:15) and the eternal covenant (13:20). Implied in all of this is that Jesus's suffering has enabled him to become the perfect savior.

III. WHY THE HUMANITY OF JESUS MATTERS

Based on the preceding survey, I would like to draw two preliminary conclusions. After that, I will revisit the three themes that have been used to consider Jesus's humanity in Hebrews to trace out several implications and possible answers to the question, "Why the humanity of Jesus matters?"

My first conclusion involves the richness and the complexity of the Epistle to the Hebrews. When I begin thinking about the subject of this essay, I thought that I had seen a progression in Hebrews moving from *solidarity* (the first and middle parts of Hebrews 2) to *suffering* (the end Hebrews 2 and Hebrews 4), and the beginning of Hebrews 5, and finally onto *salvation* (in Hebrews 5 and beyond). It quickly became apparent, however, that these themes are interwoven in rich and complex ways that defy any linear progression. These three themes are often mixed, with themes briefly appearing in the midst of other themes only to reappear as the focal theme in a later passage. For example, in the citation of Psalm 8 in Hebrews 2, *solidarity* is evident, followed by *suffering*, and exaltation, only to be followed in the next section of Hebrews 2, where *suffering* mixes with exaltation and glory, followed by *solidarity* and *salvation*, only to be followed by *suffering* again at the end of the chapter. In other words, these three themes are so inextricably interwoven that it is virtually impossible to place them in discrete categories without diminishing the impact of the text.

---

27. See esp. Peterson, *Hebrews and Perfection*.

This leads to my second conclusion. This same overlap is apparent when we try to identify elements or roles that pertain to Jesus's divinity and elements or roles that pertain to his humanity in Hebrews. For example, the subjugation of all things by the messianic Son in Ps 110:1 is only achieved by the perfect human being of Psalm 8. The exalted Son becomes the perfect human being to restore God's glorious intentions for humanity, and because he has done this, he is now exalted at the right hand of Majesty. Or consider the solidarity and perfection achieved through the suffering of the Son in his incarnation that enables him to fully represent humans to God. At first glance, this seems to be associated with his humanity. And yet this great high priest has passed through the heavens and is seated in glory. Once again, this stresses the uniqueness of Jesus's high priesthood, since a Levitical high priest never sat at God's right hand to perform his priestly duties. And yet, seated as the exalted Son is the great high priest who perpetually intercedes with empathy and mercy. In her work on the identity of Christ in Hebrews, Katherine Grieb captures this well when she notes the paradox of a "crucified high priest," one who is both the victim and the priest.[28] She adds that "preexistence/exultation Christology is combined in Hebrews with radical human solidarity and empathy hard-won through participatory suffering and death as 'flesh and blood.'"[29] Richard Bauckham is also helpful here: "[The Son's] completed work of atonement is now permanently part of the divine rule over the world. In this way, *this* high priesthood, unlike the Levitical one, [belongs] to the unique identity of God."[30] He adds: "It is no longer simply the sovereignty he shared with his Father from eternity, but now a sovereignty exercised in human solidarity with humans."[31] Fully divine and fully human, united together in rich, complex, mysterious, and glorious ways.

With these two conclusions in mind, I want to revisit to the three themes used to explore Jesus's humanity in Hebrews in order to address the question: "Why the humanity of Jesus matters?"

We begin with the theme of *solidarity*. Jesus's incarnation is the greatest possible affirmation of the goodness of God's original creation of humanity. His humanity shows that physicality—embodiment—is good; indeed it is very good (Gen 1:31). This is an affirmation of doctrines relating to creation

28. Grieb, "Time Would Fail Me to Tell," 204–5.

29. Grieb, "Time Would Fail Me to Tell," 212.

30. Bauckham, "Divinity of Jesus Christ," 33.

31. Bauckham, "Divinity of Jesus Christ," 26.

and theological anthropology. Not only does Jesus share in this humanity, the flesh and blood of the children, but he is not ashamed to do so. Do *we* share in this same view of the goodness of our humanity? Of course, we need to acknowledge the distinction between our humanity as originally created by God and our humanity as distorted by sin. Even so, we need to recognize that to be *human* is very good; to be a *fallen, sinful* human being is to stand in need of redemption. This is why Jesus's incarnation is so staggering—in the same event, Jesus affirms the goodness of *humanness* and accomplishes the work of the great high priest whose perfect sacrifice, in his *humanness*, brings about the complete forgiveness sins and concurrent cleansing of the conscience that now enables redeemed humanity to enter into the very presence of God, which had been their station in the first place.

This is remarkable! I think sometimes that we, as followers of Jesus, are actually ashamed of our humanity. In her essay, Fleming Rutledge speaks powerfully against the dangers of "spirituality" as fundamentally a gnostic type of spirituality that denies the embodied aspects of the Christian faith.[32] She observes that the church in Corinth had this type of spirituality and consequently denied fundamental aspects of what it means to have a *body*. Paul corrected them by showing that followers of Jesus might use their *bodies* to glorify God. I especially appreciate her remarks on Hebrews 10, which demonstrate how Jesus honored God with his physical *body*. As a result, his entire, physical being was given to the will of God.

There are numerous areas in which we need to reclaim a robust understanding of what it means to be human, such as current discussions about transhumanism, where the lines between human and nonhuman are increasingly blurred. The solidarity of Jesus with the daughters and sons has important implications for this question and other issues in bioethics.

Moreover, if Jesus is not ashamed to share in the flesh and blood of the sons and daughters, are *we also* unashamed to share in the flesh and blood of our brothers and sisters? Realizing the dignity that Jesus's humanity restores to all humanity, do we extend that same value horizontally to others who share in this humanity? Do we see the *other* as partaking in *our* humanity?[33] These are just a few of the implications that come from reflect-

32. See pp. 14–16.

33. See esp. the chapters by Christopher Hays and Milton Acosta Bénitiz, Darrell Bock, and Robin Jensen in this volume.

ing upon the full and yet unique humanity of Jesus and his "radical human solidarity" (Katherine Grieb) with those who also share flesh and blood.

We move now to the theme of *suffering*. None of us can even begin to imagine the suffering that Jesus endured on the cross and the events leading up to his crucifixion. Throughout the centuries, as followers of Jesus have meditated on his suffering and death, they have been moved to repentance and then to worship as they (and we) consider fully what Jesus willingly endured on our behalf. But there are additional implications that we can draw out concerning his suffering, beyond his death. Put simply, Jesus knows what it means to be human. He was fully tempted and endured tremendous suffering. But his suffering brings out the emotional component of his humanity. A survey of the Gospel accounts reveals the full range of human emotions and the reality of human condition that Jesus experienced in his humanity.[34]

Jesus's suffering affirms the value of human emotions and moves us beyond any triumphalist view of Christianity in which Christians are always supposed to be happy and rejoicing. Instead, his suffering opens up a healthy space for grief and lament, emotional responses that are entirely appropriate as we view the sin and evil deeply entrenched in our world—a world in which we do not see things as they should be but we see Jesus, the one who suffered and who now intercedes on our behalf.

Once again, Jesus's humanity and divinity are inseparable. I have often reflected on how Jesus suffered when he saw the distortion of humanity because of sin and disease through the eyes of the one through whom human beings were created and the one who knew the glorious design and intent for humanity. Or consider his suffering in his resistance to sin—never once availing himself of the release valve of succumbing to the temptation to alleviate the pressure—but rather experiencing the full brunt of temptation and resisting to the end.

This leads us to our final theme, *salvation*. The one who shared in our flesh and blood has rendered powerless the one who enslaves humanity by means of fear of death. I would suggest that we live in a society that is permeated by a fear of death. We have only to consider the tremendous effort and expense undertaken to look young and to continue to look young for as long as possible. This, I suggest, reflects a tremendous fear of death that enslaves with an unnatural obsession on youth and a denial of mortality. But the one who shares our flesh and blood and who suffered on our behalf

---

34. This is well discussed by Peeler, "With Tears and Joy," 12–26.

has nullified the devil and sets us free from this obsession. Physical death is not the end, which leads to my final point.

The one who shares our flesh and blood is also our great high priest, who has passed through the heavenlies and is interceding on our behalf. Through his sacrifice and his mediation of the new covenant, the promise of complete forgiveness of sin and of a cleansed conscience has been fulfilled. Because of his priestly work, we can boldly enter into the very presence of God. The Son, who shares our flesh and blood, is leading the daughters and sons to the glory that was always intended for them . . . for us. Like Abraham, our eyes are on the city of God that we can only see from afar right now, but one day we will join the Son in joyful celebration in the heavenly Zion. This is why the humanity of Jesus matters, yesterday, today, and forever. Amen!

4

Jesus From the Earth Up

Thinking About Jesus's Humanity in the Canon

DARRELL L. BOCK
Dallas Theological Seminary

I begin with an interesting statistic. Today there are around 360,000 births a day. That works out to 15,000 an hour, 250 each minute, and 4 every second worldwide.[1] Why does this matter? Stretch that statistic, at not quite as high a rate but as an ongoing event over the history of humanity and it begins to dawn on you just how unusual Jesus is. In the first-century world, the estimated population of the Greco-Roman world was around 70 million people. It was and is the church's claim that Jesus is unique among all of these numbers, *all of them*, whether we think in the present or the past. And this is the church's dilemma. How do we proclaim a unique Jesus who is truly one in a gazillion (and that is a very large number)? How do you talk about someone who is like everyone and unlike everyone at the same time?

I submit to you today that the canon understood this problem, even as we often forget it. Here is the idea I want to focus on. Our canon has four Gospels, often broken down into John and the Synoptics. The Synoptic Gospels, of course, are Matthew, Mark, and Luke. I am going to argue that the Synoptics tell Jesus's story "from the earth up," while John tells it "from

1. "World Birth and Death Rates."

60

heaven down." Think about it. Mark starts with John the Baptist, and Matthew and Luke start with the birth of a baby, the infancy story. Granted that birth is most unusual, a hint of things to come, but we watch the identity of Jesus dawn on people as we read the Synoptics. Who is this man who commands the wind and the waves (Matt 8:27) is a key question that the disciples ask, even after having been with him for a time. Lights come on slowly for them in the Synoptics, just as it does, or did, for us. In contrast, there is John 1:1. In a CNN-like manner it announces, "In the beginning was the Word and the Word was with God and the Word was God." I can hear James Earl Jones in the background. From verse 1 we know where Jesus fits.

That three of our Gospels work from the earth up is no accident, as everyone who comes to Jesus comes to him that way. No one implicitly understands that Jesus is the second person of the Trinity or a divine person. That always has to be explained by someone. The church has largely forgotten how to tell this story in an "earth up" way. We love John because he does all our heavy lifting for us. However, to fail to know how to tell the story from the earth up means we are asking people to leap tall theological buildings in a single bound. And in a culture that has lost, or is losing, its Judeo-Christian net and in a globe where many areas never had it, this is a crucial error that needs rectifying. The Synoptics let the story of Jesus unfold one step at a time. We need to recover how to tell the story that way. In this essay, I hope to trace how this is done in some detail. The story is a combination of a linked up narrative flow (a cumulative argument if you will), surprising acts of a person, and cultural scripts. It is less about claims, that is an appeal through the use of titles of self-identification. This account is much more about display, showing and pointing to who one is by what one does. The advantage of telling the story this way is that it starts where people start, with Jesus. He was a human like us. Yet as much as he was like us, he also was, and is, very unique, one in a gazillion. Before we take a look, I need to introduce two ideas that are key to this approach.

First, Jesus *showed* who he was more than talking about who he was. Think for a minute with me about a question John the Baptist asked (Matt 11:2–6/Luke 7:21–23), "Are you the one to come or should we expect another?" Jesus answered not "yes" or "no" but with a list of actions. He affirms his identity and the nature of the time by pointing to the acts that God is working through him, appealing to the language of the prophet Isaiah in the process set in the hope of the arrival of the eschaton (26:19; 29:18;

35:5–6; 42:18; 61:1). The elements of the reply point to the new era of deliverance. Jesus answers the question positively by pointing to what God is doing through him. This is a clue as to how the earth up story works.

Tied to this emphasis on actions is the second feature: understanding cultural scripts. These are elements of background embedded in the text that the author and original audience share that we as readers may not. Let me give you two examples. "The Bears are going up to the frozen tundra to melt the Cheeseheads." Now what is that sentence about? It touches on American football, but the only way you know that is to be aware of the clues in the text that come from the culture. A Saudi learning English in Arabia as a second language and working with a full Arabic-English lexicon would have no clue what the topic was. Or a second example, "Ian Botham walked to the crease to defend the Ashes on behalf of the Queen." This is another perfectly beautiful, very English sentence, but if you do not know the name Ian Botham or what the Ashes are, you have no idea that sentence is about the game of cricket at a test match level between the UK and Australia, a storied sports rivalry in Commonwealth history. It is living in the culture that unlocks cultural scripts. Authors can go there because the writer and original reader share that cultural world. Cultural scripts are shorthand evoking a world with what they portray. In our two examples stadiums and particular sports fill out the reference. Those in the culture know what is being said while others are at a loss. The Gospels work similarly in a Jewish and Greco-Roman world and the "earth up" story builds on actions and scripts, sometimes assuming them and at other times challenging them. These actions point to a unique authority, some of which are so unique that only God was viewed as being responsible for executing them. In order to articulate this view of "earth up," I will examine eleven distinct acts that display Jesus's identity in light of the cultural scripts within which they are located.[2]

---

2. Gorman likewise provides a list of eleven acts of Christ ("Work of Christ in the New Testament," 72–84). This chapter will focus more specifically on Jesus's identity and specifically look at Jesus's acts "from the earth up" paralleling Gorman's helpful and broader chapter.

1) ASSOCIATION WITH TAX COLLECTORS AND SINNERS

We begin with one of the more relational and controversial aspects of Jesus's ministry: the way he opened himself up to the fringes of society, especially with those marked out as unrighteous.

Jesus's approach brought controversy because his ways were different from many of the pious within Second Temple Judaism. He challenged the cultural scripts of many leaders in Judaism. Here his actions stand in stark contrast to the community at Qumran, for example. That separatist society restricted access to God on the basis of ritual washings and a strict community code, including a long probationary period for prospective members. They had to prove their worth to be members of this community. Only those who rigorously kept the Torah could sit in God's presence. Although Jews were not unified in how they looked at sin and purity—the Qumranians often fused sin and impurity, while the Pharisees did not in some instances[3]—still the expectation was that righteousness led to the extension of grace, and the righteous were to maintain a distance from the unrighteous.

In contrast, Jesus did the exact opposite. He sought out, or was responsive to, the unrighteous as well as the "impure"[4] and argued that grace leads into righteousness because forgiveness engenders love. He noted that everyone qualifies for God's grace because no one is exempt from the need for forgiveness. Numerous texts report his controversial connections. His associations or positive examples appear with tax collectors (Mark 2:17 par.; Luke 18:13; 19:7), a sinful woman (Luke 7:34, 37, 39), Samaritans (Luke 10:29–37), and even Gentiles (Matt 15:21–28/Mark 7:24–30). When Jesus went to a banquet held by the tax collector Levi/Matthew (Matt 9:9–13/Mark 2:13–17/Luke 5:27–32), he described his mission in terms of outreach as a physician coming to heal and call the sick. Luke adds the note that the call is to repentance. Jesus observes that his controversial associations have led some to reject him (Matt 11:19/Luke 7:34). The parables of

---

3. On the Jewish views tied to sin, purity/impurity, and righteousness, see Klawans, "Moral and Ritual Purity," 266–84, esp. 278 and 281. In the Old Testament, some impurity was simply the product of events in life (e.g., childbirth impurity tied to blood) versus being about the presence of sin. So not all uncleanness is about sin, though much of it was.

4. For a detailed examination of this theme, see Blomberg, "Authenticity and Significance of Jesus," 215–50; and Blomberg's monograph *Contagious Holiness*.

Luke 15 make a similar point, again explaining the associations in terms of seeking the lost. The call is to take the first steps toward those who are wandering and point them to God. Take, for example, Jesus's initiative to Zacchaeus (Luke 19:1–10). Also, Jesus's willingness to encounter lepers and the blind is a part of this ministry emphasis. This portrait of Jesus is widely attested and expresses one of the fundamental values of his ministry.

This feature of Jesus's ministry challenged the portrait of who could belong to the community of God and also transformed the perception of how one gained righteousness. Did a person earn it, or did one receive it by grace? Was full transformation in practice required before entering into God's presence, or was this personal transformation a response of gratitude for having experienced God's grace? In contrast to the Jewish officials around him, Jesus emphasized access to God in the context of a gracious forgiveness available even to the most unrighteous. This acceptance of God's kindness was the ground for divine provision and transformation. The point is that by his own authority and in distinction from surrounding tradition, Jesus defined who it was that God accepted. Such a definition of access to God by grace alone and the claim of authority over righteousness that it represented became an irritant for the Jewish leadership. It also showed one aspect in which Jesus was enacting divine authority, earth up teaching resting in authority normally attributed to God.

2) FORGIVENESS OF SINS

As much as Jesus's associations were an irritant to the leadership, his claim to be able to forgive sins was one of the major objections they had to his ministry. On this issue, two passages are key. One is the text of the sinful woman anointing Jesus (Luke 7:36–50). The other is the healing of the paralytic (Matt 9:1–8/Mark 2:1–12/Luke 5:17–26). In both cases, the declaration of forgiveness of sins brings a reaction from the observers that is rooted in cultural scripts. In an irony of the text, the complaint by the theologians in these scenes is presented as an accurate reflection of the issue Jesus is raising. Only God forgives sin, but if this is so, then how can Jesus perform this act? The challenge of these two scenes is the same.

Since they question anyone being able to do this but God, those who raise the question have only two options. Either they believe that Jesus has lied about his identity and blasphemed by assuming a prerogative that is God's alone (Mark 2:7 par.), or they believe he is truly one who can speak words of forgiveness (Luke 7:49). Although Jesus does express the declaration with a passive idea ("Your sins are forgiven" [presumably by God]), his remarks are exceptional in that there is no declaration that God is responsible for this utterance, as in the case of Nathan to David in 2 Sam 12:13 ("The Lord has taken away your sin," NASB). Nathan, speaking as a prophet for God, can make the remark, but he explicitly gives the credit for the declaration to God. Jesus's declaration is less explicit about this affirmation that God forgives and thus represents a more direct claim, implying his own authority and making it more offensive to the leadership. It is this direct declaration that raises a problem for the Jewish leaders, who desire that God be acknowledged when sin is forgiven.

The question posed in Luke 7:49, then, is precisely that which Scripture wishes to raise for reflection by Luke's reader: "Who is this, who even forgives sin?"[5] The question is posed, but not answered, at the literary level to allow reflection about the text. The scriptural portrait of Jesus makes forgiveness of sins one of the major irritants in the Jewish officials' reaction to Jesus. To them, he was claiming an exclusively divine prerogative. The irony of the text is that their observation about the significance of Jesus's act is accurate, even as they reject it. If Jesus is able to forgive sin directly, then once again we have an act that raises the issue of how one should view Jesus, taking us from the earth up.

3) SABBATH INCIDENTS AND HEALINGS

The issue of Jesus's healing on the Sabbath and of his disciples' breaking the Sabbath also produced controversy and raised the question of Jesus's authority. Again a cultural script is in view—that is, a special day that helped to define Judaism itself. Jesus is claiming authority over holy time and the divine calendar, with a promise rooted in the commandments. The Sabbath and the day of rest that accompanied it represented a key distinctive within Judaism. Its observance was a point of piety and reflected covenant faithfulness. It is in this light that these actions must be seen. Jesus is viewed as reorienting a sacred day whose careful observance characterizes faithful Jewish living.[6]

---

5. What is important to remember about this question contextually is that the possibility of Jesus being a prophet had already been raised and rejected (Luke 7:39), so it looks as if some other role is implied by this question.

6. For a thorough treatment of this theme and its background in Second Temple

The key passage is a paired set of controversies in the Synoptic tradition that link the incidents of the plucking of grain on the Sabbath and the healing of the man with the withered hand (Mark 2:23–3:6/Matt 12:1–14/ Luke 6:1–11). In addition, Luke reports two other Sabbath healings (Luke 13:10–17, crippled woman; 14:1–6, man with dropsy). John also tells of healings on the Sabbath (John 5:1–18, man with paralysis; 7:22–23, looking back to John 5; 9:1–17, man born blind). As such, this kind of controversy is multiply attested across the tradition. Interestingly, the only two miracles that John's Gospel has in Jerusalem proper are these two Sabbath miracles.

So what is the point of such incidents? What do they tell us about Jesus? Witherington summarizes well: "The categories of teacher or prophet are inadequate to explain such a stance [toward the Sabbath]: We have here either a lawbreaker or one who stands above the law and uses it to fit his mission and the new situation that results from that mission."[7] The fact that the topic swirls around one of the Ten Commandments underscores Jesus's claim to authority even more. For who has the authority to adjudicate over core, divinely authorized Torah commands? The fact that in one of these incidents Jesus claims to be "Lord" of the Sabbath underscores the approach (Matt 12:8/Mark 2:27–28/Luke 6:5). This is yet another earth up claim.

4) EXORCISMS

The texts discussing exorcism include cleansing the demoniac in the synagogue (Mark 1:21–28/Luke 4:31–37), the Gerasene demoniac (Mark 5:1–20/Matt 8:28–34/Luke 8:26–39), the Syrophoenician woman's daughter (Mark 7:24–30/Matt 15:21–28), and the epileptic boy (Mark 9:14–29/Matt 17:14–20/Luke 9:37–43). Interestingly, John's Gospel has no exorcisms. The exorcism accounts are reflected in the Markan strand of the tradition, with Matthew and Luke each using three of these accounts, but not the same three.[8] Numerous other texts assume such a ministry (Matt 12:24/Luke

---

Judaism, see Hagner, "Jesus and the Synoptic Sabbath Controversies," 251–92. Key Old Testament texts for observance of the day are Exod 20:8–11 and Deut 5:12–15. A vivid Jewish text showing what was prohibited on the Sabbath is known as the forty less one, *m*. Šabb. 7.2. It lists thirty-nine things characterized as "work" and therefore prohibited on the Sabbath. A look at the Sabbath at Qumran, in the *Damascus Document*, and in the book of *Jubilees* shows how important the day was for many Jews. Also significant is the study by Tuckett, "Jesus and the Sabbath," 411–42.

7. Witherington, *Christology of Jesus*, 69.

8. For a defense of the historicity of this class of texts, see Twelftree, *Jesus the Miracle*

11:15/Mark 3:22; Luke 13:32; Mark 9:38–40/Luke 9:49–50; Matt 9:32–33; Luke 8:2). Again, this theme is multiply attested across the tradition strands. Note something else of importance: The challenge to Jesus is not a denial about what is happening (as many Bible critics argue today), but a debate about the transcendent source of his actions. There is an irony in this: by the Jewish leaders raising the specter of Beelzebul, there is an admission from them that the authority transcends human practice.

A final key text is a part of the Matthean-Lukan teaching tradition (Matt 12:28/Luke 11:20). Matt 12:24/Luke 11:15 makes clear that this healing of a mute man also is seen as an exorcism. This is a key text because it is a miracle account in form but it reverses the normal emphases. Most miracle accounts spend the time on the details of the healing and note a reaction in passing. This text does the reverse. The miracle is briefly summarized, and then the reaction is where the account spends its time. The scene is designed to portray the significance of Jesus's healings as a whole and the reaction to them.

So what were the views that rotated around Jesus's activity? Some were open but skeptical, wanting to see more in a specific sign from heaven. Others already had an opinion. They claimed that Jesus healed by the power of Beelzebul, but Jesus explains it in a completely different way. Jesus acts by the power of God. In fact, Jesus goes through and argues that Satan healing is a contradiction in action. If that is the case, Satan would be working against himself, and his kingdom of destruction cannot stand. That leaves the action as explicable only as an act of God's presence and power.

This text is important because it explains the significance of such healings in terms of the arrival of kingdom rule and authority. Jesus says, "If I cast out demons by the finger [Luke], or Spirit [Matthew], of God, then the kingdom of God has come upon you" (NASB). In both accounts this is followed by a parable where the house of a strong man (Satan) is plundered by a stronger man (Jesus), pointing to his victory over the forces of evil. Thus, the exorcisms are graphic acts by Jesus to demonstrate that he has come to overturn the presence and authority of evil. More important than any theological debates he may have with the Jewish leadership is his battle to overturn the hidden presence of evil, which shows itself in tearing down people. He came to give us victory over evil from beyond, the hidden

---

Worker, 282–92. One should recall that even the Jewish materials recognized that Jesus performed such works, calling them "sorcery" (*b. Sanh.* 43a). Also, there is a thorough discussion on authenticity and Jewish background by Evans, "Exorcisms and the Kingdom," 151–79.

cancer that deceives and destroys people. The exorcisms portray this battle in the most direct way. They also raise the question of who has the authority to exercise such power. Someone with such power over transcendent forces is making an earth up claim.

5) THE SCOPE OF JESUS'S MIRACLES

When given the chance to confess who he is, Jesus points to the miracles as his "witness" and explanation. Several texts are important here.

In Matt 11:2–6/Luke 7:18–23, when John the Baptist sends a message asking if Jesus is "he who is to come," the miracle worker replies that John should be told what is being done: "The blind see, the lame walk, lepers are cleansed, the deaf hear, the dead are raised, and the good news is preached to the poor" (AT). Jesus replies in the language of hope, Isaiah's prophecies about the coming period of God's great work of salvation. These miracles point out Jesus's identity and mission as well as the time of deliverance God has now brought. The reply shows how Jesus pointed to the display of what he is doing versus being focused on titles. Miracles are key to this action-oriented approach.

The next text is associated with Jesus's nature miracles. After the stilling of the storm, the disciples ask themselves, "What sort of man is this that even winds and sea obey him?" (Matt 8:27). The question is raised because the creation was seen to be in the hands of God (Job 40–42; Ps 107:23–29). For a similar miracle in Matthew 14, where Jesus walks on the water, the resulting confession is combined with worship: "Truly you are the Son of God" (14:33). This miracle, showing Jesus's authority over creation, is another factor to consider when thinking about Jesus from the earth up.

Another text is tied to Jesus's power over life itself. This is most dramatically developed in the story of Lazarus, in which Jesus is portrayed as "the resurrection and the life" (John 11). Other resuscitation texts include Jairus's daughter (Matt 9:18–26/Mark 5:21–43/Luke 8:40–56) and the widow of Nain's son (Luke 7:11–17), yet another multiply attested theme. Being the source of life is another divine prerogative pointing from the earth up.

Finally, there is a sequence of texts in Mark 4:35–5:43/Luke 8:22–56. Jesus's miraculous power is summarized in a linked series of four miracles: calming of the sea, exorcism, healing a woman with a hemorrhage, and raising the dead. This sequence covers the whole scope of Jesus's power, from creation to supernatural forces, human well-being, and life itself. It goes from decree over creation to defeating demons, disease, and death. It shows that Jesus has the power to deliver, and to do so comprehensively. It also raises the question of what human being is like this.

Thus, the scope of the miracles indicates the comprehensive extent of Jesus's authority. The power over life, demons, and creation indicates a scope of authority in one person that can exist only because he shares in divine power. Again, we summarize from another study of the topic. Graham Twelftree concludes his study of Jesus's miracles with this note: "In short, for Jesus and the Gospel writers, a miracle performed by Jesus is an astonishing event, exciting wonder in the observers, which carries the signature of God, who, for those with the eye of faith, can be seen to be expressing his powerful eschatological presence."[9] Prophets may have done some of this, but no one else performed the scope of these miracles.[10] This is another earth up claim.

6) PURITY PRACTICES

This issue primarily involves two texts (Mark 7:1–23/Matt 15:1–20). Cultural scripts of religious practice are in view as these are the only Gospel texts where the question of what is "common" or "profane" (κοινός [i.e., unclean]) comes up. Pharisees and scribes challenge Jesus for the disciples' failure to keep "the tradition of the elders." They fail to wash their hands to prevent uncleanness in their handling of food.[11] Other texts address Jesus's relationship to fasting and his critique of the religious practices of the Jewish leaders (Luke 5:33–39; 11:37–54/Matt 23:1–39). Again, the theme is multiply attested. These texts do not so much challenge purity practices as reprioritize them, making true piety a reflection of more than one's ability to follow detailed practices on the basis of specific legal stipulations.

What Jesus responds to, then, is the tradition built around uncleanness. He highlights the biblical call for love and a pure heart, not just the Torah per se. Jesus's challenge makes it clear that he rejected the use of

9. Twelftree, *Jesus the Miracle Worker*, 350.

10. It is, therefore, the scope of the miracles and the inclusion of these acts in an inductive argument with the surrounding evidence which direct me to a different conclusion than Daniel Kirk, even though we are working from the same evidence. For his treatment of the exorcism and healings of Jesus in the synoptics see Kirk, *Man Attested by God*, 415–88 (esp. 416, 486–88).

11. For discussion of the Jewish practice here, see Booth, *Jesus and the Laws of Purity*, 155–87.

oral law, which, with its extra requirements beyond Scripture, was said to build a fence around Torah. However, when Jesus goes on to elaborate upon his response, he does comment on matters of "defiling" that Torah does treat. He opts for a priority on the ethical dimensions of the law, stressing personal behavior. Both the rebuke that confronts them on how parents are dishonored and the emphasis on defiling coming from the heart show this focus on the law as it relates to one's interpersonal actions. When Mark adds the narrative comment that the effect of Jesus's remarks was to make all foods clean (7:19), he shows Jesus's emphasis by reconfiguring how the law is seen and prioritized in relationship to other scriptural themes. Reading Matthew gives one the same sense, but to a lesser degree. The emphasis on the interpersonal relationships is still there, but the explicit statement of foods being declared clean is lacking.

Jesus's comments are not merely those of a prophet commenting on the law, nor are they the work of a scribe interpreting the law. Jesus does not argue as later rabbis did, citing the precedent of other rabbinic opinions. Rather, the point is that Jesus, in light of his authority, has the right to comment and even to prioritize matters tied to purity. Ben Meyer speaks of an "eschatological ethic" at work here as the arrival of the new age brings a fresh look at the law and its priorities: a standard of righteousness to which the law always aimed is being more effectively worked out in conjunction with the promise of the new era.[12] Jesus's remark in defense of his lack of his disciple's fasting—that new wine requires new wineskins—makes the point explicitly (Mark 2:22/Matt 9:17/Luke 5:38). This kind of wholesale newness over common piety also must point to the revealer. As Meyer states, "Since the Mosaic code was conceived to have been divinely revealed, any code claiming to supersede it had somehow to include the claim to be equally revealed—indeed, to belong to a superior revelation."[13] The new era promised in Jer 31:32–33 was not to be like the one revealed on the mountain. The law would be lodged in the heart by being written there.

This also had implications for the revelator. Who could emphasize and reveal the scope of the law and practice that God gave through Moses in this fresh way? It is someone through whom God brought a time that transcended that of Moses and who transcended Moses himself. Here Jesus

---

12. Meyer, *Aims of Jesus*, 138–39. He goes on to say, "Jesus was not a rabbi but a prophet and, like John, 'more than a prophet.' He was the unique revealer of the full final measure of God's will" (151).

13. Meyer, *Aims of Jesus*, 152.

did not claim to go up the mountain to get the revelation of God as Moses had. Rather, he spoke directly of what "*my* Father" would do and what he requires. There is a directness to this sending and revealing. Thus, these acts inherently present a claim of authority and divine insight. Purity and fasting were not the only areas tied to the law and handled in this way by Jesus; but they show Jesus's authority over the law God gave to Israel to make her distinct.

7) OTHER ISSUES TIED TO LAW

This is a large topic so I limit myself to one example: the antitheses of the Sermon on the Mount (Matt 5:21–48). Sometimes it is argued that Jesus is merely rejecting oral law in his "you have heard it said, but I say to you" remarks (5:21, 27, 33, 38, 43). In part, this position is taken because Jesus introduces the antitheses with the remark that he came to fulfill the law and the prophets and that one should not teach anything that alters a jot or tittle of it (Matt 5:17–20). However, this argument does not work. Verse 20 makes it clear that one's righteousness is to exceed that of the scribes and Pharisees, not have a different type of righteousness. Jesus then expounds what this means in the antitheses. The result is that this exceeding righteous standard comes from reading the law not for its letter but for what it asks of the heart, as all the following examples show.

The antitheses intensify each command, pressing it in terms of its internal intent. The issue is not just murder, but also anger that leads to murder. The issue is not just adultery, but also lust that leads to adultery. The issue is not thinking through how one can get out of marriage, but taking one's vow seriously in order to keep it, recognizing also that God is involved in bringing a couple together. The issue is not how an oath is worded, but the integrity that makes oath-taking unnecessary. The issue is not eye-for-eye retribution, but a kind of nonretaliation that keeps the spiral of violence from spinning out of control.[14] This last example is particularly revealing, showing Jesus's emphasis on the relational dimension of the law and a refocus on a fresh hub for it, so that relationships do not break down. Absence of retribution is the point in Jesus's stepping back from the call to hate one's enemy. The standard may not be what is "fair" or "equal," but what goes beyond the call of normal duty to reverse the cycle that causes relationships

14. Note how this antithesis simply cites Exod 21:24 or Lev 24:20. There is no oral law mentioned here.

to be destroyed. The outcome is clear: the standard of righteousness that Jesus's reading of the law calls for exceeds that of the scribes and Pharisees. Jesus's standard operates at a higher level than the one the world or the Jewish teachers live by. It reflects God's character in the process, for in the call to show mercy and love, the example of God is invoked, and those who live this way are called sons and daughters of God (cf. Matt 5:45).

All of this raises questions: Who has the authority to open up the inner character of the law in this way? Who gets to discern what is to be kept and what is less important? Who decides when certain legal limitations apply and when they do not? There is an authority here over the law that raises questions about who it is who reveals this interpretation of the law. Again, a quotation from Witherington pulls all the strands of this section together:

> Jesus seems to assume an authority over Torah that no Pharisee or Old Testament prophet assumed—the authority to set it aside. . . . In short, he feels free not only to operate with a selective hermeneutic but also to add and subtract from Scripture. All of this suggests that Jesus did not see himself as a Galilean Hasid ["holy man"]. . . . He saw himself in a higher or more authoritative category than . . . types familiar to Jewish believers.[15]

This summary is well stated and correctly surfaces the question of what kind of person Jesus saw himself to be by assuming such authority. Jesus had no doubt that he could serve as a revelator like God, speaking and revealing the divine way and will. How Jesus handled the law is another example of actions revealing Jesus from the earth up. The handling of God's law in this way reflects divine prerogatives. The scope of how Jesus did it points in the same direction.

Jesus's way of reading the law as well as the tradition tied to it, shows his authority over it. If I may paraphrase, it shows that the Son of Man is not simply Lord of the Sabbath; he also is Lord over the reading of the law. In this, Jesus reveals not only his authority, but also his wisdom as the interpreter of the law *par excellence*. Jesus functions here as Word and revelator. As revelator he makes an earth up claim.

15. Witherington, *Christology of Jesus*, 65.

8) REDESIGNING LITURGY

Underscoring what has been said about the law is how Jesus handles sacred liturgy rooted in the law, as evidenced by the Last Supper (Matt 26:17–30/ Mark 14:12–26/Luke 22:7–23). The appeal is to a cultural script tied to the exodus. What appears to be a Passover meal is reinterpreted in terms of Jesus's approaching death (Mark 14:12, 22–24; Luke 22:15). At minimum, we have a meal offered during Passover season that evokes the establishment of a new relationship with God on terms that Jesus creates. The connection to Passover imagery is likely, given that they are eating the meal as pilgrims in Jerusalem for Passover, even if we cannot be absolutely sure that a Passover meal was the occasion.[16] A sacred meal, or at least imagery tied to a sacred event, the exodus, is completely reshaped into a message about the new era of eschatological deliverance.[17]

What does this recasting in terms of sacrifice and covenant show about Jesus? The remarks about the meal clearly present Jesus as a sacrifice who opens up the way to the new covenant relationship with God. According to Luke and Paul, Jesus's sacrifice, as represented in the cup, established the "new covenant in my blood" (Luke 22:20/1 Cor. 11:25).[18] Jesus is the means through which forgiveness is given on the basis of that death. Jesus then stands at the hub, or base, of a new era and makes provision for establishing a fresh way of relating to God in a fresh context of forgiveness. Just as blood on the doorposts covered and protected the Israelite families when the tenth plague roamed through Egypt and led to the nation's deliverance, so Jesus's death covers and provides a way of salvation for those who share in covenantal faith.

That Jesus could take sacred exodus imagery rooted in Torah and refill it speaks to his view as interpreter of both God's law and plan. It also points to his ability to take on a creative role in that plan, to author and perfect a traditional act of worship. He acts as the unique sent revelator of God. It is like the authority he exercised over the law. It is also like the authority he

16. There is debate whether a Passover meal is at the base of the Last Supper, although this does seem likely. The classic work arguing for a Passover meal is Jeremias, *Eucharistic Words of Jesus*; cf. Goppelt, *Theology of the New Testament*.

17. For other details about the event, see the discussion in Bock with Simpson, *Jesus According to Scripture*. Here our concern is the import of the event.

18. Matt 26:28 and Mark 14:24 speak only of the "blood of the covenant," but the fact that a covenant is established by the shedding of blood means a new covenant is being inaugurated. Luke and Paul write "new covenant" and thus make explicit what Matthew and Mark leave implicit.

asserts in the temple. Jesus is expanding and reshaping most of the major images of Judaism. All of this activity raises a chief question: What sort of person is able to recast old sacred rites?[19] Jesus is not merely establishing a new rite; he is modifying one of the most sacred rites of Israel, a rite tied to the nation's origin. Jesus's belief that he can do this shows how in tune he was with God's way and will, another earth up claim.

9) TEMPLE AND TEMPLE CLEANSING

The temple cleansing represented a direct challenge to the authority of the Jewish leadership, especially the Sadducees who controlled the temple area. Here, the cultural script draws from the Jewish expectation that Jerusalem and the temple would be part of what would be renewed in the last times (1 En. 90.28–30, 40; Zech 14:21; Shemoneh Esreh, benediction 14). These factors appear to suggest that Jesus cleansed the temple with a prophetic-like call to the nation to behave appropriately in the temple. There is no doubt that if covenantal unfaithfulness continued, then judgment would come (Mark 13:2/Matt 24:2/Luke 21:5–6; Luke 13:34–35/Matt 23:37–39). However, it is better to see Jesus acting as a messianic claimant bringing eschatological renewal. The act comes on the heels of riding into Jerusalem on a donkey and accepting praise as a king. Here is an example where the combination of the narrative sequence and the cultural script reveals the action's import. Jesus is making his action statement about the need for reform of the temple to prepare for the new era. This is like the prayer in benediction 14 of Shemoneh Esreh, which links messianic hope and the temple, just as the later inquiry of Jesus before the council moves from temple to messiahship. It also reflects the picture of *Pss. Sol.* 17–18: that the messiah to come would purge Jerusalem, cleanse it, and make it righteous. The fact that this is Jesus's first act after entering the city as a messianic claimant argues for a messianic intention to purge the temple over a mere prophetic act.[20] If this claim is met with rejection, then the nation stands culpable for rejecting messiah and the approach of the new era.

---

19. Goppelt, *Theology of the New Testament*, 220, says it this way: "Jesus now vouchsafed forgiving fellowship by giving himself as the One who died for the benefit of all others. It is not a heavenly body, not a pneumatic substance, that was given, and also not only an atoning power, but Jesus as the One who died for all."

20. For a detailed consideration of the significance and authenticity of Jesus's entry into Jerusalem, see Kinman, "Jesus' Royal Entry into Jerusalem," 383–427.

Again, to make such a move by itself could have been seen as merely prophetic, but placed alongside the other eschatological claims of Jesus and his other actions that touched on the law, this messianic claim surfaces with implications for the kingdom's arrival. Jesus is challenging holy space by what he does here. The temple is Israel's most sacred spot and the most holy place on earth for a Jew. To see oneself as having the authority to exercise judgment over the central religious symbol of the nation and the most sacred spot in the world was to perform an act that assumed a claim to divinely connected authority.[21] It is another earth up act. And the series of actions in an array of areas, many of them falling at the end of his ministry, further develops a narrative string about Jesus and his work that points to who he is.

This is precisely why the cleansing raises the leaders' question after the event about the source of Jesus's authority (Matt 21:23–27/Mark 11:27–33/ Luke 20:1–8). It was exactly the right question to raise. Even the way Jesus plays with the "temple" image, fusing his body as temple with the physical temple, suggests a level of holiness associated with his presence that links it to God's presence (John 2:19, 21). So, like the handling of the law, the treatment of the temple suggests an authority over the most sacred of Israel's sites, the very place where God dwells. Jesus is the Messiah and, more than the temple, functions as the hub and residing place of the coming promise. To claim authority over the most sacred of earthly spaces is to make an earth up claim.

10) SUFFERING AND CROSS

Jesus's experience of the cross takes on many dimensions. He is rejected and regarded as unrighteous, yet he is an innocent sufferer (Luke 22–23). The actual descriptions of Jesus's death on the cross and the Scripture he cites from the cross point to this portrait. The injustice of the cross will be vindicated when Jesus is raised up like the rejected stone of Ps 118:22–23. John's Gospel also supports this idea when it speaks of the Son of Man being lifted up. Here the cross is seen not as a defeat, but as the means of glorification for the Son (John 3:14; 17:1–5). Neither Jesus nor the evangelists say much in describing how forgiveness comes through Jesus's work,

21. These acts regarding the temple, liturgy, law, and purity practices drawn from the Gospels complement and supplement Tilling's account of the believer's relation to Christ as evidence of Christ's identity from Pauline texts. Tilling, *Paul's Divine Christology*.

but the texts that do treat it view his death as a sacrifice, opening up the way to a new covenant. In a larger context, this prepares for the coming of the Spirit, the sign of the new age (John 14–16).

Thus, in terms of Christology, Jesus's suffering and cross mark him out as one whom God vindicates even as he suffers an unjust and heinous death born out of rejection. He suffers primarily as the Son of Man, but the portrait is drawn from texts depicting the righteous sufferer and the Suffering Servant. That his sacrifice is worthy of establishing a new covenant also speaks to the greatness of his person, as does the nature of the vindication that God gives to him. Who else is worthy to sit at the right hand of God but one who shares divine status and authority? Jesus's death sets up the final act that identifies who Jesus is: the resurrection. Here we consider an act that Jesus does not perform in the Gospels' language, but one where God acts for Jesus, the force of the consistent reference to Jesus being "raised" in the passive (also Acts 2:24), clarifying who he is in the midst of a dispute about whether he is sent by God or a blasphemer. In the act of resurrection, God himself takes Jesus from the earth up and shows who Jesus is. This act of God is the divine vote in the current dispute between his being a blasphemer or one worthy to be exalted to God's side. This is a different sense of earth up than our claim about reading Jesus this way, but it vividly also pictures how we are to see Jesus and ultimately why we cannot leave Jesus to be a mere earthly figure.

11) VINDICATION IN RESURRECTION, ASCENSION, PROVISION, AND JUDGMENT TO COME

In the Gospels at his Jewish examination, Jesus develops the significance of his resurrection at the very moment when he is being condemned to the cross (Mark 14:55–64/Matt 26:59–66/Luke 22:66–71). It appears in Jesus's reply to the question of whether he is the Christ, when he predicts divine vindication for himself. The moment of seeming defeat is the very opportunity for disclosing how God will bring him victory. Upon being asked if he is the Christ, Jesus appeals to Ps 110:1 and points to God's vindicating him and giving him a seat at God's right hand.[22] One day he will also ride the clouds as Son of Man, an appeal to another cultural script. Riding the clouds is key because in Scripture only God rides the clouds (Ps 104:3; Isa

22. For a discussion on the christological use of this Psalm see Bauckham, *Jesus and the God of Israel*, 21–23.

19:1), so we have a human who will ride the clouds like God. Jesus is claiming that rather than being the defendant before the council, he one day will be their judge, operating from the very side of God.[23] One day they will see the Son of Man seated at the right hand of the Father. Matthew and Luke intensify this remark, noting that "hereafter" (Matthew), or "from now on" (Luke), they will see this exercise of authority. They will not have to wait to see this. The vindication comes soon—in the empty tomb.

Additionally, the promise of provision of the Spirit becomes important as evidence that the Christ is present (Luke 3:15–17) in the new era (Luke 24:49; Acts 1:4–8; John 14–16). Acts 2 explains the significance of what Jesus declared. Peter points to the distribution of the Spirit as a sign of messianic authority and the arrival of divine promise. Jesus's questions about Ps 110:1 and his initially cryptic claim for vindication at his trial are resolved in Acts 2. Peter's speech refers to Ps 110:1 (Acts 2:34) as clarifying the resurrection-ascension that Jesus implied through the psalm. Peter's speech in Acts 2 also explains that the resurrection is evidence, along with the distribution of the Spirit, that Jesus is Lord and Christ, the bearer of a new era with its long-promised benefits.

In sum, the resurrection leads to Jesus's being given a place at God's side. His resurrection not only means that there is life after death and a judgment to come, for which all people are accountable to him, but it also points to the identity of the one who brings the promise of life and the Spirit. He is the one qualified to share the throne with God's very presence, distribute God's blessing, and execute divine judgment. By taking Jesus from the earth up, God showed who Jesus is, clarified why he was sent, and acted to vindicate Jesus's claims. In the context of a Judaism that held to monotheism, this claim showed a intimately connected identity between Jesus and God, a unity that John's Gospel expresses as a oneness between the Father and Son. It resulted in a confession of Jesus that made him a coregent in heaven, sharing in the divine identity and worthy of confession (John 20:28) and worship. As we have seen throughout this section on Jesus's activity, appreciating who Jesus is does not emerge so much through his verbal claims. The key is to apprehend what his array of acts, and the events tied to them, tell us about his unique human-divine identity as the Son of Man, who is Son, Messiah, Lord, Servant, and Judge. This is an earth up Christology.

23. The detailed explanation and defense of the historicity of this scene is the burden of Bock, *Blasphemy and Exaltation in Judaism and the Final Examination of Jesus.*

SUMMARY

It is the scope and ultimate unity of all of these acts that point to Jesus's uniqueness. Taking most of these categories one by one, we see that parallels with activity by other human agents can be found. Moses worked with the creation. Prophets revived the dead. Elijah ended a drought. However, no one attempted or achieved the combination of acts that Jesus performed. It is the scope of these acts and their theological significance that establishes his uniqueness. The directness of his involvement with salvation—in the forgiveness of sins, the sacrificial provision for life, and the giving of the Spirit—tells us that Jesus is more than a human agent commissioned with divine authority. The Gospels argue that the full array of Jesus's acts explain that Jesus, the promised Messiah, is also the divine Lord. He is the Son of Man who combines humanity and divine prerogatives in unique ways. This is Jesus from the earth up. The portrait relies heavily on the background tied to cultural scripts to make its points. Jesus shares not only in divine authority but also in divine identity, essence, and being. Whether one thinks of the Sabbath, the law in general, the changed imagery of the Passover, the temple purging, exorcisms, raising people from the dead, controlling creation, or forgiving sin—Jesus is doing things that God does while exercising authority over things God has set up. The crucifixion is the ground from which God builds his plan of redemption through a uniquely worthy sacrifice. The miracles, and especially the exorcisms, show the scope of Jesus's authority and the enemies against whom he is battling to bring victory. The reconfiguring of imagery tied to feasts shows that a new era has come. The work undertaken is greater than that of a religious teacher, ethicist, or prophet.

Confirming all of this are some sayings that highlight Jesus's unique authority at the hub of divine activity.[24] Numerous texts declare the authority that Jesus has to judge and acknowledge others before God (Matt 10:32–33; Mark 8:34–38; Matt 10:40/Mark 9:37) or that blessing comes from not being offended at him (Matt 11:6). The apocalyptic Son of Man sayings fit here as well. Jesus stands at the center of divine blessing in several "I" sayings that show his authority (Matt 11:28, over rest; 5:17, over law; Mark 2:17, over forgiveness; Luke 19:10, over the lost; 12:49, to bring fire). He is greater than Abraham (John 8:58), than Jacob (John 4:12–14),

---

24. See Stein, *Method and Message of Jesus*, 122–24, identifying two categories of sayings here: (1) the totalitarian claims of Jesus; and (2) Jesus comparing himself with Old Testament saints. This paragraph reflects these sections.

than Solomon and Jonah (Matt 12:38–42/Luke 11:29–32). He is greater even than the temple (Matt 12:6). Several sayings point to his having come or having been sent from heaven.[25] The parable of the wicked tenants pictures Jesus as the sent Son (Mark 12:1–12/Matt 21:33–46/Luke 20:9–19). In sum, Jesus is unique as the revelator of God, standing in the middle of divine deliverance, a human who does divine things.

The crucifixion of Jesus demonstrates how earthly powers are threatened and reject these claims, but the resurrection-ascension is God's ultimate vindication of these claims. The judgment to come will be the ultimate proof that Jesus possesses absolute authority. However, in the current era, it is the provision of the Spirit, as the enabler of his children, that points to this uniquely authoritative Jesus. His seated position at the side of God shows that he shares completely in divinity and divine activity. He is the one who is both Lord and Christ. In an ultimate way, the resurrection takes Jesus from the earth up, adjudicating the dispute between Jesus and the Jewish leaders with a divine vote of action. This act is the ultimate reason to read Jesus in such an earth up light. Jesus cannot merely be left to his earthly ministry. From the very side of God, Jesus has brought the promised new era and with it a new community filled with new promise. That is Jesus from the earth up, one in a gazillion. The church needs to learn how to retell that story with clarity so people will ask, "So who is this man . . . ultimately?"

25. For example, Matt 5:17; 10:34–35, 40; 11:19; 15:24; Mark 9:37; Luke 4:18, 43; 5:32; 9:48; 10:16; 12:49; 19:10; also in John, often as the sent one, 5:23–24, 30, 37, 43; 6:29, 38, 39, 42, 44, 57; 7:29; 8:16, 18, 26, 29, 42; 9:4, 39; 10:10, 36; 11:42; 12:44–45, 49; 13:20; 14:24; 15:21; 16:5; 17:3, 8, 18, 21, 23, 25. Simon Gathercole shows the burden of what these texts teach in terms of Jesus's self-understanding as seen in his mission texts (*Preexistent Son*). In tracing this theme, Gathercole is arguing that, in their portrayal of Jesus's self-understanding, the Christologies of the Synoptic Gospels are not as distinct from John as some contend. What this chapter has tried to show is that when one adds to this the significance of Jesus's acts, especially those we see in the Synoptics, the distance shrinks even more, so that the difference becomes more one of rhetorical strategy versus substance. The Synoptics tell the story more from the earth up, while John tells it from heaven down. Each narrative takes one to the same conclusion about Jesus's uniqueness.

That Which was Seen

Art and the Humanity of Jesus

5

Portraits of Jesus in Christian Art Through the Ages

ROBIN M. JENSEN
University of Notre Dame

In his treatise on the Holy Trinity, St. Augustine of Hippo observed that when we hear or read about people who exist but have not seen for ourselves, we inevitably produce images of them in our minds. He adds that whether or not such imaginings bear any resemblance to actuality is unimportant, so long as we realize that our mental pictures are fundamentally unreliable. He warns that we should be wary of fabricating false images and then placing our hope or trust in them. By contrast, we can love and believe in God, whom we cannot see, but only grasp intellectually. Yet, Augustine acknowledges that we cannot help but fabricate pictures in our imaginations when we think, and he offers the example of visual portraits of Jesus (along with Paul and the Virgin Mary) to clarify and adds words of caution:

> Even the physical face of the Lord is pictured with infinite variety by countless imaginations, though whatever it was like he certainly had only one. Nor as regards the faith we have in the Lord Jesus Christ is it in the least relevant to salvation what our imaginations picture him like, which is probably quite different from the reality. . . . What does matter is that we think of him as a man; for we

have embedded in us as it were a standard notion of the nature of a man.[1]

Augustine, continues, saying that it would be a miracle if any of the many diverse appearances we humans imagine of Christ was even roughly correct. In any case, we could not discern between a true image and a false one because we have no way of verifying its accuracy.

Furthermore, external appearances, whether imagined or actually perceived are unreliable, largely because they are transitory but also because they can be obscured, mistaken, or simply illusory. As Augustine noted, different viewers perceive differently or invent quite different mental conceptions. Truth is obtained through faith and not by sight (2 Cor 5:7).

While Augustine's examples reveal his distrust of imagined appearances, they also tell us that portraits of Jesus, the apostles, and the Virgin Mary both must have existed in his time and that his audience would have been aware of them. Moreover, these portraits apparently varied, so no established artistic conventions as yet existed to convey identity via familiar attributes. For Augustine, the limited validity of a depiction of Christ does not depend on whether it faithfully followed a received portrait tradition (since none existed), but simply because it demonstrated Christ's human incarnation. Beyond that, individual imaginations fill in what cannot be known, and everyone will have different notions. The one requirement is that Christ be imagined—or depicted—with a *human* face and body.

Augustine could have pointed out the simple fact that the New Testament nowhere provides a description of Jesus's appearance. This omission raises the question of whether the authors of the four Gospels intended it, or simply overlooked any account of his physical appearance. Because of this, one may wonder how an artist could portray him at all without at least some verbal guidance and this leads us to wonder why artists eventually came to describe him according to certain iconographic patterns: wavy dark hair, full beard, slender nose, generally Caucasian features, etc. Since the sixth century, most artistic depictions of Jesus are instantly recognizable. But one should ask, how did these depictions come about? And, perhaps even more, whether they are legitimate.

Surprisingly, this question is rarely asked. However, around twenty years ago in the final run-up to the turn of the millennium, media outlets along with art museum officials experienced a sudden interest in portraits of Christ, especially as it was his two thousandth birthday. The events

1. Augustine, *On the Trinity* 8.4.6–7 (246–47).

associated with this development provided the opportunity to ask the question, "What did he look like?"

Fernando Yáñez de la Almedina, "Head of Christ," 1506.

Among these events was an exhibit held in London's National Gallery, titled "Seeing Salvation: The Image of Christ." The popularity and impact apparently surprised then Museum Director Neil MacGregor and his co-curator Gabriel Finaldi. With the exhibit widely acclaimed as a triumph, the two subsequently produced a BBC television series, accompanying book, and a full-color, best-selling catalog.[2] Mounted in seven galleries and thematically organized, the objects came largely from works already held by the museum. They dated from the third to the twentieth century and were more or less grouped according to theological motifs: Sign and Symbol; The Dual Nature; The True Likeness; Passion and Compassion; Praying the Passion; The Saving Body; and The Abiding Presence. Because the show drew more than five thousand visitors a day and was the fourth most popular in the world during the time of its run it was a sensation of its kind. Theologians and sociologists alike analyzed this amazingly positive response in a country where attendance in Christian churches appears to be rapidly waning.

The BBC series based on the National Gallery exhibit may have inspired a similar PBS special, which aired months later (around Christmas 2000) and was titled *The Face: Jesus in Art*. The momentum continued well into the next decade and beyond. Perhaps wanting to replicate the huge London success, the Philadelphia Museum of Art mounted a similar exhibit, *The Face of Jesus* (2011), which focused mainly on Rembrandt's seven portraits of Christ, made between 1643 and 1655. From Philadelphia, this exhibition traveled to Detroit and then to the Louvre in Paris.

A more audience-participatory event was staged by the *National Catholic Reporter*—"Jesus at 2000." The journal invited contestants to submit

2. MacGregor and Langmuir, *Seeing Salvation*; MacGregor and Finaldi, *Image of Christ*.

original artwork in response to the question, "What would Jesus Christ look like in the year 2000?" The panel of judges assigned to rank the nearly seventeen hundred entries from nineteen different countries included Sister Wendy Becket. The winning image, "Jesus of the People," submitted by Janet McKenzie was praised and panned alike.[3] The fact that McKenzie's rendering makes Jesus's ethnicity and gender ambiguous prompted hate mail and even personal threats. A Jesus who did not appear to be clearly male and certainly not Caucasian, and moreover surrounded by symbols that suggested some kind of religious syncretism really drew some viewer's ire. Others, including Sr. Wendy, praised the image for its inclusivity, dignity, and haunting beauty.[4]

Clearly, the question of how Jesus has been—or should be—depicted in art is controversial. A few months ago, I exchanged rather tense e-mails with a reporter who wrote to ask me why images of Jesus are usually light-complexioned, blond, and blue-eyed. I responded that while such depictions are common, many more, perhaps even the majority, actually don't show him this way. I presumed that my correspondent was bothered that pictures of the historical Jesus, a first-century Palestinian Jew, did not show him as looking somehow Middle Eastern. Evidently, I missed his point, because I finally grasped that my questioner had something else in mind: the figure in the Book of Revelation—the Ancient of Days—"one whose hair is white as white wool, with eyes like flame of fire and feet were like burnished bronze (Rev 1:13–16), an image based on Dan 7:9 (the ancient One with hair like pure wool).

Setting aside this apocalyptic vision of the Ancient One, Scripture never describes Jesus's physical appearance, before, during, or after his earthly life. Various non-canonical gospels portray Jesus in variety of changeable forms, sometimes as a boy or even as a woman (e.g., *Acts of Peter* 20–21; *Acts of John* 87–89). Some early writers cite the description of the suffering servant in Isaiah 53, who has "no form or majesty—nothing in his appearance that we should desire him" or contrast that with of Psalmist's ode to the "most handsome of men" (Ps 45:2).

Interestingly, along with these ambiguous references, the canonical Scriptures almost imply that Jesus's appearance was at times indiscernible.

---

3. "Jesus 2000."

4. Since then several other works have appeared in print, including my own, *Face to Face*; Williams, *Faces of Christ*; Lucie-Smith, *Face of Jesus*; and Taylor, *What Did Jesus Look Like?*

For example, Luke's post-resurrection narrative implies that the risen Jesus was unrecognizable to his followers on the road to Emmaus until he broke bread with them (Luke 24:13–43). The long ending of Mark, which probably post-dates the rest of the Gospel, specifically says that Jesus first appeared to Mary Magdalene and then—*in another form*—to two of his disciples (Mark 16:12). According to the Fourth Gospel, Mary Magdalene mistook the risen Christ for a gardener; it was only when he spoke that she realized who he was (John 20:15–16). Later in that Gospel, the risen Christ appeared to the disciples on the beach, but they didn't immediately recognize him (John 21:4).

The Transfiguration event is another example in which Jesus's physical appearance changed as his garb became suffused with light. According to Origen of Alexandria, only Peter, James, and John were able to witness this, as they alone had the capacity to perceive his luminous glory.[5]

Each of these instances should suggest that artists should not be too sure that they could achieve anything like a "realistic" portrait of Christ in his life on earth or after his resurrection and ascension. In fact, it almost seems that the obfuscation is deliberate. Perhaps the parallel fact that we have different textual presentations of Jesus in the four Gospels similarly contravenes our efforts to be comprehend Jesus's person or earthly mission in any simplistic manner.

Nevertheless, around the year 2000, a forensic anthropologist attempted to produce an historically accurate rendering of Jesus's face. Originally commissioned for the BBC, the image appeared on the cover of *Popular Mechanics Magazine* in December 1999, just in time for Christmas.[6] Trying for a scientific approach to reconstruct Jesus's physical appearance, the artist used the skull of a Palestinian male from the first century. Although the comparison is something of a stretch considering the differences of time and place, the idea bears some similarity to Rembrandt's choice of a young Jewish man to be his model for his small portraits of Jesus, one of them titled, *Head of Christ, Done from Life*—one of the paintings featured in the Philadelphia Museum exhibition. While Rembrandt obviously did not believe he was creating an actual from-life likeness, scholars have suggested that he used a young Sephardic Jew from his neighborhood in Amsterdam as his substitute model especially in order to create an ethnically accurate image.

5. Origen, *Against Celsus* 2.64.
6. See Legon, "From Science and Computers, a New Face of Jesus."

Despite these efforts to be scripturally, scientifically, or historically accurate, they are motivated by some dubious assumptions. We certainly do not believe that all first-century Palestinian men looked alike—or that just any young, Dutch Jew, especially of Spanish or Portuguese descent, would be the obvious model for Christ. Almost any artistic work is inescapably influenced by its cultural context, intended audience, and personal vision. Portraits of Jesus are no exception. Nevertheless, people regularly express a wish that artists would depict an authentic or truthful portrait of Jesus, without really specifying what that might be or how someone could go about it. Objections to blond, blue-eyed Jesus images may be understandable, but that would also rule out most other ethnically-specific portraits. The problem of trying to produce a faithful or historically accurate likeness actually presupposes a prior question. Can we—or should we—make pictorial images of Jesus at all? While Augustine thought it might be done—albeit with conditions and cautions—according to several other early Christian writers, any visual depiction of Christ would be impossible, heretical, or essentially blasphemous.

One of the most commonly cited treatments of this problem comes from a letter purported to be from the fourth-century bishop and historian Eusebius of Caesarea to the Emperor Constantine's daughter, Constantia. According to the document, she had written to him requesting a portrait of Jesus for her personal devotion. His reply expresses some outrage—as well as the nub of the problem:

> What sort of image of Christ are you seeking? Is it the true and unalterable one which bears his essential characteristics, or the one which he took up for our sakes when he assumed the form of a servant [Philippians 2:7]. . . . Granted, he has two forms, even I do not think your request has to do with his divine form. . . . Surely, then, you are seeking his image as a servant, that on the flesh which he put on for our sake. But that too, we have been taught was mingled with the glory of his divinity, so that the mortal part was swallowed up by life [2 Cor 5:4].[7]

A less famous story concerns "from life" portrait of Jesus. The second-century church father, Irenaeus, complained that some gnostic groups (the Carpocratians) possessed images of philosophers, including one of Christ made by none other than Pontius Pilate.

---

7. Eusebius, *Letter to Constantia*, 16–17.

They treated these portraits in the way that pagans customarily venerated idols—with garlands and lit candles. Irenaeus clearly believed that the practice—if not also the portraits themselves—were the products of a heretical sect.[8]

This critical report of portraits made by sectarian groups was reprised in a comment attributed to the late second-or early third-century Roman teacher, Hippolytus, who likewise claims that followers of the gnostic teacher Carpocrates possessed images of Christ fashioned by Pilate.[9] The story also found its way into the work of the fourth-century heresy-fighter, Epiphanius of Salamis who repeated the assertion that Carpocratians had images of Jesus made by Pilate out of precious materials and they venerated them, after the manner of the "heathens" alongside of images of Pythagoras, Plato, and Aristotle.[10]

A different fourth-century text also has been attributed to Epiphanius. Although some have questioned the document's authenticity, it raises a significant issue. In a letter addressed to Emperor Theodosius and found among the records of the ninth-century iconoclastic debate (thus read out by the critics of images), Epiphanius (or Pseudo-Epiphanius) expressly denies that any ancient Christian "father" could have painted an image of Christ either for a display in a church or in a private house. The rest of the text provides some interesting details: that those who do such things "lie" by representing the Savior with long hair, which they do "by conjecture because he is called a Nazarene, and Nazarenes wore long hair." Epiphanius objects to identifying Jesus as a Nazarene because Jesus drank wine, while the Nazarenes do not.[11] Epiphanius asserts that artists who make these pictures invent physical types according to their whims, and that simple logic contradicts them. How could the Savior have had long hair he asks, when his disciples all had short, cropped hair? This would have made him look different from the others, rendering it unnecessary for Judas to identify him with a kiss. The Pharisees, he concludes, could have saved their money! This difference of appearance is actually quite evident on early Christian depictions of Jesus from Rome's catacombs and early sarcophagus reliefs, on which Jesus's long curly hair and lack of beard easily distinguish him from his disciples with their beards and cropped hair.

---

8. Irenaeus, *Against Heresies* 1.25.6.

9. Hippolysus, *Refutation of All Heresies* 7.32.8.

10. Epiphanius, *Refutation of All Heresies* 27.6.9–10.

11. Epiphanius, *Letter to the Emperor Theodosius* 41–42.

Early Christian Sarcophagus with scenes of Christ and Peter, ca. 325–350.

Other early writers include similar references to Pilate and the Carpocratians. Epiphanius's disapproved details have parallels in another specious letter—this time reported to include an eyewitness description of Jesus from Pontius Pilate's predecessor as governor of Judea, Publius Lentulus. Lentulus's supposed letter, addressed to the Roman people and senate is of mysterious origins, possibly translated from Greek into Latin in the thirteenth century. It survives in several fifteenth-century Florentine collections as well as in Ludolph the Carthusian's *Life of Christ*, published in Germany in 1474.

According to the document, Lentulus perceived Jesus as "somewhat tall in stature with a comely appearance; his hair the color of an unripe hazelnut and smooth down to his ears, but then somewhat curled, darker, and shinier, waving about his shoulders, curly." It was parted in the center "after the pattern of the Nazarenes." His brow was smooth and unwrinkled, his complexion ruddy, and his expression cheerful. He had an abundant (but not particularly long) brown beard that divided at his chin. His eyes were blue grey, clear and quick. Finally, the description concludes with a reference to Psalm 42: "He is the most beautiful among human beings (*pulcherrimus vultu inter hominess satos*)."[12]

Note that the Lentulus letter does not criticize the portrait's existence or its rendering of Christ's appearance. By the date of this surviving manuscript, paintings of Jesus were widely accepted, and his facial features were relatively consistent. Yet, the question remains. How did artists come to depict Jesus in this conventional way? Augustine, evidently unaware of any supposed from-life portraits (including any made by Pilate), insisted that since Jesus was human, minimally he must at least be imagined (or imaged) with a human face and physique. But he clearly still supposed that the

12. Dobschütz, *Christusbilder*, 308–29.

imagined images would diverge. An examination of the art of his time, however, reveals that representations of Christ were becoming established, traditional, and show almost no significant variation.

One answer is the existence of a miraculous portrait, actually made from life, that served as the prototype for all subsequent depictions. Aside from the dubious, above-referenced Pilate-made portrait, a group of well-established traditions assert the existence of portraits of Christ, made without human hand (*achieropoietos*). The most famous of all is the one known as the Mandylion, obtained (as the tradition says) by the first-century King of Edessa who sent a servant out to ask Jesus to come and heal him. Rather than arriving himself, Jesus obliged the servant with an image of his face, imprinted on cloth that he used as a towel.

The earliest known version of this tale appears to date to the sixth century, however, so it is difficult to anchor in any historical record. It has an obvious parallel in the story of Veronica's veil or the miraculous image

Detail from an icon depicting the Story of King Abgar receiving the Mandylion, ca. 940 CE, from the Monastery of Saint Catherine, Sinai, Egypt.

of Kamouliana, which is less well-known to western Christians. Other examples include the Shroud of Turin and the so-called Holy Faces of Manoppello and Lucca.

However one regards these stories of miraculously produced images, it is significant that their depictions in art show Jesus's facial appearance fairly consistently—with dark, shoulder-length hair parted in the center, a pointed beard, a long, narrow nose, and a small mouth under a drooping mustache. They have marked similarities to the well-known sixth-century Christ icon from St. Catherine's Monastery in Sinai for example, and to almost every subsequent depiction of Jesus in art. The power of this traditional portrayal is so great that viewers often resist alternatives, like the

Caravaggio painting, *The Supper at Emmaus*, which still confounds the viewing public for its strange presentation of a beardless Christ. Neverthe-

less, a remaining question is whether those likenesses said to be produced "without hands" were influenced by representations that already existed, or the opposite: that they served as authorizing models for subsequent images of Jesus.

As I have already pointed out, the oldest surviving images of Jesus show him as distinctly youthful, beardless, and with long curling hair. As such, he looks quite different from his apostles. With extremely rare exceptions, depictions of Jesus as bearded and more mature in physique do not pre-date the mid to late fourth century. For a while both types occurred simultaneously, but by the sixth century, the bearded type became dominant. By the Middle Ages, it was essentially the only that artists represented Jesus.

The earlier type, however, in which Jesus assumes a beardless face, long curly hair, and a graceful (if not sinuous) body conforms to the way artists had always depicted the younger

Icon of Christ, Pantocrator. Sinai, Monastery of St. Catherine, Egypt. Sixth century.

gods and heroes of the classical pantheon (cf. figure of Belvedere Apollo). Apart from the fact that Jesus is never shown nude, his youthful appearance might be intended to suggest his status as the Son of the Supreme Father—a distinction that would align with Arian conceptions of the Son as a creature and not equal in nature or eternity to the Creator. Furthermore, in almost all of these early images, Jesus appears in scenes from his earthly life: being baptized, healing, teaching, working wonders, and entering Jerusalem. Very few images of his death, resurrection, or ascension can be dated prior to the fifth or sixth centuries.

The iconographic similarities of Christ with the younger Greco-Roman gods and heroes should not surprise us. Christian writers, beginning with Justin Martyr, recognized the parallels of the Jesus story with the myths of these gods and the possibility of conflation or confusion.

Christian apologists, like Justin, similarly acknowledged that the healing gods, human magicians or itinerant wonder workers like Aesclepius, Simon Magus, or Apollonius of Tyana, could be compared with Jesus and so tried to use this to their advantage in order to make positive connections for their pagan audiences.

Adapting the iconography of the junior gods, or semi-divine heroes, particularly those who work wonders, shepherd souls through the underworld, bring light from

Belvedere Apollo, Roman, ca. 120–40 CE., now in the Vatican Museum.

the darkness, are born through miraculous or divine conception, or die and then rise again makes sense as a strategy for evangelizing adherents to the traditional cults. Jesus is like these gods—only better (or truer). As Justin Martyr proclaimed in his address to the Roman emperor, Christians propose nothing different from those things Romans believe regarding the divine sons of Jupiter.[13] This type is also appropriate for a Christology that regards Christ as a Son, subordinate to his divine Father. He is not the equal to the supreme Deity, but rather the mediator between the distant, invisible, and transcendent One and his earthly creation.

The later type—the bearded figure—occurs in rare examples of Jesus teaching his apostles or transmitting the New Law to Peter and Paul. The first type parallels the iconography of ancient philosophers, surrounded by their disciples. The second usually shows him either standing on the rock of Eden (Paradise) or seated on a throne as the ruler of the universe. In these representations, his facial type parallels the iconography of the "senior" or "father" gods, especially Jupiter. This iconography is also appropriate to a Christology that regards Christ as equal in nature, activity, and power to the First Person of the Holy Trinity. No longer the younger and subordinate Son, he is now

13. Justin Martyr, 1 *Apology* 21. See also Justin Martyr, *Dialogue with Trypho*, 69.

co-eternal and consubstantial with the heavenly Father. His image has been transformed from that of a divinely empowered miracle worker to a supreme ruler of the cosmos.

Early Christian sarcophagus with Christ giving the New Law to Peter and Paul, mid-fourth century.

Jesus as Teacher Surrounded by His Apostles. Mosaic apse from Sta. Pudenziana, Rome, ca. 400 CE.

For a century or so, a mixture of both types might even occur on the same monument. For example, two distinctly different images of Jesus appear in adjacent apses in Rome's fourth-century mausoleum of Ste. Costanza. This also occurs in the sixth-century program of nave mosaics in Ravenna's basilica of Sant' Apollinare Nuovo, where the left side of the nave displays images of Jesus in his earthly ministry, calling disciples and working miracles, whereas the right side shows scenes from the Last Supper, arrest, and trial through his post-resurrection appearance to the apostles. Although it is difficult to date all of these images precisely, in each instance the distinct presentations are more or less contemporary to one another. Their similarities in overall composition strongly suggests that they were done by the same workshop of artisans and so the differences in the ways they show Jesus were evidently intentional. Moreover, we have no evidence that these differences made them puzzling or problematic to viewers.

Bronze statuette of Jupiter, second half, second century, Rome.

Jesus Healing the Paralytic, mosaic panel from Sant'Apollinare Nuovo, Ravenna, ca. 500 CE.

95

Last Supper, mosaic panel from Sant'Apollinare Nuovo, Ravenna, ca. 500 CE.

One possible explanation for the distinct depictions in the Ravenna mosaics is that they prompt viewers to perceive a transformation in Jesus's status as he transitions from his earthly ministry to his Passion. According to organization of the Fourth Gospel, which has often been described as having two parts: a Book of Signs and a Book of Glory. The evangelist describes his first miracle at Cana as the first of his signs (John 2:11), followed by the healing of the royal official's son at Capernaum (John 4:54) and many others (e.g., John 6:2, 14, 26, etc.). Jesus then announces the commencement of his glorification immediately after he dismisses Judas from the table (cf. John 13:31). This commences the so-called Book of Glory, which narrates Christ's Passion and Resurrection, which includes with his final discourse with the twelve, including his priestly prayer that opens, "Father, the hour has come; glorify your Son so that the Son may glorify you" (John 17:1). This transformation, from a compassionate miracle worker and teacher to the exalted savior and world conqueror (cf. John 16:33) could have been indicated by a change in his appearance—from youthful and beardless to mature and fully bearded. In the Ravenna program Jesus is beardless in all the depictions of his miracles and only appears bearded in the images that proceed from the Last Supper to his post-resurrection appearance.

It may also be that this early art simply allows Jesus to take on more than one external appearance for the sake of viewers who find him manifest in different ways at different times or circumstances of their lives. This idea was articulated by Cyril of Jerusalem in the fourth century:

> The Savior comes in various forms to each person according to need. To those who lack joy, he becomes a vine, to those who wish to enter in, he is a door; for those who must offer prayers, he is a mediating high priest. To those in sin, he becomes a sheep, to be sacrificed on their behalf. He becomes 'all things to all people' remaining in his own nature what he is. For so remaining, and possessing the true and unchanging dignity of Sonship, as the best of physicians and caring teachers, he adapts himself to our infirmities.[14]

Bishop Cyril's argument suggests that diverse, perhaps even age-, race- or even gender-ambiguous depictions of Jesus are acceptable. Artists need not be expected to produce historical or ethnically accurate portraits. In fact, one could argue that variances in the way Christ is portrayed is theologically true and pastorally beneficial. Humans imagine, make, or choose different, but equally proper images for Jesus in different places, eras, and situations, affirming his variety of roles as healer, teacher, miracle worker, cosmic judge, law giver, enthroned Lord, or returning savior. Moreover, this iconographic inconsistency undermines idolatry by resisting a single, cult image. Resisting a single, human-made portrayal as if it were somehow uniquely correct or truthful is not just scripturally and theologically correct, it also reflects and respects the freedom of an artist to express an idea rather than just making accurate renderings of external appearances.

Let me conclude with a caveat. Recalling Augustine's admonition that depictions of Christ must minimally make him look human, Cyril of Jerusalem's description might be best taken metaphorically. Picturing Jesus as a gate or even a sacrificial lamb might undermine the doctrine of the Incarnation. A canon of a late seventh-century council, the Council of Trullo that proclaimed that representations of Christ would render in human form addresses this concern:

14. Cyril of Jerusalem, *Catechetical Lecture* 10.5 (198). See also Origen, *Against Celsus*, 2.64.

In order that 'that which is perfect' be delineated to the eyes of all, at least in colored expression, we decree that the figure in human form of the Lamb who takes away the sin of the world, Christ our God, be henceforth depicted in images, instead of the ancient lamb, so that all may understand the depths of the Word's humiliation, and that we may remember his conversation in the flesh, his passion and death, and his redemption that was for the whole world.[15]

Christian visual art is not the only place one finds varying imagery for Jesus. Christian hymns similarly proclaim him "Beautiful Savior," "Lover of my soul," "Brother kind and good," and "Judge Eternal, enthroned in splendor." An enormous variety of representations have emerged from two thousand years of Christian artistic imagination, and almost every one of these diverse images contains some distinguishing element that—almost mystically in some cases—identifies it as a portrait of Christ. Consistency and much less ethnic or historical accuracy is not required.

When it comes to Jesus, a portrait is not an achievement of external verisimilitude, but a way for its viewers to engage, encounter, or discover something with their eyes that their mind may not grasp alone. Seeing is not a reason for believing, as Augustine insisted. However, seeing can inspire prayer and foster devotion. The important thing is not to become idolatrously attached to any single image for, as the Bishop of Hippo maintained, everyone will envision Jesus differently. The important thing is to see him as he looked in his earthly life—as a human man.

15. Quinisext Council, "Canon 82," 139–40.

6

Seeking Mystery in Material

Reflections on the Making of *Corpus*

DAVID J. P. HOOKER
Wheaton College

THE ASK

The party was winding down before I had a chance to talk to Jeff. Dr. Jeff Greenman was the chair of Biblical and Theological Studies at Wheaton, and the department was in the midst of designing their new digs in the fifth floor of the Billy Graham Center. As part of the renovation they had asked a few members of the art department, including myself, if we would be interested in a creating a commissioned work for the space. They were looking for work that would reflect biblical themes. I had never directly tackled biblical narrative before, but I was intrigued with the possibility. As we sat, Jeff broached the subject, "Hey David, have you had a chance to think about what you might do for the new space?"

"I have. I was thinking about a piece based on Elijah and the crows. Elijah as a full-sized ceramic figure pressed against the wall, completely covered in birds. A murder of crows. I think it would be a piece about submission and faith; the tension, and the trust."

Slight pause . . .

"Well, that's interesting, but we have a few gaps in the biblical narrative we'd like to address. I was wondering if you might be willing to pick up one of those themes."

"Oh, OK. What kind of gap did you have in mind?"

"The death and resurrection of Jesus."

Considerably longer pause. . . .

"No way." I thought to myself. "There's no way I'm going near that. It's too . . . big. Too impossible, too many land mines."

"I'll think about it," I said.

That was the beginning of a journey that has led me here today.

The piece that arose from that conversation is *Corpus*, which is at the east end of the main hall on the fifth floor of the Billy Graham Center. For this work I used an antique sculpture of the body of Jesus (a corpus) from a decommissioned Crucifixion and ritualistically covered it with the contents of vacuum bags collected by the college's custodial staff. These bags contained dirt, fiber, bits of paper and other detritus as you might expect. They also contained bits of people from this community: hair and skin cells.

PROCESS RATHER THAN MEANING

"So, tell me, David, what is *Corpus* about? What does it *mean*?"

Ah, the dreaded artist question.

I get this question a lot. Artists get this question a lot. Usually from very well-intentioned people. People who genuinely want to connect with the art, but do not know where to begin. Maybe some of those people have no interest in connecting with the work at all, either through disinterest or laziness, and are just being polite: but on the whole I'm going to go with well-intentioned.

It is, nonetheless, an impossible question for me to answer.

It was not, by the way, the question that the editors asked of me when they invited me to contribute—I wouldn't want to give you that impression. It is, however, a question that, like our new puppy at home, feels always underfoot: eager for attention, wanting to please, but ultimately a stumbling block. So let me address it right off.

The issue within the question is that it makes an assumption about the nature of art and art making that (in my experience) is patently false, even though it has been promoted by artists for centuries under the "artist as genius" model. The assumption looks something like this: The artist, having won the favor of the muse, or the gods, or God, has an inspiration, some core idea that sparks her or him into frenetic artistic activity. This activity results in a work of art (preferably in a form heretofore unknown to humankind), which contains the original idea/inspiration in a way that can touch the viewer in some manner beyond words. It is a transcendent experience. The viewer or viewers (preferably plural, the more the merrier) heap praise on the artist. The artist then goes dormant for an undisclosed amount of time, waiting to hear from the muse again. Illicit substances, as well as all kinds of lasciviousness, may be involved.

OK, I mock. But still, I suspect if you consider yourself "not artistic," or if you've ever uttered the phrase "I don't know if it's art, but I know what I like," then I suspect this model is not too far from the one you have inherited. It is the one I absorbed in my formative years. To be fair, it is the model many artists advocate for still. Artist as genius. Artist as the outsider (or in the church "artist as prophet"). Art as inspiration. Art as communication. To be honest, I would be rid of the whole mystique.

There are much better models out there. One of them was proposed by Dorothy Sayers in her book *The Mind of the Maker*. Sayers, a well-known fiction writer and theologian, superimposed her two interests, using a trinitarian model to describe the process of making. In her model, the idea or concept for the work is like God the Father. The activity or energy of making, that which makes the work incarnate, is like God the Son, and the power of the work, how the work effects the viewer is like God the Holy Spirit.[1] There are a few caveats here, and more to explore in this model than there is time for (I highly recommend the book), but I want to highlight how this model changes the focus from meaning to process. There is nothing linear about the Trinity. You cannot say that one divine person exists before the other, or one is more important than the other, or one can be understood without the other two. Everything is relational. And cyclical. There is no beginning and no end. While I want to come back to this model at the end of this chapter, but for now I hope this might encourage you to think about the artistic process differently. Particularly note that the "power" part of this trinity, what happens when the work is encountered by the viewer, is an open invitation for you, as a viewer, to become part of the creative process for any work of art. Your role is not passive, it's participatory.

Rather than try to explain *Corpus*, then, I think it is a better strategy to explain something of my artistic practice, and how *Corpus* fits into that practice. I use the term artistic practice deliberately. The emphasis is not on results, but on process. There is no "finished." A practice requires a different mindset. It shifts the emphasis from inspiration to repetition. Or rather inspiration comes from repetition. I don't believe in "Inspiration" so much

1. Sayers, *Mind of the Maker*, esp. 33–47.

as I believe in momentum. This is not to say I don't believe a Corpus was inspired; I do. I just think of inspiration as something that happens in the middle of a bigger practice, not as an origin event. Practice requires work, commitment, and continuity. Success in practice is not defined by exterior measures, such as critical acclaim, academic standing, or even the ability to make a living from one's work. Success is defined by faithfulness. In this way artistic practice mirrors sanctification.

With that in mind, let me say that my prime motivation for making *Corpus* was to explore a set of ideas through materials, engaging those materials through ritualistic action. I strongly believe in art as a way of knowing, a way of being, a way of interacting in the world. This is what I mean by the title of my essay, "Seeking Mystery Through Material." My approach to art is like a science experiment with an impossible to prove hypothesis about the nature of beauty. I approached making *Corpus* pretty much the same way I approach making anything else: I try to make something beautiful, out of things that I think are beautiful, with a process that I find beautiful.

Now, I suspect vacuum debris is not a material that comes immediately to mind when you hear the word "beautiful." Fair enough. It's a tough sell. My understanding of beauty has been influenced and broadened by a number of different factors, more than I have time to address, but a crucial influence comes from the discipline of pottery. While I work in a variety of media, pottery remains at the conceptual heart. Pottery allows me to think about material and process, about ritual and history, about place and community. These are all terms I would use to describe my approach to *Corpus*. Pottery also taught me how to broaden my understanding of beauty through the Japanese aesthetic of *wabi-sabi*.

WABI-SABI

Wabi-sabi is a Japanese term used to describe an understanding of beauty that has been cultivated there for over 600 years. That is to say, *wabi-sabi* started in Japan about the same time as the Italian Renaissance—which largely defines our sense of beauty—started in the West. The two aesthetics could not be more different. Our culture tends to think of the high-water mark in visual art as defined by people whose names you associate with a Teenage Ninja Mutant Turtle (Leonardo, Donatello, Raphael, and Michaelangelo); work that we recognize and celebrate as one-of-a-kind masterpieces. In Japan, beauty is commonly defined by modest craft objects by unknown makers; works designed for the home rather than for public spectacle. Irregularly shaped pottery, for example, became the basis for Japanese tea ceremony.

The Kizaemon Ido tea bowl, originally made as a simple rice bowl, is considered by many the finest tea bowl in the world. It is a Japanese national treasure. *Wabi-sabi* is an aesthetic that celebrates irregularity, simplicity, timelessness, and humility, rather than symmetry, complexity, novelty and ambition.

Tellingly, there is no equivalent for the term *wabi-sabi* in any Western language. To give you an understanding of *wabi-sabi,* listen to the writing of Yanagi Soetsu, founder of the mingei "folk-craft" movement and writer of *The Unknown Craftsman:*

> For a long time I wished to see this Kizaemon bowl. I had expected to see that 'essence of Tea,' the seeing eye of Tea masters, and to test my own perception; for it is the embodiment in miniature of beauty, of the love of beauty, of the philosophy of beauty, and of the relationship of beauty and life. . . .
>
> When I saw it, my heart fell. A good Tea-bowl, yes, but how ordinary! So simple, no more ordinary thing could be imagined. There is not a trace or ornament, not a trace of calculation. It is just a Korean food bowl, a bowl, moreover, that a poor man would use everyday—commonest crockery.
>
> A typical thing for his use; costing next to nothing; made by a poor man; an article without the flavour of personality; used carelessly by its owner; bought without pride; something anyone could have bought anywhere and everywhere. That's the nature of this bowl. The clay had been dug from the hill at the back of the house; the glaze was made with the ash from the hearth; the potter's wheel had been irregular. The shape revealed no particular thought: it was one of many. The work had been fast; the turning was rough, done with dirty hands; the throwing slipshod; the glaze had run over the foot. The throwing room had been dark. The thrower could not read. The kiln was a wretched affair; the firing careless. Sand had stuck to the pot, but nobody minded; no one invested the thing with any dreams. It is enough to make one give up working as a potter. . . .

> But that is how it should be. The plain and unagitated, the
> uncalculated, the harmless, the straightforward, the natural, the
> innocent, the humble, the modest: where does beauty lie if not in
> these qualities? The meek, the austere, the un-ornate — they are
> the natural characteristics that gain man's affection and respect.[2]

Can you see the difference? In the West, we largely associate the word
beauty with things that have grandeur, complexity, transcendence. In Japan,
beauty is associated with the humble, the simple, and the ordinary. Perhaps,
like me, you may hear a whisper of Christian virtues in the embrace of this
sense of beauty. I think there is real wisdom in *wabi*, a wisdom we need to
hear in the West.

My work has been heavily influenced by the *wabi-sabi* aesthetic. It
was not so much an intellectual attraction as that it felt right. In many ways
I still try to find a way to bring that aesthetic into my work, and it shows
up in *Corpus* in the way I think about the materials I use. I am interested
in ordinary materials, ordinary objects, ordinary places, and ordinary rou-
tines. What makes something ordinary suddenly have great value? What
stories, what histories, what extraordinary beauty is there to be seen in the
ordinary, if we only have the patience, and the humility, to look carefully?
This is the mystery I seek through my artistic practice.

CONNECTION TO CHRISTIANITY

I find in an echo of the *wabi-sabi* aesthetic in a rather unexpected place:
Martin Luther's Heidelberg Disputation, Thesis 28. In this disputation Luther puts forth his "theology of the cross" which he contrasts with a "theology of glory." Thesis 28, the final thesis of the document, reads as follows:
"The love of God does not find, but creates, that which is pleasing to it. The
love of man comes into being through that which is pleasing to it."[3]

If you will allow me a little wiggle room in interpretation, if I flip the
two sentences and update the language a little, I get this: *Humans love things
they find already lovely,* that is to say the loveliness of the object creates the
love in us. That's an observation. *But God, in contrast, loves things that are
unlovely, and through his love 'makes' them lovely.* God transforms things
by loving them. Take a second to absorb that. That is a revelation. It is also,
I think, a challenge. If we take seriously our calling to be co-creators with

2. Souetsu, *Unknown Craftsman*, 191–92.
3. Luther, "Heidelberg Disputation," 57.

God, made in the image of God, what does this thesis say about the way we should approach the world? Even more so, I wonder what this says to me as an artist of faith; how I see the world, and how I understand beauty? Can I as an artist seek to work with materials and processes that are "un-lovely," common, or overlooked, and through my love of them, make them "lovely?"

MATERIAL AND PLACE

I hope you may be beginning to see now how I might think about vacuum debris as more than "filth." I have a personal story that is also relevant. When I was in college, I spent the better part of a summer selling vacuum cleaners door to door (I was not very good at it, and eventually gave up, not having sold a single vacuum). Anyway, it was my job to try to sweet talk my way into a house, vacuum a portion of the rug, and show the owners how much dirt I could get out of it, holding it out for them to see on a little white linen cloth. Of course, they were supposed to be startled by it, but I have to admit I found it fascinating. It was oddly beautiful. The dust and fibers told a story about place, about objects, about human activities. When I was in training, a veteran salesman I was paired with convinced a perspective buyer to let him vacuum their mattress. When he was done and pulled out the linen cloth, it had a small collection of something pale yellow and translucent in the middle of it. "Skin cells," he announced. Naturally, the customer was supposed to be disgusted by the revelation (and I think she was), but it was a kind of epiphany for me. I went home and tried it on my bed. It was amazing for me to think about how we leave bits of ourselves in the places we inhabit.

When I was asked to make a piece about the death and resurrection of Jesus for the college that experience came back to me. I realized that the vacuum debris could serve a dual purpose: it could both be a metaphor for our sins and it could also represent the way we as a community are grafted onto the body of Christ. Two Scripture verses became key references for the piece.

> For our sake he made him to be sin who knew no sin, so that in him we might become the righteousness of God (2 Cor 5:21 ESV).

> Now you are the body of Christ and individually members of it (1 Cor 12:27 ESV).

Still, I was not sure how to collect the debris. Should I just bring a vacuum and go to town? So I called Paul Dylan, head of custodial services at Wheaton College, and told him my idea. I suspect Paul has never gotten a more unusual phone call. "Hi Paul, this is David Hooker from the art department. Will you collect bags of vacuumed dirt for me? It's for an artwork." I wasn't sure what kind of response I would get, but Paul was immediately on board. He got eleven full vacuum bags for me. He even made sure to get them from different places from all over campus. In doing so he added something to the concept beyond my own imagining. In a way he, and by extension the rest of the custodial staff, with their ritualistic daily routine of cleaning the campus, became collaborators in the making of *Corpus*. I find that very gratifying and very humbling.

MATERIAL AND HISTORY

While the first reaction to the artwork is usually related to the debris on the surface, to me the specific Corpus—the antique statue underneath the debris—is just as significant. I knew instinctively that I wanted to work with an existing Corpus, or body of Christ, from a crucifix that had once been in a church. If I made the statue myself it wouldn't have the same impact. There were two main reasons for this: first, I didn't want to the work to become about me and my skill, rather I wanted the emphasis to be on the material. Secondly, I wanted the history. It is not enough that we see ourselves as connected to Christ in this place and time, but we also need to see ourselves as part of the larger body of Christ, extending well beyond Wheaton College, through time and space, standing with faithful witnesses all the way back to the very beginnings of the Early Church. Communing with the saints. There is no better way I can think of to do that than to use something from the past. You cannot fake history.

But this was also a problem. Tracking down a decommissioned corpus that was right for the project was not easy. It took a while to find one that was the right scale and with the right visual theology. And I wanted one that was as close to life-sized as possible, as it was going to hang low in the space, confronting the viewer face to face. Finally, I found one just outside of Kansas City owned by a small family-run company that salvaged decommissioned religious items from churches for resale.

When it arrived and I was able to examine it closely, I found that the history I was looking for was visible in ways I had not expected. I noticed an odd striped grey discoloration running the length of each arm. I was mentally debating if I should clean them or not when I realized what the stripes were. They were carbon marks from candles that had been placed at the foot of the cross. As such they were physical manifestations of people's prayers. Seeing that, and thinking about the meaning in that carbon, and thinking about the possibility of covering it, was powerful. It was not easy to do emotionally, but I ultimately felt it was the right thing. There is a powerful presence in the material, and in those prayers, which are still there, even though you cannot see them. Prayer is like that sometimes. Prayers also build on themselves, layer after layer, generation after generation. I am so glad those prayers are part of the piece, that material connection to the Communion of Saints.

ONGOING REVELATIONS

Working with the corpus, this figurative form of the body of Jesus, was also powerful, but in ways that I did not expect. I expected that the ritualistic act of covering the corpus; painting on a layer of adhesive, sifting on the debris, brushing off what did not stick, and repeating, building up multiple layers, would allow me to feel a deeper, visceral understanding of the humanity of Jesus. Most of the time I didn't. It was cold to the touch, so clearly plaster and not human, so that much of the time I was able to keep a kind of conceptual detachment. I thought I might feel a greater emotional connection at the head. Covering it with the debris as if pulling up a shroud, an announcement of death. But no. It was not the head, but the feet, surprisingly, that held the emotional charge. There is something about the feet that seemed more vulnerable, more intimate, more human, than the face. I'm not sure how to describe that exactly. While working I also became conscious of the biblical account of Mary anointing Jesus's feet with oil, and how my action, covering his feet with debris, was the exact opposite. I found my hands shaking. I had to stop working for about 20 minutes before I could continue. This was the visceral knowledge I was seeking, but perhaps more than I bargained for.

It may surprise you to know *Corpus* continues to reveal itself to me in new ways. While making the piece I felt more of the "Lenten" side of the concept, that is, the parts that are reminiscent of our sin and Christ's sacrifice for those sins. However, over time I am becoming more and more aware of the way the piece speaks to the "Easter" side of the equation. Some of this I intentionally hinted at by removing the cross and having the corpus seem to float in midair—a posture which I was hoping would seem more like a lifting up than a weighing down. But I am also more aware of the organic material in the debris, the skin cells and the hair, a metaphorical compost: fertilizer added to the soil to feed the next generation. In that way *Corpus* also reminds me of a passage in John 17, when during the High Priestly prayer Jesus prays for all people:

> My prayer is not for [the disciples] alone. I pray also for those who will believe in me through their message, that all of them may be one, Father, just as you are in me and I am in you (John 17: 20–21 NIV).

It was even revealed to me that the piece interacts with the cosmos in a way that was completely unexpected. My colleague John Walton, clearly an early riser, told me that the sunrise on the Autumnal Equinox sends a shaft of light down the hall that frames *Corpus* perfectly. The effect only lasts a couple of days each year. That sounded pretty awesome, but it turns out the event was much more glorious than I imagined. I am still not sure what to make of that, but I believe there is an invitation in there somewhere.[4]

4. Special thanks to Greg Halvorsen Schreck for this photo.

EMBRACING THE MYSTERY

We now come full circle, back to Dorothy Sayers, her model for creative process based on the Trinity, and the theme of this conference: why the humanity of Jesus matters. While I don't presume to have a perfect answer to that theological question, I think there is at least some insight available to us in Sayers' model.

In the past year it has struck me in a new way what it means to believe in the Trinity, in a God that is three in one. God is by nature relational, existing in perfect communion. This is a mystery beyond my capacity for understanding. As I reflect on the question of why the humanity of Jesus matters, I am struck by how I am always tempted to answer that question from my point of view, the point of view of the created, and not consider that question from the point of view of the Creator. What radical love is this, what radical communion, that invites the created into relationship with itself by becoming part of its own creation?

> Dear friends, let us love one another, for love comes from God. Everyone who loves has been born of God and knows God. Whoever does not love does not know God, because God is love. This is how God showed his love among us: He sent his one and only Son into the world that we might live through him. This is love: not that we loved God, but that he loved us and sent his Son as an atoning sacrifice for our sins. Dear friends, since God so loved us, we also ought to love one another. (1 John 4:7–11 NIV)

Amen

That Which was Testified to

History and the Humanity of Jesus

7

Bodies Transgressing Boundaries

in *Imitatio Christi*

GEORGE KALANTZIS
Wheaton College

"The body never lies"

– Martha Graham, *Blood Memory*

"The body never lies" is one of Martha Graham's (1894–1991) most oft-quoted aphorisms. Perhaps the greatest American dancer and choreographer of the twentieth century, Graham reshaped the art-form and inaugurated an unprecedented era of imagination and vitality. In her autobiography, *Blood Memory*, Graham describes her identity as a dancer in a way similar to how I propose we, too, ought to enter into our relationship with history, and indeed, Christianity itself: "Sometimes, it's blood memory that guides you—not the blood your mother and father gave you, which animates you now, but that which stretches back two or three thousand years. A movement comes to you, and suddenly, you realize this is a very, very serious thing—you are dealing with the past."[1]

1. Kriegsman, "Martha Graham Her Magical Muse."

Telling the stories of the past frames our present, informs our future, and makes us into the people we are: it's *blood memory*, indeed. But how do we tell the stories of the past? How do we remember our mothers and fathers, stretching two or three thousand years back? Storytelling is identity-formative. It forms the teller, it forms the hearer, but it also forms the very story itself. Every time we narrate, we enter a psycho-social transaction of power that forms us into the people we are—or, at least, into the people we wish to be. That is why *how* we tell "the story" is equally as important as *which* stories we choose to tell. As Palestinian poet Mourid Barghouti has famously said, "If you want to dispossess a people, the simplest way to do it is to tell their story and to start with, 'secondly.'"[2]

Take the history of monasticism, for example. It is customary to date the beginning of Egyptian monasticism to the life of St. Anthony who—as St. Athanasius, his biographer, says—was willing to sell all his possessions and depart for the desert. Heroic, pious, godly, worthy of imitation as Anthony's example may continue to be, this telling of the story usually leaves out one crucial detail: Anthony had a sister. Before he could pursue his monastic life, Anthony placed his sister in a *parthenion* (a place where virgins lived) where she eventually became the abbess. As Sister Lois Farag, notes, her name is never mentioned. "The account indicates that all decisions were made by Anthony. The nameless sister was the dutiful subject of those decisions." Farag continues: "There is no indication of her consent to such a decision. . . ."[3] And though

> monastic institutions for women were well established long before Anthony decided to go to the desert . . . monasticism is always dated from the beginning of Anthony's flight to the desert. Women's lives and spiritual activity do not count as the beginning of the spiritual movement of total devotion to God that came to be known as monasticism . . .
>
> This propensity of neglecting the stories of women persists in most narratives and is a major challenge to recording the story of women, including monastics, in history.[4]

Start with Basil of Caesarea and Gregory of Nyssa and not with Macrina, their sister, the theologian who influenced and guided both of her

2. Quote Adichie, "Danger of the Single Story."

3. Athanasius, *vita s. Antoni* 54: "And his sister grown old in virginity, and that she herself also was a leader of other virgins."

4. Farag, "Beyond Their Gender," 112–13.

brothers, and one ends up with a truncated understanding of asceticism or the knowledge of God permeating Cappadocian theology. Start with Augustine the bishop and not with Monica's influence on her son, and one will scarcely understand the persistent love of God of the *Theologian of the Heart*.

This is the danger of the self-formative "single story" that Nigerian author Chimamanda Ngozi Adichie has highlighted. The consequence of the single story, Adichie insists, is that "it robs people of dignity."[5] People become tropes. They disappear. They remain nameless; and mute.

Doing history well ought to begin with, "firstly." In the academic fields of inquiry and research, in patristics and early Christian studies, no less than in biblical studies, we are fortunate that there are some who have taken on the task of looking back into that memory that we call *History*, lifting up the names and the stories of those often marginalized and forgotten. Their scholarship helps us see the often overlooked protomartyrs, theologians, teachers, apostles, ascetics, and politicians of the early church, the dispossessed—usually women—whose stories animated the imagination of Christians for centuries and whose influence, authority, and legacy has been preserved in the literary and material record. This is not an easy task, for, "doing history well . . . is irreducibly a moral affair."[6]

BODIES AS SPECTACLE AND SYMBOL:
STORYTELLING IN TWO SCENES

Scene I: Amphithéâtre des Trois Gaules, Lugdunum (Lyons, France)—177–178 CE

In his *Ecclesiastical History* volume 1, Eusebius preserves a riveting account of a trial and execution, a martyrdom, that took place during the reign of Marcus Aurelius (177–178 CE) in Roman Gaul (modern France). Swept in one of the local pogroms that dotted their times, a group of Christians in the cities of Lyon and Vienne were arrested and brought to trial in front of the magistrate. Featured prominently in the account are the deacon Maturus, "a late convert," Attalus, who had "always been a pillar and a foundation," Sanctus, who "endured marvelously and superhumanly all the outrages which he suffered," and Blandina, a slave woman "through whom Christ

5. Adichie, "Danger of the Single Story."
6. Williams, *Why Study the Past?*, 24–25.

showed that what men think lowly God deems worthy of great glory." Following their trial, the condemned were brought to the arena where they were expected to yield under unimaginable torture. They were expected "to blush, to sweat, to show signs of fear and shame, bowing, scraping, and weeping to proclaim their repentance and remorse and to ask for forgiveness and life."[7] They were expected to renounce their faith, and to confess in public the prescribed words that attested to the supremacy of Rome, what the Stoic philosopher Seneca has described as the "recoil effect."[8] Yet, Blandina did not recoil:

> Blandina was filled with such power that those who tortured her from morning to night grew exhausted and admitted that they were beaten, for they had nothing left to do to her. They were astounded that she was still alive even though her whole body was smashed and cut open... But the blessed woman, like a noble athlete, gained strength while confessing the faith and found comfort for her sufferings by saying, 'I am a Christian and nothing wicked happens among us.' ...
>
> After their long ordeal, [the martyrs] were finally sacrificed, ... Blandina was hung on a stake and offered as food to the wild beasts that were let loose. *She appeared to be hanging in the shape of a cross,* (σταυροῦ σχήματι κρεμαμένη) *and her constant prayers greatly inspired her fellow athletes* (ἀγωνιζομένοις), *who saw the One who was crucified* (ἐσταυρωμένον) *for them in the form of their sister.* ... Small and weak and despised as she was, she had put on the great and invincible athlete: Christ.[9]

Scene II: Roman Amphitheater in Carthage, Tunis, Tunisia (203 CE)

A generation after Blandina, in 203 CE, in Carthage, on the North African side of the Great Sea, Vibia Perpetua, a young married woman and a mother from a good provincial family, was arrested along with her young slave girl, Felicity (who herself would give birth to a baby girl in the midst of their ordeal) and a number of their fellow Christians—many still catechumens. Eventually, after the customary interrogations by the local magistrate, they

---

7. Shaw, "Body/Power/Identity," 302–3.

8. Seneca, *Epistle* 14.4–6.

9. Eusebius, *Ecclesiastical History*, NPNF2 1.16–56, emphasis mine.

were all condemned to face the beasts and the gladiators because they refused to renounce their faith.

The first part of the account, known as the *Passio Perpetua et Felicitatis* was, purportedly, a diary written by Perpetua herself while in prison.
Through a series of charismatic visions that frame the ordeal, Perpetua
becomes increasingly conscious of a deep transformation. The vivid character and unexpected content of her interactions with the divine empower
Perpetua to break with conventional societal norms that were considered
natural for a Roman woman (mother, wife, daughter fully subordinated
to paternal authority, etc.) and move towards the ultimate expression of
her victory—perhaps even *virtue*—against the forces of evil. In the final
vision, right before her execution, Perpetua comes to reject any conception
of herself as a victim. She sees herself as a gladiator in the arena, facing a
"mighty Egyptian gladiator," a stand-in for Satan, as an equal. As she read-
ies herself to face her opponent, she is raised to her feet and is transformed:
"my clothes were ripped off, and suddenly I was a man" (10.7). And even
though it is as a *man* that Perpetua conquers the Egyptian, she is ultimately
recognized as her true self: "Then I walked up to the trainer and took the
branch [of the victor]. He kissed me and said to me: *'Peace be with you, my
daughter!'*" The trainer, of course, is God.

In her study of self-understanding and the narrative representations of the self as sufferer in early Christianity, Judith Perkins notes that:
"From the outset, Perpetua presents herself as an unruly woman, a woman
who refuses to bow to society's expectations. The unruly woman is a trope
often employed in texts 'to rehearse a hierarchical revolution.' Usually by
the text's closure, however, the woman has been put back in her place and
the gendered hierarchical system safely affirmed."[10] In the classical Greek
stories contemporary to the accounts of the Christian martyrs, "looking
at women is a male's privilege. Even for women themselves, being looked
at defines their place; in the classical Greek romances contemporary with
[these stories], women are presented as essentially passive, objects existing
for the male gaze."[11]

10. Perkins, *Suffering Self*, 105.
11. Perkins, *Suffering Self*, 112.

TAMING THE UNRULY WOMAN?

Like Blandina, Perpetua was a great woman, but a woman nonetheless. Blandina, Perpetua, Felicity, and the other women martyrs, were lauded to be great *because* they were women, and these actions were not expected of them. As women, Gail Streete argues, they were "doubly dead: [their] female flesh and [their] female gender are erased and only so can [they] be valued as male."[12] Streete reminds us that even though it may perhaps be irresistible "to applaud the depiction of Perpetua and Felicitas thrusting away social roles that define and confine them as women in a patriarchal society . . . we must also remember that these women are depicted as praiseworthy but 'unnatural': their actions are 'masculine,' and in the world of late antiquity, the home of emerging Christianity, manly women are no better than effeminate men."[13] As Sebastian Brock and Susan Harvey note of Syriac Christianity, accounts of female martyrs are stunning for the regularity with which they depict either "sexual mutilation" of "sexual violence" against women or the "transvestite motif," in which women "destroy their identity as women" and take on that of men:

> The sexual mutilation of women by torture and the sexual annihilation of women by the taking of the male identity are both about the same issue—namely, power and dominance in the relationship between men and women. And these events are found in hagiography about women, both legendary and historical. The events described in each given instance may or may not be true. But men are telling these stories to women as their audience and to men about women, and they tell them as if they were true. What are we to hear?[14]

Hanne Sigismund-Nielsen's careful analysis of the *Passio* has shown that there is an important point to be made in connection with Perpetua's transformation, namely that "Perpetua does not at any moment see herself as a *delicata* [a tender, delicate girl]. She sees herself as the daughter of God. As the daughter of God she can speak with God and interceded for her deceased brother."[15] It is the male narrator and redactor who takes over the narrative after the group leaves the prison for the arena, who speaks

12. Streete, *Redeemed Bodies*, 71.

13. Streete, *Redeemed Bodies*, 71.

14. Brock and Harvey, *Holy Women of the Syrian Orient*, 25.

15. Sigismund-Nielsen, "Vibia Perpetua—An Indecent Woman," 105–6.

of Perpetua as a *pulla delicata*—and this twice. I do not believe this was accidental. And it is the hand of the narrator that continues to emphasize not only the female bodies of the protagonists, "but also a female sensibility on Perpetua's part that is appropriate to an upper-class matron."[16] Right before they were to enter the arena, the Christians were ordered by their jailers to don the clothing of the priestesses of Ceres and reenact some pagan folklore for the entertainment of the crowd. Perpetua and Felicity refuse to do so and are stripped naked, forced to enter the arena dressed only in nets. The crowd "is aghast to note that one is a 'tender girl' [*puellam delicatam*] . . . : God's beloved is naked, as is Felicity, whose dripping breasts are also mentioned [for she had given birth only recently]. This exposure is even too much for shameless pagans,"[17] and the women are brought back and reclothed in simple, unbelted tunics. From that point on, the narrator presents Perpetua behaving appropriately to her "worldly and heavenly station," as a woman, a married woman, a *matrona*. She fastens up her ripped tunic to cover her thigh, *"thinking more of her modesty than of her pain,"* asks for a pin to fix her untidy hair: *"for it was not right that a martyr should die with her hair in disorder, lest she might seem to be mourning in her hour of triumph,"* and finally dies in a classically feminine way: *"She screamed as she was struck on the bone; then she took the trembling hand of the young gladiator and guided it to her throat,"* the woman's "weak spot."

What is unusual in the *Passio* and the *Acts of Lyons and Vienne*, however, is that the "unruly women," the *patrona* Perpetua, and the slave girls Felicity and Blandina, have not been put back in their hierarchical place: society's power was not affirmed, like the classical stories that preceded them, but rather it was the very concept of *power* itself that was radically reinterpreted. When we pay attention to their *own* voices, we see that these women defy cultural objectification. And even though it strains credulity to imagine that someone like Perpetua, who was unafraid to face down both the Roman magistrate and the towering Egyptian gladiator had gone to her death in a fit of prudery, these women are represented as acting agents until the very end—even appointing their own death.

From the period of the Christian tradition, the accounts of the martyrs are almost sacramental in character, rich sacrificial narratives that reject the dominant religio-political paradigm and reinterpret assumed

16. Streete, *Redeemed Bodies*, 70.
17. Streete, *Redeemed Bodies*, 70.

perceptions of power dynamics.[18] Martyrdom was a baptism of blood that brought forgiveness of sins to the martyr,[19] and a Eucharist, in which one drank the cup of sufferings of Christ (Matt 20:22). Paul had also spoken of the redemptive role of suffering for the faith in his letter to the church in Philippi (Phil 3:10–11)[20] and again in 2 Cor 4:8–10: "*We are* afflicted in every way, but not crushed; perplexed, but not driven to despair; persecuted, but not forsaken; struck down, but not destroyed; *always carrying in the body the death of Jesus, so that the life of Jesus may also be made visible in our bodies.*" The martyrs were filled by the Holy Spirit, who gave them words to say to the authorities and to each other, visions of heaven, and supernatural strength to endure sufferings.[21]

This was a realized eschatology in which the martyr participated already in the events of the eschaton. In place of a sacrifice of incense and grain demanded by the State (as signs of the loyalty expected from those living under the protection of the gods who promised *Roma aeterna)*, the Christian martyrs offered an alternative sacrifice that rejected these illusory claims and guaranteed true eternal life: they offered themselves. In imitation of Christ (1 Cor 11:1).[22]

TAMING THE UNRULY GOD?

For martyrdom to be—not only to be seen to be—in *imitatio Christi*, Christians have to hold fast to the confession that the first body to transgress our boundaries was that of God the Son, the Word of God who became one of us: "*And the Word became flesh and lived among us*" (John 1:14). The story of Jesus is the unusual story of the *unruly* God, through whom society's gestures of dominance and claims of power are not affirmed but rather

18. *E.g. M. Polycarp* 12; *Acts of the Scillitan Martyrs*, 3–4. Also, Tertullian, *Apology* 10 says that the chief charge against Christians was that they refused to sacrifice. Cf. Kalantzis, *Caesar and the Lamb*, 21–34.

19. Ignatius, *Romans*, 5–6; also, Tertullian, *On Baptism*, 16.

20. Tertullian, *C. Marcion* 4.39.5, followed the same principle when he presented martyrdom as atonement for sin.

21. Matt 10:19; Mark 13:11; Luke 12:11–12. See, for example, Perpetua's account of her visions in "Passio Sanctarum Perpetua et Felicitatis," 3–9.

22. Jacob, "Le Martyre, épanouissement," 57–83, 153–72, 177–209; Ferguson, "Spiritual Sacrifice in Early Christianity and its Environment," 1169–70, 1180, 1186. Also, *M. Dasius.* 5.2; *M. Polycarp* 14; *M. Conon* 6.7; *M. Felix the Bishop.* 30. See also, Ignatius's letter *To Polycarp*, 3.1–2.

radically reinterpreted. Through the story of Jesus in the New Testament, the world "as is" is subverted and set upside down.

Yet, as the story of Jesus is told and retold, as Roman society becomes Christianized, the secular becomes sacred and the sacred secular, the old values, the old gods, are reasserted, and there is no room for this unruly God. The result is the transformation of a *religio*, the communal "binding together" of the people of God into *Platonized* eschatologies, *moralized* anthropologies, and inevitably *paganized* soteriologies (to use N. T. Wright's tripartite lament).[23] And Jesus becomes mythologized. Ethereal, an Idea, a symbol, or worse yet, a transaction.

This domestication, this taming of the unruly God in Christ has led us to a place that is far removed from the genuinely biblical notions of the revolutionary kingdom of God. For it moves us far away from the one *"who in every respect has been tested as we are"* (Heb 4:15), the one who *"bore our sins on his body"* that *"we might live"* (1 Pet 2:24).

An axiomatic first principle in the Christian story is that *quod non est assumptum non est sanatum*.[24] It is axiomatic because it changes everything. The physical, particular, actual body of this Jewish man, Jesus, Mary's baby, changed everything. Jesus's body healed ours—and it also healed our embodied relationships. Don't miss the *sanatum* in the axiom above: because of Jesus, the old values of male and female are healed and reoriented. As theologian Cherith Fee Nordling so often reminds us, "In Jesus we get our bodies back!" It is in Jesus that we are able to be truly women, truly men, truly Jews, and truly Greeks (Gal 3:28), not having to morph into the other in order to be seen or have value. That "dividing wall of hostility" that frames our experiences with one another, the power polarities and binaries that define our relationships, has been broken down "in his flesh" (Eph 2:14). With St. Athanasius we can assert that because the Word of God became human (ἐνηνθρώπησεν), because he assumed our human nature for his own, we can now become partakers of divine nature (2 Pet 1:4), albeit as creatures. "For we were the purpose of his embodiment, and for our salvation he so loved human beings as to come to be and appear in a human body."[25]

---

23 Wright, *Day the Revolution Began*, 147.

24. Meaning, "whatever [part of our humanity] is not assumed [by Christ during the Incarnation] is not healed."

25. Athanasius, *On the Incarnation*, 4.

In this season of Lent, as we approach Easter Sunday, we cannot forget that the descriptions, the narratives of the Gospels are stories, stories about bodies, *bodies* as spectacle and symbols. Jesus's story is about bodies. He was born, to an actual woman. I wonder, did Mary hurt during childbirth? Did her back ache during the pregnancy? Did she have morning sickness? Or get up umpteen times at night to go to the bathroom during the last trimester? Did Mary comfort Jesus when he was crying at night as "she treasured all these words and pondered them in her heart" (Luke 2:19)? Jesus ate and grew up, "he increased in years" not just simply "in wisdom and . . . in divine and human favor" (Luke 2:52). Did Jesus suffer from dysentery, like his neighbors? Were his hands callused and scared from manual work? Was there dirt under his fingernails? What did Jesus smell like?

In his *Commentary on the Gospel of John*, Theodore, the bishop of Mopsuestia (ca. 350–428 CE) gives us a most moving reading of Jesus's visit to the home of his friends, Martha, Mary, and Lazarus in John 12: "As usual, they welcomed Him with great enthusiasm, and they were preparing supper and Martha was serving. Lazarus, in the meantime, was reclining with Him. '*Mary took a pound of costly perfume made of pure nard, anointed Jesus' feet, and wiped them with her hair. The house was filled with the fragrance of the perfume. But Judas Iscariot, one of his disciples (the one who was about to betray him), said, 'Why was this perfume not sold for three hundred denarii and the money given to the poor?'* Instead of accusing the woman of wastefulness, Judas ought to have been impressed by her faith, for by wiping the feet of the Lord with her own hair she hoped that the smell of his body would cling to her own flesh, yearning, somehow, to preserve his scent even when he was not there."[26]

What did Jesus smell like? Ask Mary.

---

26. Theodore of Mopsuestia, *Comm. on John*. 102, XII.3; adapted from Kalantzis, *Theodore of Mopsuestia*, 96–97.

8

Astonishing Fulfillment

Irenaeus and Origen on the Humanity of Christ

BRIAN E. DALEY, SJ
University of Notre Dame

It is almost a truism that Christian faith is based on a paradox: the stunning proclamation that "God is with us." For virtually all forms of religion, the prime object of faith and veneration is assumed to be what philosophers call a "transcendent" reality: a Being beyond being who is the source of all other beings—for Biblical traditions this is God, the invisible and ultimately unknowable creator and constant guide of the world and its history, who has spoken to humanity through chosen servants, and has formed a special people to seek him and represent him on earth. Yet since the first century, Christian disciples have, with increasing clarity, proclaimed that Jesus of Nazareth, their ultimate prophet, was not simply a man inspired by this God to announce God's coming kingdom, but that he *was*, at the core of his reality, a constituent part of what we mean by God; that his identity was to be God's eternal, invisible, creative Word, who, in the person of Jesus, has "become flesh and dwelt among us" (John 1:1–2, 14–18). Like all paradoxes, this proclamation seems to be self-contradictory, yet Christian preaching and theology largely rest upon it.

In the first few centuries of Christianity, this affirmation of the Incarnation of the Son, or Word, of God was regarded by many outside Christianity, like the Platonist philosopher Celsus, as the root absurdity of this new, hybrid religious movement. "Gnostic" versions of the Christian message, too, began to proliferate: revisionist versions of the Christian narrative that claimed that Jesus revealed to a select few a further, more ultimate message. This was that the present world, including our own physical existence, is the result of a cosmic mistake, or a series of cosmic deceptions, that took place long before the biblical story began; and that salvation from our misery comes only to those enlightened few who have managed to learn "the real story," and who can simply disregard the world's history and physicality as irrelevant to long-term human welfare. Some have argued that the ancient gnostic urge to seek our salvation in an "insider's" escape from the harsh facts of existence remains the driving force behind American religion.[1] We want to know the truth, so we can manage it, and sometimes we seek it in our own fictions.

Much of the driving force behind early Christian development of an outline for what constitutes genuine faith developed out of the intuition that such gnostic versions of the church's narrative were radically mistaken; instead, early Christian theologians attempted to set the paradox of God's meeting us in time—of the "Word made flesh"—in terms that would work out its implications without emptying the gospel message of its unique challenge.

Two thinkers, from the end of the second and the beginning of the third century, who left a deep and lasting influence on how we think of the man Jesus as God were Irenaeus of Lyon and Origen of Alexandria: both Greek speakers from the eastern part of the Roman empire, both well-trained in the traditional disciplines of classical learning, and both heavily engaged in communicating an understanding of the Christian faith to adults of ordinary background. Despite their similarities of time and education, however, they approached the underlying Christian paradox in quite different ways; their very differences can be instructive for us as we continue to struggle with the same problems.

---

1. See, for instance, Bloom, *American Religion*.

I. IRENAEUS

The best-known early critic of gnostic Christianity, and perhaps the first Christian writer to attempt to oppose those gnostic systems systematically and at length, was certainly Irenaeus of Lyons. A native of Smyrna, a city on the west coast of Asia Minor with an ancient Christian community, Irenaeus seems to have had a thorough and traditional education in rhetoric, and probably also knew the Greek philosophical tradition well. For unknown reasons, he migrated west after the death of his friend and local bishop Polycarp in the mid-150s; he apparently spent some time in Rome, and eventually settled in the Gallic city of Lyons, on the Rhone near the frontier of the empire, where the growing Christian community probably included many Greek-speaking *émigrés* like himself. Among them, there were also probably a variety of gnostic sectarians and teachers. Irenaeus seems to have become bishop of Lyons, after the death of his aged predecessor Pothinus, in the persecution of Marcus Aurelius in 177, and to have lived until early in the third century. His writings probably come from this final quarter-century of his life.

In his monumental refutation of the major gnostic interpretations of Jesus and his message, his five books *Against the Heresies* (or "sects"), Irenaeus unequivocally insists that the Son and Word of God, who shares God's being and role as the source and fulfillment of all else that is, truly and fully became a human being. In doing this, God the Son set right what had gone amiss, sharing and—as Irenaeus so characteristically puts it— "recapitulating" in his own story our human history since Adam. He writes, near the beginning of his synthetic treatment of the person of Christ in Book III, that Jesus of Nazareth is not called "the Christ" because a heavenly figure from some primordial cosmic family, called "the Christ," descended on him at his baptism, as some of the gnostic teachers suggested, but because his very identity as both divine and human, as Son of God and son of Mary, "anointed" or spiritually dedicated him to bring history to its climax.

> There is, therefore, as I have pointed out, one God the Father, and one Christ Jesus, who came by means of the whole dispensation, . . . and gathered together all things in himself. But in every respect, too, he is human, the formation (*plasma*) of God; and thus he took up humanity into himself, the invisible becoming visible, the incomprehensible being made comprehensible, the impassible

becoming capable of suffering, and the Word being made human, thus summing up all things in himself. . . .[2]

For Irenaeus, as he often repeats, this clearly implies that God the Son became what we are, taking on himself real human flesh in a way that "sums up" the whole story of human existence on earth:

> For if he did not receive the substance of flesh from a human being, he was neither made human nor [was he] Son of man; and if he was not made what we are, he did nothing great in what he suffered and endured. But everyone will agree that we are [composed of] a body taken from the earth and a soul that receives spirit from God. This, therefore, the Word of God was made, recapitulating in himself his own handiwork; and for this reason he confesses that he is the Son of Man. . . .[3]

The purpose of this historical arrangement of events or "dispensation [oikonomia]" was clearly that God might save fallen and alienated humanity, even give our race a new start.

> For unless humanity had overcome the enemy of humanity, the enemy would not have been legitimately vanquished. And again: unless it had been God who had freely given salvation, we could never have possessed it securely. And unless a man had been joined to God, he could never have become a partaker in incorruptibility. . . . For it behooved him who was to destroy sin and redeem humanity, which was under the power of death, that he should himself be made that very thing which it was: that is, a human being . . . so that sin should be destroyed by a human being, and humanity should go forth from death.[4]

The goal of the whole plan, in fact, was nothing less than "the promotion of human nature into God,"[5] a process of hoped-for identification

2. Irenaeus, *Against the Heresies* [= AH], III, 16.6 (ANF 1:442–43 [alt.]).

3. Irenaeus, AH, III, 22.1 (Roberts and Donaldson 454 [alt.]). Here as elsewhere, Irenaeus suggests that the human person, on his or her own, consists of body and rational soul; "spirit," the other human component referred to in Scripture (e.g., 1 Thess 5:23), he normally takes to mean the Holy Spirit: given by God as primordial grace, and received by the created soul for his or her salvation, but not strictly a part of human nature. Nevertheless, the human person or "Adam" was created, Irenaeus argues, with the incarnate Christ in view, "that the first man, of animal nature [i.e., body and rational soul] . . . might be saved by the spiritual one" (AH, III, 22.3).

4. AH, III, 18.7 (Roberts and Donaldson 448 [alt.]).

5. AH, III, 19.1 (Roberts and Donaldson 448 [alt.]).

of creature with creator which already, at the end of the second century, anticipates the classical Eastern Christian hope for "divinization."[6]

To bring this process about, Irenaeus argues, the incarnate Son of God must communicate to his human brothers and sisters some share in God's own qualities: incorruptible life, a share in that radiant beauty of the divine Being that Irenaeus characteristically—and perhaps mysteriously—refers to as God's *glory*. God's glory is revealed to creatures especially through the gift and the promise of Christ's human existence. Irenaeus writes:

> The glory of the human creature is God, but the human person is the recipient of God's activity, and of all his wisdom and power.[7] Just as a physician is proved by his patients, so is God also revealed through human beings. . . . For anyone who holds, without pride or boasting, the true opinion regarding created things and the Creator, who is the almighty God of all . . . shall also receive from him the greater glory of promotion (*provectus*), looking forward to the time when he shall become like the One who died for him . . .[8]

Irenaeus goes on, in a famous passage in *Against the Heresies* IV, 20, where he speaks of the transforming effect on the human creature of seeing God's beauty, to identify the revelation of this vision as the main purpose of the incarnation of God the Son:

> For the human creature does not see God by his own powers, but when God pleases he is seen by humans: by whom he wills, and when he wills, and as he wills. For God is powerful in all things; having once been seen proleptically through the Spirit,[9] and seen too adoptively through the Son, he shall be seen paternally in the Kingdom of heaven, the Spirit truly preparing us in the Son of God, and the Son leading us to the Father, while the Father confers upon us incorruption for eternal life, . . . which comes to everyone from the fact of seeing God. . . . Those who see God are in God,

---

6. See the preface to book V of *Against the Heresies*, which boldly ends by speaking of "the Word of God, our Lord Jesus Christ, who did, through his transcendent love, become what we are, that he might bring us to be what he is himself" (AH, 528).

7. My translation of the Latin text: "Gloria enim hominis Deus; operationis vero Dei et omnis sapientiae eius et virtutis receptaculum homo" (AH, III, 20.2). The Roberts and Donaldson translation is puzzlingly incomplete here.

8. AH, III, 20.2.

9. Presumably in the prophetic visions of the old covenant.

and receive of his splendor; but his splendor vivifies them. Those, therefore, who see God receive life.[10]

Earlier in this same important chapter, echoing the Johannine Apocalypse, Irenaeus identifies the revelation of God the Father as the reason for the Son's becoming human and sharing God's life-giving glory with us:

> For no one was able, either in heaven or on earth or under the earth, to open the book of the Father, or to behold him, with the exception of the Lamb who was slain and who redeemed us with his own blood, receiving power over all things . . . that even as the Word of God had the sovereignty in the heavens, so also he might have the sovereignty on earth . . . : that all things, as I have said, might behold their King, and that the paternal light might meet with and rest upon the flesh of our Lord, and come to us from his resplendent flesh, and that thus the human person might attain to immortality, having been invested with the paternal light.[11]

Christ, as God's creative Word made flesh, now gloriously raised from the dead, reveals to angels and humans God's paternal love and power. That vision of God in a human form, speaking to us in human words, itself confers this immortality.

Irenaeus gives the reason a few chapters earlier in this same Book IV:

> The Father has revealed himself to all by making his Word visible to all, and conversely, the Word has declared to all the Father and the Son, since he has become visible to all. . . .[12] For by means of the creation itself, the Word reveals God the Creator; and by means of the world he declares the Lord the maker of the world. . . . But by the law and the prophets the Word preached both himself and the Father; and all heard him, but not all believed. And through the Word himself, who had been made visible and palpable, the Father was shown forth, although all did not equally believe in him; but all saw the Father in the Son. For the Father is the invisible of the Son, but the Son is the visible of the Father.[13]

In these and many similar passages of the *Adversus Haereses*, Irenaeus communicates the main point of his argument against gnostic Christianity:

---

10. AH, IV, 20.5.

11. AH, IV, 20.

12. Irenaeus seems to mean here that the relationship of Father and Son, and ultimately the whole saving Mystery of the Trinity, is revealed only by the Incarnation.

13. AH, IV, 6.5–6 (Roberts and Donaldson 468–69 [alt]).

that the salvation of the human race from its historic alienation from its creator is achieved not simply by learning a new way to understand the world, but by entering into a new, life-giving relationship with God that is based on our human sharing in the filial relationship of the Incarnate Son, Jesus, with his eternal Father. Salvation comes through our seeing God's glory, God's radiant being, now humanized, and in that very vision sharing the Sonship of our brother Jesus. Those who reject such a direct relationship to the divine glory . . .

> defraud human nature of promotion (*provectus*) into God, and prove themselves ungrateful to the Word of God, who became flesh for them. For it was for this end that the Word of God was made human, and he who was the Son of God became Son of man, that the human person, having been taken into the Word and receiving adoption, might become the son of God. For by no other means could we have attained to incorruptibility and immortality, unless we had been united to incorruptibility and immortality. But how could we be joined to incorruptibility and immortality, unless first incorruptibility and immortality had become that which we also are. . . .[14]

Putting his point more briefly later in Book IV, Irenaeus suggests that although God has always revealed himself and realized his creative and saving purpose through his Word and his Spirit, whom he calls God's two "hands," now, "in the last times, [the Word] was made human among humans, that he might join the end to the beginning—that is, humanity to God."[15]

Characteristic of Irenaeus, however, is the recognition that this fulfillment of God's purpose has not taken place all at once: that even if God had foreknown and intended the unity of his creatures with himself always, still creatures needed to be prepared for their salvation gradually, pedagogically. Even the Incarnation itself is but the penultimate stage in the union of God and humanity. "The Word of God, who dwelt in men and women . . . , became the Son of man, that he might accustom humans to receive God, and God to dwell in them, according to the good pleasure of the Father."[16] For Irenaeus, the growth of the human race toward the fulfillment of God's purpose in creating us is, at its heart, a gradual process: not because God

14. AH, III, 19.1 (Roberts and Donaldson 448–49 [alt.]).

15. AH, IV, 20.4 (Roberts and Donaldson 488 [alt.]).

16. AH, III, 20.2 (Roberts and Donaldson 450 [alt]).

lacks power to realize his intentions, but because humans were initially unable to grasp and hold the gift that is promised.

> It was possible for God himself to have made the human person perfect from the first [Irenaeus argues at the end of Book IV], but the human could not receive this, being as yet an infant. And for this reason our Lord, in these last times, when he had summed up all things in himself, came to us not as he might have come, but as we were capable of beholding him. . . .
>
> For the Uncreated is perfect: that is, God. Now it was necessary that the human being should in the first instance be created; and having been created, should receive growth; and having received growth, should be strengthened; and having been strengthened, should abound; and having abounded, should recover [from sin]; and having recovered, should be glorified; and having been glorified, should see his Lord. For God is he who is yet to be seen, and the beholding of God produces immortality, but immortality renders one close to God. . . .[17]

Because God is infinite, full union with him always lies to some extent in the future for finite creatures, however filled with faith and hope they may be. So time, history, and human growth are central dimensions of Irenaeus's conception of salvation; and the historical humanity of Jesus, although it is the summit of the way God has chosen to unite the human race with himself, must itself be gradually recognized within the world's history, must even "recapitulate"—sum up and repair—the stages of that history, if it is to be effective at all.

II. ORIGEN

A younger contemporary of Irenaeus, Origen was born in the great cultural center of Alexandria around 185—the same time that Irenaeus seems to have begun composing his massive refutation of gnostic Christianity. Like Irenaeus, Origen had received a high-level education in grammar, rhetoric, and Platonist philosophy; like Irenaeus, too, he was keenly aware of the challenge posed to the church's faith by the current gnostic reinterpretation of the biblical message and of the person of Jesus. But although he was himself highly sophisticated philosophically, Origen's life-work came to be centered more and more on the public interpretation of the Christian

---

17. AH, IV, 38.1–3 (Roberts and Donaldson 521–22 [alt.]).

Scriptures: on developing and using a method for understanding and preaching the scriptural message that would be consistent with—and ultimately formative of—the faith of the whole community.

In the chapter of his treatise *On First Principles*, that deals most explicitly with the central Mystery of the Incarnation of the Word, Origen begins by emphasizing Christ's mediating position between creatures and the transcendent God. Almost immediately, however, he goes on to register, with surprisingly deep feeling, his amazement that this mediation involves Christ's full, personal participation in both those realms of reality. He writes:

> Of all the marvelous and splendid things about him there is one that utterly transcends the limits of human wonder and is beyond the capacity of our weak mortal intelligence to think of or understand, namely, how this mighty power of the divine majesty, the very Word of the Father and the very Wisdom of God, in which were created 'all things visible and invisible' (Col 1:16), can be believed to have existed within the compass of that man who appeared in Judea; yes, and how the wisdom of God can have entered into a woman's womb and been born as a little child and uttered noises like crying children; and further, how it was that he was troubled, as we are told, in the hour of death. . . .
>
> When, therefore, we see in him some things so human that they appear in no way to differ from the common frailty of mortals, and some things so divine that they are appropriate to nothing else but the primal and ineffable nature of deity, the human understanding, with its narrow limits, is so baffled, and struck with such amazement at so mighty a wonder, it knows not which way to turn, what to hold on to, or where to betake itself. If it thinks of God, it sees a human being; if it thinks of a human being, it beholds him returning from the dead with spoils, after vanquishing the kingdom of death. For this reason, we must pursue our contemplation with all fear and reverence, as we seek to prove how the reality of each nature exists in one and the same individual.[18]

---

18. Origen, *On First Principles* II, 6.2 (Butterworth 109 [alt.]). Origen's treatise *On First Principles*, written around 230–31, as he was preparing to move from Alexandria to Caesarea in Palestine, seems to be a formal exposition of the contents of the Church's "rule of faith," derived from the Bible but expressed in simple statements, which Origen presents (in Book IV of the work) as the hermeneutical framework for interpreting the whole Bible in an authentically Christian sense. See my article, "Origen's *De Principiis*."

Origen situates the paradox of Jesus's existence, then, precisely in his role as mediator between the transcendent being of God—the source, sustainer, and goal of all finite things—and God's creation itself. God's Word and Wisdom, eternally generated in a non-material way, dwells in created souls in proportion to their merit and their commitment to the Good.[19] As God's Word and invisible image (see esp. Col 1:16), the Son communicates to rational creatures—angels and human souls—"a participation in himself (and so in the divine life) . . . proportionate to the loving affection with which [that creature] had clung to him."[20] So it became possible, in Origen's view, in the age before cosmic creation, for the personified Word and Wisdom of the transcendent God to be, by exclusive participation, a single agent with a human being; the soul of Jesus—created, Origen supposes, like all spiritual beings, before the existence of a material world[21]—was always united to the Word by love and desire, making it functionally (if not strictly ontologically) one with the Word, capable, precisely as a soul, eventually of being embodied in matter as well. He conjectures, in the same passage of *De Principiis*, that the soul of the one we know as Christ,

> clinging to God from the beginning of creation and ever after, in a union inseparable and indissoluble, being the soul of the wisdom and word of God and of the truth and the true light, and receiving him wholly and itself entering into his light and splendor, was made with him in a pre-eminent degree one spirit. . . . This substance of a soul, then, acting as a medium between God and the flesh (for it was not possible for the nature of God to mingle with a body apart from some medium), is born, as we have said, as the God-man; that substance existed as the medium, to which it is surely not against nature to take on a body.[22]

For Origen, as this passage shows, it is essential to have an ontological scheme of spiritual mediation between God and the created world if we are to grasp the full meaning of the humanity of Christ. And to see that mediation as realized precisely in Jesus's created soul, which can enter into genuine spiritual unity with other beings freely, through love, seems to have provided him with the answer. He writes:

---

19. Origen, *On First Principles*, IV, 4.1–2.
20. Origen, *On First Principles*, II, 6. 3 (trans Butterworth 110 [alt.]).
21. Origen, *On First Principles*, I, 4–5; II. 9.
22. Origen, *On First Principles*, II, 6.3 (Butterworth 110 [alt.]).

> It cannot be doubted that the nature of his soul was the same as
> that of all souls; otherwise it could not be called a soul, if it were
> not truly one. But since the ability to choose good or evil is within
> the immediate reach of all, this soul which belonged to Christ so
> chose to 'love righteousness' as to cling to it unchangeably and
> inseparably in accordance with the immensity of its love. . . . Thus
> we must believe that there did exist in Christ a human and rational
> soul, and yet not suppose that it had any susceptibility or possibil-
> ity of sin.[23]

In his free and unwavering desire to "love justice and hate iniquity," in
the words of Psalm 45 (44), the soul of Jesus was, before the creation of the
material world, united irrevocably and freely to God, the absolute Good;
and like a lump of iron placed in the fire, it glows so steadily with a light
and heat that is not strictly its own, that it comes to be seen as naturally
transformed.[24] In practical terms, Jesus's soul is both divine and human. It
is the mediator between these totally disparate realms.

It is by our imitation of Christ, who is both God and a human being,
that we, too, can freely walk the way that leads us to endless and loving
union with God. Christ reveals our own fulfillment to us, calls us to imitate
him, and in this way becomes, by his very position in the world, the proof
and effective force of God's salvation. Origen writes:

> This is why Christ is set forth as an example to all believers, be-
> cause as he ever chose the good, even before he knew evil at all
> . . . , so, too, should each one of us, after a fall or a transgression,
> cleanse himself from stains by the example set before us, and tak-
> ing a leader for the journey proceed along a steep path of virtue, so
> that perchance by this means we may, as far as possible, become,
> through our imitation of him, "partakers of the divine nature" (2
> Pet 1:4).[25]

And Origen conceives of our individual contact with Christ and love
for him, as the ensouled and incarnate Word of God, often in very concrete,
even physical terms. In an almost casual remark in the first book of his
Commentary on John, for instance, Origen underlines the unique depth
of insight into the person of the Savior conveyed in the Fourth Gospel by

23. Origen, *On First Principles,* II, 6.5 (Butterworth 112–13 [alt.]).

24. Origen, *On First Principles,* II, 6.5; see below, for Origen's use of the same image
in *Homilies on Leviticus* I, 4 (SChr 286.82).

25. Origen, *On First Principles*, IV, 4.4 (Butterworth 319 [alt.]).

insisting that "the Gospels are the first-fruits of all the Scriptures, but of the Gospels, that of John is the first-fruits. No one can apprehend the meaning of it, unless he has lain on Jesus' breast and received from Jesus Mary to be his mother also."[26] In other words, to understand John's Gospel, one must make personal contact with Jesus, as the beloved disciple did; one must "become another John, and have shown to him, like John, by Jesus himself, Jesus as he is."[27]

In his fourth *Homily on Leviticus*, commenting on the "cereal offerings" of the Levitical tradition, which only the "sons of Aaron" may eat— because "anyone who touches [these offerings] shall become holy" (Lev 6:18), and so ritually set apart—Origen suggests that the same mysterious, sanctifying power inheres in the flesh of Christ, which the Son took on in order to be sacrificed for us. "Whoever touches the flesh of this sacrifice," Origen remarks, "will be made holy immediately if he is unclean, will be healed if he has any disease." He continues:

> So the woman understood, who 'suffered from the flow of blood,' that he was himself the flesh of sacrifice, and that his flesh was the 'holy of holies'; and because she truly understood that his flesh was the 'holy of holies,' she therefore drew near him. And she did not dare touch that holy flesh—for she had not yet been cleansed, nor had she laid hold of what is perfect (see Phil 3:12)—but she 'touched the fringe of his garment,' with which his flesh was covered, and by her faith-filled touch she drew forth power from his flesh, which sanctified her from her uncleanness and healed her from the illness from which she suffered. . . . If anyone, as we have said, should touch the flesh of Jesus in that way that we have just explained—should draw close to Jesus in full faith and complete obedience, as to the Word made flesh—he has touched 'the flesh of sacrifice' and has been made holy.[28]

To "touch the flesh of Christ" and experience its cleansing power as the "flesh of sacrifice," in other words, one need not make actual physical contact, but must simply grow close to him in faith, know who he really is, and follow him.

---

26. Origen, *Commentary on John*, 1.6 (300).

27. Origen, *Commentary on John*, 1.6 (300). A profound study of Origen's characteristic emphasis on the importance for salvation of our affectionate contact with the human Jesus remains Bertrand, *Mystique de Jésus chez Origène*.

28. Origen, *Homilies on Leviticus* IV, 8 (SChr 286.188–90).

Origen refers also to this same encounter when he turns, in his *Fifteenth Homily on the Gospel of Luke*, to the scene of the presentation of the infant Jesus in the temple, and describes the child's meeting there with Simeon and Anna. The aged Simeon's contact with Jesus, Origen points out, was even more direct and intimate than that of the woman with the hemorrhage.

> If she derived such profit from simply touching the end of his garment, what should we think about Simeon, who 'took the infant to his bosom" and held him in his arms with joy and gladness, seeing that the child who was being carried by him had come to release prisoners, and would set him free from the bonds of his body, knowing that no one could free anyone from the prison of the body with a hope for eternal life except the one whom he held in his arms.
>
> So [Simeon] says to him: "Now, Lord, let your servant go in peace; for as long as I did not hold Christ, as long as I did not press him in my arms, I was locked in prison and could not escape from my chains." This should be understood not only of Simeon, but of humans of every kind. If anyone will "depart in peace" from this world, if anyone will be released from prison and from the place where we are held chained, to come to share in the Kingdom, let him take Jesus in his hands and wrap him in his arms, let him take him completely into his bosom. Then he will be able to go rejoicing wherever he will.[29]

Origen's point in these reflections is certainly to draw out the powerful implications of the imagery of the Gospels for personal meditation on Christ's importance in the believer's release from what holds him or her captive. Central here, too, however, is his stress on the full humanity of Christ as the channel through which the dynamic, healing energy of God reaches each of us in our need and transforms us, if we earnestly reach out to him.

Jesus, in the anthropological scheme elaborated in *De Principiis*, is first of all a preexistent created soul, who remains so uniquely faithful to its creator, the divine Word, that it alone is not separated by the primal fall of creatures from God. As a soul, however, Jesus too is capable of being united with flesh or embodied, as well as united with God by contemplation and love. So Jesus takes on a body in the material world, as other, "fallen" souls have, in order to communicate to the others, by human means, his own

29. Origen, *Homilies on Luke*, 15.1–2 (178–80).

vision and love of the transcendent God. And it is through contact with Jesus as a complete human being—through drawing near and "touching" his flesh, as well as forming a conscious friendship with his soul—that the rest of humanity learns of God's saving activity, and is able to embrace it.

III. COMPARING IRENAEUS AND ORIGIN

How can we compare the role of Christ's humanity in the versions of the Christian story of salvation offered by these two giants of early Christian theological synthesis? Both of them, as we have mentioned, lived at a time when revisionist, "gnostic" retellings of the church's gospel narrative— a term both of them used without hesitation to designate the version of Christianity they opposed[30]—presented the most immediate challenge to mainstream Christian faith. "Gnostic" groups like the Valentinians (on the less obviously radical side), the Ophites, or the Sethians, claimed to be able to draw on an intellectualizing imagination and to set the Christian gospel in the context of an esoteric "back-story" of creation, fall, and redemption that shifted the blame for our alienation from God, our enslavement in this dense and resistant material world, to the scheming of a band of self-preoccupied or benighted pre-cosmic agents, which eventually produced a world of matter and chaos in which intelligible meaning, and real contact with or progress toward God, became impossible. The release of the sparks of enlightened, self-conscious spirit caught up in this material world could only be achieved by telling them the hitherto secret truth about their own origin, enabling them to disregard their opaque and oppressive, emotionally charged surroundings and be united with intelligible reality. Knowledge of how mind became embroiled in matter, for gnostic Christians, was the key to setting the mind free.

Opposition in the main Christian communities to this type of dualistic, radically mythological reinterpretation usually consisted in telling again the biblical story of humanity's creation, fall, and redemption in simpler terms. Creation of the material world, and of the spiritual beings embodied in material flesh, whom we call humans, was central to the early church's understanding of the intentions of the supreme God. Irenaeus and

---

30. For a recent study questioning the appropriateness of categorizing some early Christian writings and groups as "Gnostic," see Williams, *Rethinking "Gnosticism."* The dubiousness of the label seems not to have been obvious to second-century critics like Irenaeus and Origen.

Origen matter, for us twenty-first century Christians, mainly as representatives of this centrally important approach to proclaiming the faith. For both of them, the full humanity of Christ is central to that story. Yet they differ in the details they emphasize, and in the tone in which they tell it.

(1) The narrative Irenaeus proposes, in contrast to various gnostic versions, is decidedly not an attempt to clarify or alienate the story presented in the canonical Hebrew and Christian Bible with a description—however long and elaborate—of what went on in the heavenly realm "before" the formation of the present cosmos. Irenaeus contents himself with the Bible's narration, beginning with that of Adam and Eve in the first three chapters of Genesis. He implies, as we have seen, that the disobedience of the first humans to the divine command may have been due more to immaturity than to malice. So he suggests, near the end of Book IV, that the very youth of the first humans led to their imperfection and weakness:

> Inasmuch as created things are not uncreated, for this reason they come short of being perfect. Because as these things are of later date, they are also infantile; so they are unaccustomed to, and unpracticed in, perfect discipline.[31]

So the task of Jesus and Mary, the protagonists in the final part of the story, is, in Irenaeus's language, to "sum up" or "recapitulate" the human story from its earliest stages: to set it right, act out humanity's responses to God's challenges and invitations as they were meant to be acted out, by humans who are genuinely responsible and free. The characters in the drama of history are healed and rescued not by our escaping from the stage, but by our having new characters act out their roles over again, and get the story right.

Origen's anti-gnostic narrative, unlike that of Irenaeus, does reach back speculatively into an age when conscious and free souls existed by themselves, not yet burdened by a body and its appetites. But it was not an alien conspiracy, but the failure of all souls except that of Jesus to cling to God in love and obedience that led to their "fall" into the weaknesses of the present world, which was created to receive them, Origen theorizes, and it was the sole fidelity of Jesus that unites him, in permanent and transformative desire, to the divine Word. The emphasis here, unlike that of Irenaeus, is on a narrative whose shape is determined as much by Middle Platonic anthropology as by Genesis. Yet the result is similar to Irenaeus's

---

31. Irenaeus, *Against the Heresies*, IV, 38.1 (trans. Roberts and Donaldson 520 [alt.]).

story: Jesus, fully human but inseparably united in his soul's freedom to the Word, reveals and models the kind of human behavior that leads to eternal union with God, and that is grounded in his free human choice to love his creator. Salvation, then, like the fall, is not due to intervention by non-biblical agents.

(2) The goal of the biblical narrative, in Irenaeus's retelling of it, is presented as largely a *visual* experience: contemplating the "God, who is yet to be seen"[32] and discovering in that contemplative gaze eternal life, a share in the glory, the stunning beauty, that radiates from God's being.[33] But it is precisely the Son of God whose role it is to communicate that divine beauty to creatures, and so enable them to be "vivified."[34] And the chief means of that communication is through the Son's humanity, which makes incorruptibility and immortality available to us by his identifying himself with us, leading to our adoption as God's children.[35]

Origen's approach lays less emphasis on the visual revelation of the form of God as the purpose of the Incarnation, and more on his nearness and tangibility. Love, as human contact rooted in free choice and desire, is where union among spiritual creatures begins. Actually *touching* the body of the Word made flesh seems to incarnate love, to establish a contact with God that frees embodied human creatures from the long-term confinement in the material world into which our race has fallen, and gives them a new surge of healing energy. And the object of this contact is not simply vision or knowledge of God, but a fully realized, humanly fulfilled love that enkindles and consumes the creature from within, as fire consumes a log of wood. This is not simply due to the revelatory power of God's bodily presence in Jesus, but to the embodiment of his divine power in flesh like ours, "for the divinity of Christ, from which this fire draws its energy, is from above."[36]

(3) Still, for both Irenaeus and Origen, the union of the divine Word and the visible, palpable flesh of Jesus was more than simply participation, as a limited, earthly reality might be understood by the philosophical tradition to participate in the universal forms. It was, in the language of later Byzantine spiritual theology, genuine *divinization*: a transcendental

32. Irenaeus, *AH*, IV, 38.3 (Roberts and Donaldson 522).

33. Irenaeus, *AH*, IV, 20.5 (Roberts and Donaldson 489).

34. Irenaeus, *AH*, IV, 20.5 (Roberts and Donaldson 489).

35. Irenaeus, *AH*, III, 19.1–3 (Roberts and Donaldson 448–49).

36. Origen, *Homilies on Leviticus*, I, 4.

gift from God to a creature, which made the creature uniquely and permanently different: in this case, a gift that united the creature personally to God's creative, revealing Word. In the second book of his apologetic treatise *Against Celsus*, the critical Middle Platonic philosopher, Origen makes this point clearly. Celsus has attacked mainstream Christians, as Christian gnostic writers would also do, for promoting the scandalous assumption that the transcendent source of all things could be conceived of as residing within the limits of matter, inhabiting a material body in history. In response, Origen affirms that this is indeed what Christians believe, as the starting-point of the story they tell:

> Let our critics know (he says) that he, whom we think and have believed to be God and Son of God from the beginning, is the very Logos and wisdom and truth itself. We affirm that his mortal body and the human soul in him received the greatest elevation, not only by communion but by union and intermingling, so that by sharing in his divinity he was transformed into God.[37]

But Origen immediately adds that such a transformation of a finite, created thing by the presence in it of a transcendent spiritual power is really no more self-contradictory or even paradoxical than what some classical philosophical schools have assumed to hold in the general, transforming relationship of the eternal forms to matter. He writes:

> If anyone should take offence because we say this even of his body, let him consider what is asserted by the Greeks about matter: that, properly speaking, it is without qualities, but is clothed with qualities such as the creator wishes to give it, and that it often puts aside its former qualities and receives better and different ones. If this is right, why is it remarkable that by the providence of God's will the mortal quality of Jesus' body should have been changed into an ethereal and divine quality?[38]

To affirm, as both Irenaeus and Origen do, that in Christ the Word of God has made our full humanity, spiritual and physical, his own is to affirm an intimate identity between God and the world that is—at least as far as humanity is concerned—analogous to the marvels of transcendent presence we see every day in the created, intelligible, gloriously beautiful realities around us, and that we generally take for granted. In the terms of

37. Origen, *Contra Celsum* III, 41 (156).
38. Origen, *Contra Celsum* III, 41 (156).

Biblical faith, however, this presence of "God with us" is not only a philo-sophical paradox, but a promise of redemption.

And Which We Proclaimed to You

The Contemporary Church
and the Humanity of Jesus

9

Toward a Black Anthropology and Social Ethic

Why the Humanity and Jewishness of Jesus Matters

Esau McCaulley
Wheaton College

INTRODUCTION: THE PLACE OF BLACK ANTHROPOLOGY ON THE WORLD STAGE

I am a New Testament scholar by trade, equipped with the standard tools of our discipline: namely, historical investigation, linguistic examination, and literary analysis. It is true that Christology, an account of Jesus's humanity and divinity, grows out of reading of biblical texts, but the construction of a full orbed Christology is often the work of systematic or historical theologians. What's more, the task of this paper, anthropology (i.e., what it means to be human) must grow out of Christology if it is to be truly Christian, because Jesus Christ is the true image bearer. In the strangely prophetic words of Pilate, when we look upon Jesus we see the truly human person (John 19:5). Therefore, I find myself in danger on two fronts: attempting to articulate an *anthropology* that grows out of a *Christology*. I am in an area that biblical scholars have often feared to tread.

But I am weary of letting our specializations turn into bunkers from which we lob bombs from fortified positions. Each of our disciplines tends to tell the other that the interloper is not playing by the right rules or using the right language, but I think that it is important that we talk to one another from time to time.

Why does the humanity of Jesus matter? Well, it depends. There is the sense in which Jesus's incarnation effects the salvation of all who believe. Therefore, in the broadest terms, the incarnation matters in much the same way to everyone. But life is rarely that simple. Before I became a Christian, I was not a free floating "person" looking for a savior. I was a black man from the South dealing with the ongoing legacy of Jim Crow. So when I ask whether or not Jesus has anything to do with my life, I am speaking of this *black life* that I live in a country that does not always know what to do with this dark skin that I carry from city to city. What does the incarnation, Jesus's full humanity, mean to me as a black man and how does that understanding of Jesus's humanity provide me with an understanding of my own self that can help me navigate this divided and broken society?

Let me be clear. Speaking about how Jesus's humanity helps us overcome racial divisions is not my primary focus. I am not in the first place concerned with how Jesus's humanity helps me reconcile with the majority culture. I am interested in answering the question of how Jesus's humanity helps me live as a black man. To center on reconciliation with others bypasses the necessary soul work that I need to do in order to enter into a conversation as a whole and complete person. I must become fully human before I can enter into a meaningful dialogue.

Here is the problem: For African Americans, the story of Christology and anthropology in the United States is decidedly not a story of *decline* from a consensus on the worth of black bodies and souls. Instead, our story is one of the denials of our basic humanity. Our struggle is not trying to conceive of what it means to be human in light of Christ's humanity, but rather to be treated as humans.

In his book on Christian theology and the origins of race, Willie James Jennings quotes the Jesuit Alessandro Valignano, a missionary to Japan. Valignano sees Japanese converts as very valuable assets to the church, people who will make good Christians if he could manage to win them over. Conversely, in Valignano's view, the people of Mozambique (and we can assume the rest of Africa) are not as promising. He says:

> They are a very untalented race . . . incapable of grasping our holy
> religion or practicing it; because of their naturally low intelligence
> they cannot rise above the level of the senses. . . . They lack any cul-
> ture and are given to savage ways and vices, and as a consequence
> they live like brute beasts. . . . They are a race born to serve, with
> no natural aptitude for governing.[1]

If Valignano can be seen as representative of the people of his day,
then the African slave trade, which grew up around this time, was rooted in
the denial of the image of God in Black people (and for that matter a whole
host of others).

If we can skip a generation, or three, and arrive on these great shores
of the United States, we find James Henry Hammond, senator from the
great state of South Carolina saying the following during a speech before
the senate in 1858:

> In all social systems there must be a class to do the menial duties,
> to perform the drudgery of life. That is, a class requiring but a low
> order of intellect and but little skill. . . . Fortunately for the South,
> she found a race adapted to that purpose to her hand. A race infe-
> rior to her own, but eminently qualified in temper, in vigor, in do-
> cility, in capacity to stand the climate, to answer all her purposes.
> We use them for our purpose and call them slaves. We found them
> slaves by the common 'consent of mankind.'[2]

It might also be worth quoting here an excerpt from London Anthropological Society:

> The Human Family is composed of a certain number of species
> or races. . . . The White, or Caucasian, is the most elevated, and
> the Negro the most subordinate of all the Races in their organic
> structure, and therefore in their faculties.[3]

From the above, I take it that that the full humanity of people of African descent has been a question from the beginning of the slave trade, up

1. From Jennings, *Christian Imagination*, 34.

2. See also "We will not renounce our part in the mission of the race, trustee, under
God, of the civilization of the world. . . . He has made us the master organizers of the
world to establish system when chaos reigns . . . the judgment of the master is upon us:
'Ye have been faithful over a few things; I will make you ruler over many things.'" As
Albert Beverage says, justifying the US annexation of the Philippines; found in Murphy,
"Evil and Sin in African American Theology," 212–27.

3. Hunt, *Negro's Place in Nature*, 4.

through the Civil War. It was then encased in law and custom during Jim Crow. Let me just list a few of these laws:

1. No person or corporation shall require any white female nurse to nurse in wards or rooms in hospitals, either public or private, in which negro men are placed. *Alabama*

2. All marriages between a white person and a negro, or between a white person and a person of negro descent to the fourth generation inclusive, are hereby forever prohibited. *Florida*

3. The officer in charge shall not bury, or allow to be buried, any colored persons upon ground set apart or used for the burial of white persons. *Georgia*[4]

One more thing needs to be said about this as we deal with the question of the plight of a fully formed Black anthropology for a social ethic. This question is only partly rhetorical: In what year did the majority of the United States of America recognize the full dignity of Black bodies and souls? Stated differently, when did the race-based hierarchy outlined above become socially unacceptable? Regardless of how one answers these questions, it is clear that the question of a Black anthropology, an account of what makes us human, has operated along a slightly different track than the mainstream theological discourse that functions as something of a frame for this book.

To turn our attention from the European gaze upon the Black person to Black theological and cultural reflection itself, the question becomes, how have we as a people given an account of what it means for us to be human? This question will occupy the rest of this essay. I argue that, historically, African Americans have provided three answers to this question of Black identity. The first is not particularly Christian, but it is nonetheless important. Black secular scholars have used a particular reading of Black history as the basis for Black identity. Second, liberation theologians have seen the exodus narrative as analogous to the Black slave narrative and, therefore, as a starting point for our identity. The third account also draws upon the Bible, arguing that Black existence in American is utterly cruciform. We suffer unjustly, even unto death at the hands of the state. Therefore, as the one who also suffers unjustly, Jesus is black. This black Jesus then forms the basis for black self-understanding.

4. From "Jim Crow Laws."

I examine the strengths and weaknesses of these proposals before turning to two sources for a positive foundation for a Black anthropology to argue that a Black anthropology must be rooted in a messianic Christology. This messianic Christology makes much of Jesus's particularity as a Jewish person and universality as king. Second, I argue that the doctrine of recapitulation, as found in Irenaeus of Lyons, points the way toward an anthropology that unites all the people of God.

BLACK HISTORY AND OUR STRUGGLE AS THE BASIS FOR BLACK IDENTITY

So how do you form an identity when it has been systematically denied to your people? How can you understand who you are when your own name comes from your former masters? I am Esau "McCaulley" not because my family can trace their tribes to the lost tribes of Scotland, but because a minor family in Scotland, who did not even have their own tartan, wanted to make a better life for themselves.

One answer to this question of the foundation of Black identity has been to put our finger on our painful story and use that as a basis for constructing an understanding of our place in the world. In his classic, *the Souls of Black Folks,* W. E. B. Dubois speaks about the reality of being both Black and American as two-ness that we have to strive to keep intact. He says:

> The history of the American Negro is the history of this strife,—this longing to attain self-conscious manhood, to merge his double self into a better and truer self. In this merging he wishes neither of the older selves to be lost. He would not Africanize America, for America has too much to teach the world and Africa. He would not bleach his Negro soul in a flood of white Americanism, for he knows that Negro blood has a message for the world. He simply wishes to make it possible for a man to be both a Negro and an American, without being cursed and spit upon by his fellows, without having the doors of opportunity closed roughly in his face.[5]

To be black, according to Dubois, is to engage in this struggle to be free *and* black in America. But it goes deeper than this. In order to engage in this struggle for identity, we must tell the story of that struggle. This story

5. Du Bois, *Souls of Black Folks,* 2–3.

of the black struggle for personhood stands in stark contrast to the story that America likes to tell itself. Both are *theological* accounts of American history, but they have very different aims.

The story that portions of America likes to tell itself is one of discovery of an untamed land, of partnership with the original inhabitants, of the desire for freedom of religion, of the creation of the most just system of government that humanity has ever known. This version acknowledges the unfortunate reality of slavery and the treatment of the first inhabitants of this country, but it emphasizes progress. This focus on progress makes it possible to look at our supposed triumph over racism—especially with the election of a black president—as yet another glory of this country. In this reading, the bad parts were not that bad, and the glories grow in the telling. This greatness is the foundation of a certain form of American identity. I like to call this the "glory narrative" of American history. Make no mistake: this is a *theological* account, rooted in a certain understanding of God and his purposes.

Black persons can only have bit part in this narrative. We are oppressed for a short while, but now, we are finally free. We are the backdrop for someone else's triumph. Black history, as the foundation for Black identity, offers a different *theological* account of the history of this country, even when that account is completely secular. By denying the providential ordering of the "glory narrative," it calls into question the God contained in that narrative. It is a form of atheism-as-protest: "If your God told you to do this to us, then we deny him."

To be clear, this rejection of the God of the glory narrative is not a denial of the God of the Bible. Frederick Douglas, the great abolitionist and theologian, said the following toward the end of his biography:

> I have, in several instances, spoken in such a tone and manner, respecting religion, as may possibly lead those unacquainted with my religious views to suppose me an opponent of all religion. . . . What I have said respecting and against religion, I mean strictly to apply to the slaveholding religion of this land, and with no possible reference to Christianity proper; for, between the Christianity of this land, and the Christianity of Christ, I recognize the widest possible difference—so wide, that to receive the one as good, pure, and holy, is of necessity to reject the other as bad, corrupt, and wicked. To be the friend of the one, is of necessity to be the enemy of the other. I love the pure, peaceable, and impartial Christianity of Christ: I therefore hate the corrupt, slaveholding,

women-whipping, cradle-plundering, partial and hypocritical Christianity of this land.[6]

The Black account of American history, then, is a bloody and dark story that begins not on the Mayflower, but the good ship Jesus.[7] It is a story of middle passages, auctioning blocks, sexual assaults, and divided families. It is a heart-breaking tale that makes one weep to look upon it. But in the secular Black telling, it becomes a story of a people who bear up under suffering. It is the story of the constant affirmation of our humanity in the face of a system that attempted to deny it.

Some have claimed that this story unites African Americans in a way that transcends even the Christian story:

> There is . . . a shared, transcendent cultural reality experienced by black Christians and non-Christians alike: Black suffering. Black suffering bears and has borne a double burden. On the one hand, black suffering shares the suffering that is common to all human beings, sickness, broken homes, tragedies of death, accidents, wars, etc. On the other hand, black suffering has been compounded by slavery, discrimination, and racism. This sociological grid of blacks provides a solidarity that transcends even membership in the Christian religion.[8]

What makes us who we are as black people in this account? What unites us? Our suffering! We are those who have suffered and yet we live! What is the Christian to think of such things? Is it true that the suffering of my people unites us one to another more than the blood of Christ unites us to our fellow Christians?

One can see how such a statement could be concocted even if we must reject it. How much kinship did the black slave or black Christian under Jim Crow feel with his white Christian neighbor? Furthermore, the black account of American history does serve as a corrective to the glory narrative that damages so many. I contend that these two theological accounts of American history, one white and one black, continue to divide our churches. The price of admittance into the wider community of faith cannot be a story that Black Christians know is false.

Nonetheless, I wonder if a secular Black history can function as the basis for Black anthropology or social ethic. I say this for the following

6. Douglass, *Narrative of the Life of Frederick Douglass*, 117.

7. "Adventurers and Slave Traders."

8. Hoyt, "Interpreting Biblical Scholarship," 17–39.

reasons. In the secular world this account of the black struggle is without guidance. We are free by happenstance, a battle won that could have gone another way or because of a key speech there that stirred a populous. But is our present status a testament only to human strength or is there something more? Does a secular account of blackness require us to believe in an almost mystical quality to blackness that this secular account of the human person itself denies? Without God there is no "black girl magic." There is no magic at all. We are all here by chance and our survival is just that. But if God has created the very diversity that provides the richness of the human experience, then blackness becomes eschatological. More on this later. Secondly, where are we going on this narrative? Whither the black man or woman in this country? What is our *telos* and who determines it? Third, how does the black story touch on the grander human story in a way that transcends our suffering? Are we all strangers, you and I, or is there something that makes sense of the history of black versus white; Japanese vs. Chinese; Jews vs. Palestinian? Is there a universal reconciliation that is more than the sharing of our wounds?

Finally, the claim that what unites Black people is deeper than what unites us as Christians is an implicit denial of Christian eschatology, particularly the resurrection of the dead. Stated differently, it requires the falsity of the resurrection for its probative force. If there is a God who judges the living and the dead, who sent his Son so that we might live with him forever, then there is nothing grander than being a part of God's family. If Jesus is not risen, then we are still in our sins and we should eat and drink for tomorrow we shall surely die.

THE BLACK EXODUS AND THE BIBLE AS ANALOGY

If secular accounts of Black history cannot function as the basis for a Black sense of identity or anthropology, maybe the Bible as a book of liberation can. Liberation theology, of which Black theology is one manifestation, has the following characteristics: (1) preferential option for the poor, which means that the church's primary job is to side with the oppressed; (2) liberation is a vital part of salvation, meaning that God is concerned with the whole person, not just one's soul; and (3) the exodus is paradigmatic for understanding salvation, rendering salvation meaningless apart from the transformation of structures.[9]

9. Adapted from "Liberation Theology," 978–79.

At the core of liberation theology, then, is a certain Christian *praxis* that sees the exodus—even the violent elements of that narrative—as paradigmatic for the church's active engagement in the work of liberation. I will have some critical things to say about this in a few moments, but surely the magisterium was right in *Libertatis Nuntius* when it acknowledged elements of truth in liberation theology:

> It is important that numerous Christians, whose faith is clear and who are committed to live the Christian life in its fullness, become involved in the struggle for justice, freedom, and human dignity because of their love for their disinherited, oppressed, and persecuted brothers and sisters. More than ever, the Church intends to condemn abuses, injustices, and attacks against freedom, wherever they occur and whoever commits them. She intends to struggle, by her own means, for the defense and advancement of the rights of mankind, especially of the poor.[10]

The church does care about the poor, God is concerned about the whole person, and we are involved in the work of liberation. The question is *how* social and economic justice connect up with conversion to Christ and the transformation of life.

Let me, then, return to the exodus motif and black bodies. Black liberation theology has picked up on the theme of the exodus as a fitting image for the Black experience in the United States. Like the people of Israel, African-Americans found themselves enslaved in a foreign land. Like the people of Israel, African-Americans groaned under the harsh treatment of taskmasters while longing for freedom. The Negro spirituals, such as *Go Down Moses*, evoked this Exodus imagery and longing for freedom. *Go down Moses* is famous for its repeated refrain:

> *No more in bondage shall they toil*
> *Let my people go*
> *Let them come out with Egypt's spoil*
> *Let my people go*

The song is about Egypt, but it is also about Black freedom. It is a not-so-subtle call for God to do for Black people what he did for Israel. In these accounts of Black liberation, different characters have played the role of a Moses or Messiah-like figure come to lead Black people to the promised land of freedom or equality.

10. Ratzinger, *Instruction*.

The exodus reading of Black identity also focuses on suffering that is decidedly more Christian than a secular account of Black history. It is true that Blacks in North America and beyond have found comfort in the knowledge that there is a God who cares for the oppressed. We have also had a history of preaching a wholistic gospel that does not divorce the spiritual from the material. But there are limitations to these uses of the exodus analogy. First, some of these readings fail to recognize that the history of Black Christianity precedes slavery. The ancient kingdoms of Nubia and Ethiopia worshiped Jesus without having been enslaved. The Ethiopians were composing hymns to the triune God when the British were still worshiping rocks and trees.

Secondly, these readings fail to recognize the Bible's own formative impact on the whole of the lives and thoughts of African Americans. Stated differently, the Bible does not only appeal to us because elements of the Israelite story mirror aspects of the Black story. The Bible and wider Christian theology make certain claims about love, peace, justice, reconciliation, and the transforming power of the Spirit that speak to the Black soul in much the same way that they speak to the Latino soul, the Asian soul, the European soul. Here I am not far from our theme when I say that the full testimony of the Word provides us with a complete account of what it means to be human that draws us to worship like everyone else.

Slavery and oppression mark the Black interpretation of the Bible and informs the types of questions we ask. But just as slavery and oppression are not the whole of the Black experience, responding to slavery is not the whole of our interpretive method. God's love for people of color does not begin with the slavery analogy.

As I read the Bible (and here I draw on the best of the Black interpretive tradition) it begins first with universal affirmation of the *imago Dei* in Gen 1:26–28 and the claim in the table of nations that we are all interconnected (Gen 10:1–32). Furthermore, the narrative of the Bible, which climaxes in the coming of the Son, derives its energy from Gen 12:1–3. Gen 12:1–3 explicitly says that the vocation of Abraham and Israel is to bring blessings to the nations of the earth. So, while the exodus is formative, it cannot carry the weight of Black identity full stop.

I also wonder if the exodus as paradigm for societal transformation captures the heart of the biblical narrative. Moses tells Pharaoh to let God's people go so that they might *worship God*. The purpose of liberation is the formation of a people who themselves serve the nations of the world.

Exodus gives way to Leviticus, the formation of the cult. It is not a freedom simply to determine one's own socio-economic destiny, as important as that is. Liberation's *telos* is transformation and communion with the God, who created all things.

BLACK JESUS AND THE SUFFERING ANALOGY ONCE MORE

This brings us to Black Jesus. When Black theologians refer to Jesus as *black* they do not have his skin in mind, but his relationship to the experiences of Black Americans. This does not mean that the question of Jesus's actual color is not important or that presentations of him as the idealized European are not problematic, but that is a topic for another day.

According to these theologians, Jesus's blackness arises out his life as a part of an oppressed class and his status as the innocent one who was killed by the State. Summarizing James Cone, Dianna Hayes says the following: "Jesus, and therefore God are black because only as black are they in full solidarity with those who, in the United States especially, have historically been oppressed simply because they are black."[11] This idea that Jesus is black grows out of the Black Exodus. If Black folks are analogous to the Israelites, then the Messiah who comes to liberate people of color must himself be black. Jesus is black, especially in America, because to call him white is to put him on the wrong side of the power balance in this country. Jesus was a part of the oppressed class, not the privileged. Israel did not colonize Rome; Israel was colonized by Rome.

But, like the exodus analogy, this analogy limits the appeal of Christ. Yes, Black Christians, like all other Christians, are drawn to the love that God showed to the lowly and outcast in the person of his Son. But we also love Christ because he is *not* like us. To limit Jesus's appeal to what makes him near to us denies the larger claims that he makes about himself. It is precisely as the incarnate Son of God that his humility is compelling. It is the fact that God's Son did not have to be like us that makes his nearness irresistible. Finally, when he did come near, his word was not an unqualified "yes." Jesus brought a "yes" and "no" to the varied cultures of his day.

---

11. Hayes, "Christology in African American Theology," 153–61.

JESUS AS ISRAELITE AND THE DOCTRINE
OF RECAPITULATION

If Jesus as the suffering one, the exodus, and Black history are not a sufficient basis for building a Black anthropology or identity, then what is? How exactly does Jesus's humanity matter for the Black bodies that move through this world? Here I may disappoint the reader with what seems like a somewhat traditional Christian account, but I think that a traditional account might be of particular importance in the context of the issues swirling around Black identity.

My claim is that Jesus as the messianic King of Israel and Son of God, when placed in the context of the wider Christian story, can be the foundation of an affirmation of Black identity. Let me explain this position by contrasting it with a claim from F. C. Baur, that pillar of the early generation of biblical studies. When explaining the origins of Christianity, he says that he wants to show how:

> Christianity, instead of remaining a mere form of Judaism, and being ultimately absorbed in it, asserted itself as a separate, independent principle, broke loose from it and took its form as a new form of religious thought and life, essentially differing from Judaism, and freed from all its national exclusiveness.[12]

According to Baur, in order for Christianity to become universal, to appeal to every person, it had to be less Jewish. However, Baur's Jesus and the Jesus of the school of thought that followed in his wake did not become more universal. It became more white and more European. It was a Jesus particularly suited to the proclivities of Baur's day.

If Jesus becomes a liberal white Protestant and Jesus is the image of God (the basis for all our identities), then what does that mean for us? It means that the highest form of humanity is the white liberal Protestant, or those who can mimic its behaviors. Let the reader understand that the same problem holds when Jesus is present as the sole preserve of white Evangelicalism. Does one have to be culturally white to be pleasing to God? Do we have to like the same music and wear the same khakis? This is why the Black Jesus is a different form of the same mistake. When we limit the identity of Jesus solely to the things that resonate with our culture, we limit his ability to speak a word to our culture about what it means to be human.

12. Baur, *Paul, the Apostle of Jesus Christ*, 1:3.

What would it mean to give Jesus back to Israel in order to give him to the world? Affirming Jesus as Israelite affirms his particularity. He had an ethnicity and culture that formed him. The food, music, ceremonies, and stories of his people cannot be separated from his identity without falling prey to the ever-present danger of Marcionism. In the same way, our food, music, ceremonies, culture, and history are important too. The incarnation embraces culture.

There is more. Jesus's words to Israel and its particular customs were not an unqualified "yes." He saw the sin and hypocrisy of his people, the ways that they had failed to be all that God called them to be. So, his word to Israel (whose culture was rooted in the very words of God) was both "yes" and "no." This again serves as a basis for a divinely discerned "yes" and "no" to all the fallen but glorious cultures of the world. Our identities and stories are not closed off from God's judgment. Remember when Jesus said to the people of his day:

> Jerusalem, Jerusalem, you who kill the prophets and stone those sent to you, how often I have longed to gather your children together, as a hen gathers her chicks under her wings, and you were not willing. (Matt 23:37, NIV)

Jerusalem didn't want to remember herself as the city that killed prophets. But Jesus forced them to face the whole of their story, and so be saved. In the same way, Jesus calls upon us to look at the whole of our stories, the good and the bad so that we might repent and be transformed.

But Jesus, as Israelite, is not simply an affirmation of particularity; it is also a statement about universality. God's purposes in Abraham's offspring was to create a people who would themselves bring blessing to the world and undo the damage caused by the Fall. The exodus finds its meaning by looking back onto God's creational purposes and forward to his coming kingdom.

The Messiah Jesus, as King of Israel, is the fulfillment of God's desire to create a people from every tribe, tongue, and nation who will reflect him in the world. This means that our very diversity, my Africanness and your Europeanness together in one family, is a manifestation of the universal saving power of the gospel. We, together under the one true king, are the climax of the covenant and the manifestation of God's glorious grace. The gospel *demands* that my Blackness endures and be visible unto eternity. Ethnicity is eschatological (Rev 7:9). A human and Jewish Jesus, then, is the key to Black identity and anthropology. I am who I am because my people were created to offer our distinctive gifts to God.

But the narrative account of Jesus's humanity does not simply give me a Black anthropology, it also gives me a social ethic that helps me live faithfully. My goal is not societal acceptability; it is not whiteness. My goal is Christ. I have a north star.

In one of the earliest articulations of a theory of atonement, Irenaeus posits his theory of recapitulation in which Christ becomes man and passes through every stage of life and in so doing reconciles every aspect of our humanity to God. Jesus's humanity reclaims every aspect of the human experience and makes the whole of life christological. He says:

> For, in what way could we be partaken of the adoption of sons, unless we had received from Him through the Son that fellowship which refers to Himself, unless His Word, having been made flesh, had entered into communion with us? Wherefore also He passed through every stage of life, restoring to all communion with God.[13]

When the whole life of Jesus is seen as his reconciling all things to himself, then his decision not to turn Rome into an enemy—even as a child living under the thumb of an empire—becomes a part of his atoning work. His decision to love his own people who failed him deeply becomes a part of his atoning work. Stated different, Jesus gathers up all our failures and vanquishes them on the cross. Jesus's love for Rome becomes the foundation for racial reconciliation, but again, that love was not sentimental or devoid of truth-telling. It is a rugged love that told Rome and Israel the truth about themselves.

Furthermore, Jesus passing through every stage of life to reconcile us to God also reminds me that God wants to redeem my black childhood, my black teen years, and my black adulthood, and wrap them all up in his glory. It is a call to be my whole, free, redeemed black self and to see his work in every aspect of my life. Black lives, at every age, matter because Christ passed through these stages to reconcile them to God. This reconciliation again has a *telos,* to unite this distinctly black story to the grand story of what God is doing in his Son. Irenaeus one more time:

> He, appearing in these last times, the chief cornerstone, has gathered into one, and united those that were far off and those that

13. Irenaeus, *Against Heresies* 18.7.

were near; that is, the circumcision and the uncircumcision, enlarging Japhet, and placing him in the dwelling of Shem.[14]

Christ's reconciling work climaxes with the entire family of God united one to another by the blood of Christ, not as non-descript members of a faceless hoard. We are not Buddhists. We do not merge with Brahman. Instead, my blackness, which includes the story of my people, our journey to freedom from slavery, and our deep kinship with the suffering of Christ, is affirmed as a unique manifestation of God's desire to create a peculiar people drawn from every tribe, tongue, and nation.

14. Irenaeus, *Against Heresies* 5.17.

10

Jesus as Missional Migrant

Latin American Christologies, the New Testament Witness,
and Twenty-first Century Migration

CHRISTOPHER M. HAYS and MILTON ACOSTA
Fundación Universitaria Seminario Bíblico de Colombia

The émigré Holy Family of Nazareth, fleeing in Egypt,
is the archetype of every refugee family.
—Pope Pius XII, *Exsul Familia Nazarethana.*

INTRODUCTION

Last Christmas, Alexandria Ocasio-Cortez, a Latina Christian and the new darling of the Democratic party, tweeted out, "Merry Christmas to everyone—here's to a holiday filled with happiness, family and love for all people (Including refugee babies in mangers + their parents)." The criticism of new federal immigration policies—cutting 2019 refugee admissions to a mere quarter of the 2016 numbers[1]—was obvious enough.[2] In reaction, conservative Christian pundit, Charlie Kirk, fired back that Mary and Joseph were "LEGAL citizens" and charged Ocasio-Cortez with "misrepresenting the Gospel on this holy day."[3] Kirk was likely highlighting that Congresswoman Ocasio-Cortez had made a misstep in her Tweet: by referring to the refugee baby in a manger, Ocasio-Cortez collapsed the birth of Jesus with his subsequent flight to Egypt. Still, *pace* Charlie Kirk, this probably does not constitute misrepresenting the Gospel; it is common to read about the visit of the magi at Christmas time, even if it is technically an Epiphany text. But quibbles about the liturgical calendar aside, Congresswoman Ocasio-Cortez is basically right: the baby Jesus was a victim of forced migration due to violence.

Whatever one's feelings about migration, it is a defining feature of geopolitics. There are currently 244 million international migrants worldwide, a full 3.3 percent of the world population.[4] Of those 244 million international migrants, 68.5 million have been forcibly displaced.[5] What is more, these astronomical figures do not take into account the pernicious phenomenon of forced *internal* displacement due to civil violence, as a result of which, just in 2017, a full 11.8 million people became domestic refugees.[6] The US sits squarely in middle of the controversies about migration, as 14.5 percent of the US national population is comprised of migrants,[7] 11.3 million of whom (as of 2016) were undocumented.[8] Small surprise, then, that social-scientific researchers have come to refer to the present era as the "Age of Migration."[9]

So, in the age of migration, what does it mean that Jesus was a migrant? What does the humanity of the migrant Christ mean for the US church, given that nearly one in seven people in our country is an immigrant? To

1. Hansler, "US Admits Lowest Number of Refugees"; see also U.N.H.C.R., "Resettlement Data."

2. Davis, "Trump to Cap Refugees."

3. Huckabee, "So, Were Mary and Joseph Actually Refugees?"

4. McAuliffe, "Migration and Migrants," 1–5.

5. U.N.H.C.R., "Figures at a Glance."

6. International Displacement Monitoring Centre, "Global Report on Internal Displacement."

7. McAuliffe, "Migration and Migrants," 4.

8. McAuliffe, "Migration and Migrants," 9.

9. Castles and Miller, *Age of Migration*.

answer that question, the present chapter begins by surveying key christological insights from Latin American theologians, which strikes us as a fitting procedure since Latins constitute the largest group of migrants to the US.[10] It then turns to the New Testament to examine the diverse senses in which Jesus was a migrant. In light of these two sources of theological reflection, we delineate the contemporary ramifications of this fact. In brief, we argue that Jesus was indeed a migrant—both in the voluntary and involuntary senses—and that fact should transform the way that the church undertakes her mission both *toward* migrants and *with* migrants.

THE HUMANITY AND CRUCIFIXION OF JESUS IN LATIN AMERICAN LIBERATIONIST CHRISTOLOGIES

We begin with Latin American theology, specifically Liberationist Christologies, since we find the contributions of liberation theologians particularly poignant for the present discussion. To a certain degree in contrast with traditional Eastern and Western Christologies, Liberation Christologies place a high premium on the particular details of Jesus's human life (e.g., his economic location, occupation, social relationships, etc.). They do so not in order to reduce theology to sociology, but because of a conviction that social realities are themselves part of God's creation and objects of God's redemption. As such, when liberation theologians approach the christological task, they scrutinize the realia of Jesus's life and the concrete ways he intervened in the world in order to transform social realities in the direction of the kingdom of God.[11] For the present purposes, two key facets of Liberationist Christologies need highlighting: their emphasis on the particular humanity of Jesus and their interpretation of the ramifications of his crucifixion for the historical causes of justice.

Beyond Mere Human Nature: The Particular Humanity of Jesus

Liberation theologians highlight a tendency in the history of Christianity "to exalt the humanity of Jesus," to the point of portraying Jesus in glorified,

---

10. 44 percent of the total population of US migrants; Zong et al., *Frequently Requested Statistics on Immigrants.*

11. Sobrino, *Jesucristo liberador*, 14.

divinized, or hyper-spiritualized ways, even prior to his resurrection.[12] Such interest manifested itself in dogmas that highlight Jesus's divinity at the expense of his "true and concrete humanity."[13] In critical response to this historical tendency, Jon Sobrino came to emphasize that the incarnation is not an "occasional visit of God to this world disguised as a human being,"[14] precisely because of his perspective that dogmaticians seem to portray God as more or less a tourist in the human Christ, insofar as they sometimes breeze past the concrete features of Jesus's biography. Agreeing with Sobrino, Leonardo Boff holds that there has to be a real incarnation, complete with all the minutia of mundane human existence; otherwise Christology would be reduced to abstract, toothless concepts.[15]

José Comblin clarifies that Liberationist Christologies do not seek to debunk key Christian dogmas, but to provide a corrective emphasis, in order "to restore the true image of the humanity of Jesus, which is the model and path of our humanity."[16] In other words, for Jesus to be followed he has to be followable. Comblin argues that a Chalcedonian construal of Christology effectively seems to reduce the humanity of Jesus—that is, the human life that Jesus lived—to an abstract human nature. But "a human being is not just human nature. Each human being is a story, the story of a project, a story of successes and failures, a story lived in a specific context, [a story]and that gets its meaning from that context."[17] When our account of Jesus is effectively detached from the realia of his biography, we end up with human nature, but not with a true human being.

According to Sobrino, the problem with this "abstract Christ" is that the people of God end up knowing "a Christ without Jesus." This is a "scandalous situation" because in the end, the abstract Christ is most beneficial to "the powerful and the oppressors," who worship Christ while ignoring the fact that Jesus was a Jewish peasant. The scandal for Sobrino is the coexistence of poverty with the Christian faith throughout Latin America. This situation has emerged because an abstract Christ is loving and powerful, but has nothing to say about justice or the conversion of oppressors;

---

12. Comblin, "Reflexiones sobre la notificación enviada a Jon Sobrino," 62.

13. Sobrino, *Jesucristo liberador*, 25.

14. Sobrino, *Jesucristo liberador*, 66, 106.

15. Boff, *Jesucristo el liberador*, 31.

16. Comblin, "Reflexiones sobre la notificación enviada a Jon Sobrino," 64.

17. Comblin, "Reflexiones sobre la notificación enviada a Jon Sobrino," 65.

historical transformation has been skirted because the church has no Jesus, only Christ.[18]

The Crucifixion and Crucifixions of Jesus

The defining feature of Jesus's biography is of course the fact that he gave his life. Being human for Jesus did not consist of benefiting himself, but of emptying himself and giving himself unreservedly to others,[19] most consummately in the crucifixion. But Jesus's crucifiability (as it were) depends upon his humanity, for crucifiability requires humiliatability and mortality, which are exceedingly human characteristics.

Theological reflection in Liberationist Christologies places a premium not only on the fact that the human Christ was crucified, but also on the fact that, in being humiliated and killed, Jesus is united to the "millions of brothers and sisters of our peripheral societies" who are also humiliated and killed. These suffering people exemplify, in their suffering, the humanness that Jesus possessed and came to save. This is the reason why the most important question in the whole Bible is the one God puts to Cain (Gen 4:9): "Where is your brother?"[20]

The way Jesus died, by crucifixion, is for Sobrino a key point of contact between the conditions of large numbers of Latin Americans and Jesus. In his book *Jesucristo liberador*, Sobrino elevates poverty, marginalization, and violence to the category of crucifixion.[21] The premise that supports this conviction is that God is present in human suffering, particularly "the suffering of the victims of this world," as stated in Matthew 25. Human suffering is a present reality in Latin America. In contrast to so many European and US theologians, we in Latin America are not doing theology "*after* Auschwitz, but *during* Auschwitz."[22] Sobrino appeals to the assassination of some of his colleagues as an example of the crucifixion of the people of Latin America

18. Sobrino, *Jesucristo liberador*, 30–33.

19. Boff, "Cristología a partir del Nazareno," 33.

20. Campana, "Jesús, los pobres y la teología," 50.

21. There is a "historical continuity" between the suffering servant of the Lord and "the crucified people." The millions of crosses in the Latin American continent "not only make us think and move us to change our way of thinking, but unavoidably oblige us to think." For Latin American Christologies there is nothing more important or necessary than that (Sobrino, *Jesucristo liberador*, 45, 16–17).

22. Sobrino, *Jesucristo liberador*, 321.

today, for his colleagues were murdered as a consequence of their struggle for justice and righteousness, just as Christ himself was. Therefore, Sobrino concludes that these people "complete in their flesh what is lacking in the passion of Christ [Col 1:24]."[23] The logical consequence of this is that the crucified people themselves become bearers of a "historical soteriology." This is, for Sobrino, "the greatest novelty in the theological analysis . . . that is done in Latin America, as opposed to other parts of the world."[24]

In Latin America, the passion of Jesus traditionally has been a source of comfort and resignation, but not of liberation. That is why the most important date in the Latin Christian calendar, popularly speaking, is Holy Friday.[25] This observation is not intended to deny the importance of Jesus's empathy, his capacity to sympathize with those who sorrow insofar as he was himself a man of sorrows.[26] Nor should the passion of Jesus be reduced to the experience of suffering; rather, Jesus's passion has meaning because it is undertaken as "a fight against suffering."[27] The life and suffering of Jesus demonstrate how real God's love for humanity is.[28] Sobrino acknowledges that anything we say about this will always be inadequate, but he ventures to propose that "God participates in the passion of Jesus and in the passion of the world."[29] This is a crucial meaning of the incarnation: true love is expressed in solidarity. But the veracity of such solidarity requires that Jesus be truly human and his suffering real.[30]

---

23. Sobrino, *Jesucristo liberador*, 325.

24. Sobrino admits that this correlation of the crucifixion with Latin American suffering caused by poverty is done more by intuition than by exegesis. But he also argues that the alternatives are even worse: popular religiosity and useless or harmful Christologies that say nothing about "centuries of inhuman and antichristian oppression" (Sobrino, *Jesucristo liberador*, 329, 13).

25. Sobrino, *Jesucristo liberador*, 26.

26. Boff, *Jesucristo el liberador*, 105.

27. Sobrino, *Jesucristo liberador*, 307.

28. Sobrino, *Jesucristo liberador*, 294.

29. Sobrino, *Jesucristo liberador*, 310.

30. Boff, *Jesucristo el liberador*, 130.

THE MIGRANT MESSIAH: NEW TESTAMENT TESTIMONY

With the benefit of these insights from the Liberationist theological tradition, it is appropriate to shift attention to examine how the New Testament texts present Jesus as a migrant. The obvious starting point, as intimated above, is the flight of the Holy Family to Egypt.

Jesus as an Involuntary Migrant

The notion that the infant or toddler Jesus was a refugee has gained a good deal of traction in popular discourse. Matthew 2 indicates that Joseph was warned in a dream that Herod sought to destroy Jesus, such that Joseph and Mary were forced to flee from Judea to Egypt under cover of night (Matt 2:13–15). The sword fell just behind them, as Herod slaughtered all the male children in Bethlehem under two years of age (Matt 2:16). Hence the argument that Jesus was a refugee.[31]

Some fire back that Egypt was *still* part of the Roman empire, such that Jesus should not be likened to a refugee because he remained in the same empire in which he had previously resided.[32] Nonetheless, Egypt and Judea were politically distinct regions within the empire (*Aegyptus* being at that point a province ruled by a Roman procurator and Judea being part of a client kingdom governed by Herod the Great as a vassal monarch). The Holy Family geographically relocated to a kingdom ruled by a different leader, with a different culture, different religions,[33] and different dominant languages, all because they feared legitimately for the life of their child. The fact that they remained within the Roman empire hardly undermines the analogy to modern refugees, lest we would also contend that a first-century migrant fleeing from Asia Minor to what is modern England should also not be considered a refugee, insofar as ancient Galatia and Britannia were

31. Thus, e.g., Martin, "Were Jesus, Mary and Joseph Refugees?"

32. This may be mere popular discourse, and yet this sort of argument has a genuine impact on how public opinion and public policy are formed, and therefore merits a response.

33. Even if they relocated to Alexandria, where there was a large Jewish minority population, the dominance of Greco-Roman religions would have created a dramatically different religious environment than predominant Jewish monotheism of Galilee and Judea.

also distinct provinces within the Roman empire. Such a contention would seem a willful exercise in missing the point.

But . . . what is the point? What do we gain from the observation that, according to the Matthean narrative, the Holy Family was forced to immigrate to Egypt under imminent threat of violence? In popular discourse, at least, the goal of the "Jesus was a refugee" schtick is probably to arouse sympathy, to move the emotions of those who are not instinctively concerned by the plight of refugees but might nonetheless be affectively stirred if a symbolic link could be made between the Mexican child in a detention center and the little Lord Jesus. As a rhetorical maneuver, that is probably fine, but as a theologian one should be candid that the First Evangelist was not obviously making such a case in Matthew 2. The account of the flight into Egypt is part of a larger Matthean argument to the effect that Jesus recapitulates key events in the history of Israel (being carried off to Egypt like Joseph, coming out of Egypt like Moses, etc.) as evidence that he is an exemplary leader for the eschatological people of God.

That exegetical take is true enough, but the argument can be pushed a little further in the direction of relevance to contemporary displacement phenomena. Robert Myles has argued, provocatively and plausibly, that scholars have overlooked a sub-emphasis on forced displacement in Matthew's Gospel. Myles points out that, in the account of the flight to Egypt, the term ἀναχωρέω is used four times (Matt 2:12–22). Generally meaning "to depart," or more specifically to "withdraw, take refuge,"[34] ἀναχωρέω is used on various occasions in the Septuagint to describe forced displacement in situations of violence (Exod 2:15; 1 Sam 19:10; Tob 1:19).[35] Additionally, in the genealogy of Matthew 1, fifteen of the names mentioned "can be expressly connected to episodes of forced displacement, itinerancy and/or homelessness."[36] Likewise, the genealogy speaks four times of the "deportation to Babylon" (μετοικεσία Βαβυλῶνος; 1:11, 12, 17).[37] All of this prepares the reader for the fact that, in the later Gospel narrative, Jesus is frequently displaced by the threat of danger. For example, after one of his conflicts with the Pharisees, Jesus *sought refuge* in the regions of Tyre and Sidon (ἀνεχώρησεν εἰς τὰ μέρη Τύρου καὶ Σιδῶνος; 15:21); so also, when Jesus heard of John's arrest, he ἀνεχώρησεν, leaving his hometown of

---

34. BDAG, 75.

35. Myles, "Echoes of Displacement," 33–34.

36. Myles, "Echoes of Displacement," 37.

37. Myles, "Echoes of Displacement," 39.

Nazareth behind and moving to Capernaum (4:12); again, when he heard of John's execution by Herod Antipas, Jesus ἀνεχώρησεν to a desolate place by himself (Matt 14:13; cf. Luke 13:31).[38] Staying on the move and ahead of his enemies is a recurring feature of Jesus's biography, reaching its denouement in the crucifixion when Pilate and Antipas finish what Herod the Great started. Thus, as an infant and throughout his public ministry, Jesus repeatedly experienced forced migration under the threat of violence.

Jesus as a Voluntary Migrant: Itinerancy and Incarnation

In addition to being *forcibly* displaced, Jesus undertook various *voluntary* migrations, both throughout his itinerant ministry (in a terrestrial sense), and in his very incarnation (in a celestial sense).

Jesus's Voluntary Terrestrial Migrations

To begin with the mundane, it is (blissfully) uncontroversial to point out that Jesus's public ministry was largely itinerant. The Synoptic Gospels are structured around Jesus's itinerant preaching, (in broad terms) beginning in and around Galilee and then progressing south to Jerusalem; although John depicts Jesus as a frequent flier between Judea and Galilee. To characterize his own perpetual migration, Jesus commented, "Foxes have holes, and birds of the air have nests; but the Son of Man has nowhere to lay his head" (Luke 9:58), for he had left behind his home, family, and possessions to inaugurate the kingdom of God (Mark 10:28–31).[39]

In brief, throughout his preaching ministry, Jesus was a voluntary migrant, somewhat like the Roma of today.[40] While that certainly would not have entailed the sort of trauma that forced displacement often generates, his itinerancy would have nonetheless rendered him a liminal figure, an outsider to the village economies.[41] Yet it is by dint of his voluntary migration that Jesus was able to disseminate his message across Galilee and Judea within the short span of a few years, for migration (voluntary or otherwise) is a key tool for the spread of the gospel, as will be argued forthwith.

---

38. Myles, "Echoes of Displacement," 40.

39. Senior, "'Beloved Aliens and Exiles,'" 23.

40. Strine, "Migration, Dual Identity and Integration," 111.

41. Moxnes, *Economy of the Kingdom*, 52–55.

Jesus's Voluntary Celestial Migration

Beyond Jesus's voluntary perambulation around Galilee, the motif of migration aptly describes aspects of the Incarnation of the divine Logos: in taking on flesh and taking up residence among humans, there is a real sense in which God migrated.[42] John's Gospel opens by saying that the Word became flesh and "encamped" among us (ἐσκήνωσεν ἐν ἡμῖν); God came to dwell among humanity, although humanity refused the divine immigrant (John 1:11, 14).[43] The Logos left behind heavenly prerogatives and riches, humbling "himself . . . to the point of death" (Phil 2:4–8; cf. 2 Cor 8:9), precisely to facilitate our migration into the kingdom of Heaven.[44] (You could almost say that Jesus is the *coyote* of the New Creation!) In this spirit, Vietnamese migrant theologian Peter Phan riffs on John 3:16, saying, "God, in Jesus, so loved the world, that he migrated into the far and distant territory of our broken world so that we, in turn, could migrate back to our homeland (John 3:16–17)."[45]

Migration is part of Jesus's story: whether forced to flee his country before Herodian soldiers slicked Bethlehem's streets with infant blood, or voluntarily renouncing hearth and home to declare the dawning of God's kingdom, or indeed abandoning the riches of heaven to build a better life for his children, the Son of God is a migrant. This is an historical and theological truth.

MIGRATION AND THE MISSION OF THE CHURCH

Nonetheless, this christological reality has massive missiological ramifications. So, let us now examine how this facet of Jesus's identity impacts the mission of the Body of the Migrant Christ.

The Mission of the Church to Jesus the Migrant: Matthew 25:31–46

At the end of the Matthean version of Jesus's eschatological discourse (Matt 24–25), Jesus pulls the curtain back on the final judgment, unveiling

42. López, "El divino migrante," 15–16; Phan, "Deus Migrator," 860–62.

43. Phan, "Deus Migrator," 861; cf. Aymer, "Sojourners' Truths," 14.

44. López, "El divino migrante," 16.

45. Groody, "Church on the Move," 40.

something of what will transpire when all the nations gather at his glorious Parousia. This text, the "Sheep and Goats Judgment" (Matt 25:31–46), may be the Gospel pericope with the most directly prescriptive ramifications for the church's care of migrants.

In a scene reminiscent of picking teams for a terrifying apocalyptic softball game, souls are divided left and right between the righteous sheep and the wicked goats. But this eschatological draft is not conducted on the basis of whether someone had a strong batting average or was (like Christopher in Little League) paralyzed by fear of the ball; rather, teams are decided depending on whether, in Christ's time of need, a given soul had succored him.

> For I was hungry and you gave me food, I was thirsty and you gave me something to drink, I was a stranger [or "foreigner" or "alien," ξένος] and you welcomed me, I was naked and you gave me clothing, I was sick and you took care of me, I was in prison and you visited me (25:35–36, cf. 42–43).

When the righteous inquire when exactly they had cared for the Son of Man in that manner, the exalted judge responds, "Whatever you did for one of these, my littlest brothers and sisters (ἐνὶ τούτων τῶν ἀδελφῶν μου τῶν ἐλαχίστων), you did for me" (25:40, our translation). On this basis, many theologians of migration contend that Jesus is served through acts of compassion to the needy, vulnerable, foreigner (ξένος). Peter Phan's comments are exemplary as he explains,

> Jesus is the paradigmatic migrant. . . . Already as a child, he experienced migration to Egypt. . . . During his ministry, he was itinerant and homeless, having nowhere to lay his head. . . . That is why he could truly say that whoever welcomes a migrant/stranger, welcomes him.[46]

It's a stirring interpretation, to be sure, and many have found herein a broad-spectrum injunction to serve Christ by showing mercy to any and all migrants. The question is, however, whether it is good exegesis.

Some interpreters have counseled caution, not out of a lack of compassion, but in an effort to ensure that the text not be over-read. The critical point of debate is about how widely to understand the reference of "my littlest [or 'least significant'] brothers and sisters" (25:40). Without belaboring

---

46. Phan, "Migration in the Patristic Era," 58.

all the interpretive options,[47] the forefront contenders are that "my littlest brothers and sisters" denote:

A. The disciples of Jesus in the conditions of vulnerability that accompany their *missionary* activity;

B. Vulnerable Christians; or

C. Vulnerable humans, who may or may not be Christians.

Deciding between these options is not easy, since Matthew uses the word ἀδελφοί to refer sometimes to his itinerant disciples (23:11; 28:10), sometimes to non-itinerant disciples (12:48–50; 18:15, 21, 35), and sometimes just to his fellow humans (5:22–24; 7:3–5). Addressing "option A" first, some excellent scholars have suggested that τούτων τῶν ἀδελφῶν μου τῶν ἐλαχίστων are disciples of Jesus who suffer hunger and foreignness as a consequence of being traveling missionaries; accordingly, the ξένος that one is to welcome "is technically a disciple who goes to another land for ministry and thus is a foreigner there."[48] This reading has a great deal to commend it, since there are significant parallels between Matt 25:40 and an earlier discourse directed toward the itinerant disciples, in which they are told, "Whoever welcomes you welcomes me" (v. 40), after which Jesus promises to reward "whoever gives even a cup of cold water to one of these little ones" (v. 42).

Nonetheless, there are reasons to question that interpretation since an equally strong parallel to Matt 25:40 can be adduced in a text referring to *non*-itinerant disciples. In Matthew 18, the phrase "these little ones" refers to believers who are *not* among the itinerant disciples (Matt 18:6, 10, 14). Furthermore, Matt 25:31–46 is part of a larger discourse directed to the twelve disciples (24:1–3). This narrative framework militates against Interpretation A, since it would be awkward to exhort the Twelve to care for other missionaries in order to be spared eschatological perdition. It makes more sense to read the Sheep and Goats Judgment as teaching the disciples to take care of *all* their needy and vulnerable brethren, irrespective of whether that vulnerability is the consequence of a missionary vocation. On balance, then, Interpretation A seems rather less tenable than Interpretation B.

47. For a taxonomy of all interpretations, see e.g., Davies and Allison, *Gospel According to Saint Matthew*, 3:429; Hagner, *Matthew 14–28*, 744–45.

48. Carroll, *Christians at the Border*, 124. Similarly, Luz, *Matthew 21–28*, 280; Keener, *Gospel of Matthew*, 605. Naturally, these authors' conclusions are a matter of exegetical conviction and certainly do not reflect tepidity of concern about plight of migrants!

Still, perhaps the scope of this passage can be widened a bit further, such that "these my littlest brothers and sisters" could be extended to *all* vulnerable people (interpretation C). After all, sometimes Matthew does uses ἀδελφοί simply in reference to other people, who need not be Christians (5:22–24; 7:3–5).[49] So also, the narrative scenery of this passage makes it difficult to identify "my littlest brothers and sisters" exclusively with Christians, since, according to 25:32, *all nations* (πάντα τὰ ἔθνη) had been gathered for this sorting of eschatological livestock. Allison and Davies ask, "If πάντα τὰ ἔθνη be thought to include non-Christians, how likely is it that our text envisages them visiting Christians in prison?"[50] They make a good point.[51] So it may be that the "littlest brothers and sisters" in whom Jesus is welcomed are in fact any naked, hungry, or foreign persons in need of mercy.

In sum, it seems most likely that "my littlest brothers and sisters" in 25:40 refers either to vulnerable *Christians* (interpretation B) or to vulnerable *people more generally* (interpretation C), but not just to traveling Christian missionaries (interpretation A). In either of these two more plausible scenarios, the imperative to care for the ξένος *qua* foreigner, alien, and migrant, is clear; thus Matthew 25 commands compassion for the migrant, precisely because, in caring for the migrant, we care for Jesus.

The ramifications for the twenty-first-century US church are manifest. Seventy-two percent of new migrants to the US are Christians,[52] and thousands of other believers succumb to thirst in Arizona deserts, live in terror in Syria, or are murdered in Iran and Iraq, as the US slashes refugee admissions. Thus, it is difficult for the present authors not to conclude that believers supporting the ruthlessly exclusive new immigration policies are in direct contravention of Matt 25:40—and consequentially, our brothers and sisters are dying. In the language of Jon Sobrino, migrants are the crucified people of the world today,[53] and in them, God "participates in the passion

---

49. Davies and Allison, *Gospel According to Saint Matthew,* 3:429.

50. Davies and Allison, *Gospel According to Saint Matthew,* 3:429.

51. Most interpreters do understand πάντα τὰ ἔθνη to include non-Christians, given that, in the other places the phrase occurs in Matthew's Gospel (24:9, 14; 28:19), non-Christians are clearly in view; Davies and Allison, *Gospel According to Saint Matthew,* 3:422.

52. Connor, "Faith on the Move," 25. The US is the number one destination for Christian migrants (Connor, "Faith on the Move," 29).

53. Sobrino, *Jesucristo liberador,* 310. So also Miller, "Christification of the Least," 259–62.

of the world" and Jesus is crucified again and again. To riff on Hebrews 6, by neglecting our suffering siblings, we "are crucifying again the Son of God," though there is certainly time to repent, knowing that "God is not unjust; he will not overlook . . . your work and the love that you showed for his sake in serving the saints" (Heb 6:6, 10).

THE MISSION OF JESUS'S MIGRANT CHURCH

So, the humanity of Jesus *as* a migrant entails that we love Jesus *in* the migrant. Sometimes, however, when we emphasize the immigrants' vulnerability, we fall into the trap of objectifying her or him, seeing her or him as impotent, pathetic. We often fail to appreciate that migrants are also strong and have always been vital actors in carrying out the mission of the church. This, too, is clear in the New Testament.

Migrant Mission in the First Century

Not only did Jesus carry out his earthly ministry as a migrant; he made such voluntary migration a model for many of his followers. When summoning the Twelve, he told them, "Follow me"; voluntary geographic displacement was prescriptive. The Twelve were called to a sort of "migratory discipleship"[54] and thus left behind their land and homes (Matt 19:29 and parallels). Accordingly, when others wanted to join Jesus's entourage, he warned them that following him meant adopting his lifestyle as a migrant who had nowhere to lay his head (Luke 9:56–57).

This migrant mission was not merely an idiosyncratic feature of Jesus's public ministry, some sort of a Schweitzerian *Interimsethik*. The Great Commission (Matt 28:19–20) and its parallel in Acts (1:8) underscore the necessity of geographic displacement for the mission of the church.[55] "From the earliest days the Church has migrated to the end of the world to make that message known."[56] Small surprise then that Christians first characterized their sect as ἡ ὁδός, "the Way," "the Road," "the Journey" (Acts 18:25–26; 19:23; 22:4; 24:14, 22).[57]

54. So also Stenschke, "Migration and Theology," 93.

55. Cf. Escobar, "Refugees," 103.

56. Groody, "Church on the Move," 40.

57. Senior, "Beloved Aliens and Exiles," 24. Obviously, ἡ ὁδός can also communicate "way" in the sense of a "way of life" or set of teachings (BDAG 690–92); but it seems likely

Furthermore, it would be a mistake to allow the point that the Twelve were generally voluntary migrants to obscure the fact that the ancient missionary activity of the church was conducted in no small degree through *involuntary* migration, through *forced* displacement due to violence. The book of Acts indicates that the spread of the gospel from Jerusalem to Judea, Samaria, and the ends of the earth was ignited precisely when persecution in Jerusalem propelled believers into the surrounding regions (Acts 8:1–8; 11:19–21). It was persecution by Herod Antipas that drove Peter out of Jerusalem (Acts 12:1–17), quite plausibly to preach in the northern regions of Asia Minor (cf. 1 Pet 1:1). It was the expulsion of the Jews and Christians from Rome by Emperor Claudius that sent Priscilla and Aquila to Corinth (Acts 18:1).[58] It was the repeated attempts of the Jewish leaders to assassinate Paul, that took that apostle and his message right into the heart of the Roman empire (Acts 23:11; 25:11–12, 25; 28:19–20). Forced migration, flight before hostile rulers and would-be assassins, is how God has spread the gospel from the beginning.[59] And some things never change.

Migrant Mission in the Twenty-first Century

Many ancient apostles were also forced migrants, yet they were not thereby rendered impotent. Amidst all the talk of care *for* the migrant in his or her vulnerability, we cannot overlook the power and potential *of* the migrant in the kingdom of God. Lest we slide from compassion into a savior complex, it is important to understand that throughout history (in the words of Lydio Tomasi), "It's [often] not . . . the Church [that] saves the immigrant, but the immigrant who saves the Church."[60] Therefore, in the time that remains, we will highlight three ways in which migrants can help "save the Church," especially the US Church.

----

that the term was congenial to Christians because it was redolent of the various dimensions of the church as a religio-ethical sect of Judaism, as a community in significant geographic migration, and as a community on an eschatological pilgrimage.

58. Senior, "Beloved Aliens and Exiles," 24–25.

59. Furthermore, the pattern of spreading the church through migration, voluntary and involuntary, has persisted in the intervening two millennia; Phan, "Migration in the Patristic Era," 38–47; Phan, "Deus Migrator," 850–53.

60. Tomasi, "Other Catholics," 301, cited by Groody, "Jesus and the Undocumented Immigrant," 316.

Migrant Missionaries

As members of the people of God, immigrants are agents of the kingdom. Even when they migrate for economic, political, or security reasons, migrants function as missionaries—bringing the gospel to numerous other nations,[61] including our own. Christians are disproportionately represented among world migrants, constituting 49 percent of the migrant population worldwide, and the US is the number one destination for Christian migrants.[62] Small surprise, then, that the fastest-growing Christian traditions in the US are among African, Asian, and Latin immigrant communities.[63] If you want to see inner city Chicago or Detroit evangelized, then you should start praying for more Christian migrants from Africa and Mexico to move in.

Since 2014, we have run a large project called *Faith and Displacement*. Its goal has been to confront the crisis of forced internal displacement in Colombia by mobilizing local evangelical churches into holistic mission with and toward the victims of the violent conflict. In order to make sure that we were effective in our endeavors to foster the spiritual, economic, psychological, social, and political recovery of Colombian "internally displaced persons" (IDPs), we assembled a team of over 25 social scientists and theologians from four different continents. But we did not stop with that team, because a South African sociologist and a Colombian economist do not know what it is like to be a single mother who watches her husband get beheaded by paramilitary forces before being driven from her tiny rural farm and obliged to carry her children to a behemoth megacity like Bogotá, where she then has to try to feed her family, even though she cannot read and has never had to use coins to buy a banana. How could we expect to serve IDPs, or to train churches to minister to IDPs, when our reality is so distant from theirs?

So, we recruited IDPs as co-researchers, integrated them onto our teams and learned from their experiences. Then, with their help, we created curricula to train local Colombian Christians to love their migrant victim siblings. Moreover, one of the first instructions we gave to church leaders endeavoring to serve IDPs was to ensure that, on their ministry teams, they

61. See examples in Escobar, "Refugees," 103–4.

62. Connor, "Faith on the Move," 11, 29.

63. Johnson, "USA Evangelicals/Evangelicals in a Global Context." For a specific case study, see Norton, "Migrant-Shaped Urban Mission," 68–88.

included displaced people, because the best missionaries to the displaced are often the displaced themselves.

Migrant Theologians

In addition to being effective missionaries, migrants can help strengthen the theology of the non-migrant church. As Casey Strine has pointed out, the *vast* majority of scriptural books are written by migrants, about migrants, and/or to migrants.[64] Migration is at the heart of the narratives about the patriarchs, the exodus, the conquest, the exile, the return to the land, the ministry of Jesus, and the spread of the church. The majority of the Prophetic books and New Testament epistles are written by an author who was a migrant or to a migrant community, and as a result, when refugees and displaced people read the Scriptures, they understand things that non-migrants do not.

In our time working with displaced Colombians, some of us read the parable of the Unforgiving Servant (Matt 18:21–35) with victims of the violent conflict.[65] Our goal was to learn about IDPs' perceptions of forgiveness. Yet, along the way, we realized that the IDPs were reading that parable in ways that were attentive to dynamics of violence and money in the parable which are simply overlooked by Western New Testament scholars.[66] Migrants are primed to see things we miss in the Bible; and we ignore their insights to our detriment.

So also with theology. Theology cannot be just done for the poor, or with the poor in mind. They must be part of our theologizing. Gustavo Gutiérrez explains, "From the perspective of the option for the poor, theology is done not only about the migrants and their situation, but *from* their situation."[67] Naturally, the authors cannot do theology *as* a poor migrant; but we can at least do theology *with* a poor IDP. So, in the *Faith and Displacement Project*, when we created materials to help the IDPs and churches reflect and act on their own contexts, we developed Scripture studies with the input of IDPs and about scriptural texts focused on migration, in such

---

64. Strine, "Migration, Dual Identity and Integration," 105–13.

65. See Heimburger et al., *Iglesia, política y desplazamiento*, 74–77.

66. Heimburger, Hays, and Mejía-Castillo, "Forgiveness and Politics," 1–9.

67. Gutiérrez, "Poverty, Migration, and the Option for the Poor," 82.

a way as to foster IDPs theologizing independently and locally about their own lives, pasts, and futures.[68]

Migrant Prophets

Not only do migrants see things in Scripture that non-migrants miss; they also see things in the modern world to which people like us are oblivious. We have never applied for refugee status or stayed in a detainment camp. We have never suffered real hunger or worried that we won't be able to give our children water. We have never been forced into slavery as the price of a visa. But our migrant neighbors have. They have dwelt in the shadow side of our society; thus, they can give us insights into the injustices of which most non-immigrants are blissfully unaware. To cite Stephen Bevans, this

> at times, will be a real prophetic activity, since often the local church will not want to be shaken in its cultural complacency, and [recognize that it] shares the racism and xenophobia of the population at large. The duty of the receiving church nonetheless is to be open to receive these gifts and so allow itself to be transformed.[69]

In this way, migrants can help rescue the US church from our syncretism, from our tendency to collapse Christianity with America. The Scriptures teach that Christians are aliens and exiles in the world.[70] For this reason, the *Epistle of Diognetus* described early Christians as people who "live in their own countries, but only as aliens; they participate in everything as citizens and endure everything as foreigners. Every foreign country is their fatherland, and every fatherland is foreign" (*Ep. Diog.* 5:5). Nonetheless, the American church is, by and large, too comfortable in the United States. As such, we need those who are not at home in the US to remind us that we should not feel entirely at home here either, for we are a people of the Way, λαός τῆς ὁδοῦ.

---

68. See, for example, the Scripture studies created for IDPs on Jeremiah 29 and on Ezra and Nehemiah in Hays and Ramírez, *La esperanza económica*, 44–47, 61–65.

69. Bevans, "Mission *among* Migrants, Mission *of* Migrants," 99.

70. So Heb 11:13–15, "having acknowledged that they were strangers and exiles on the earth," v. 13; 1 Pet 1:1; 2:11, "sojourners and exiles."

CONCLUSION AND POSTSCRIPT: ON FEAR

Jesus was a migrant and he called others to migrate with him, both in terrestrial proclamation and in a heavenly pilgrimage. Indeed, those who are migrants in the twenty-first century are poised to help save the non-migrant church, for these migrants are uniquely equipped as missionaries, as theologians, and as prophets; they remind us that we are all migrants, a pilgrim people.

But . . . all this kumbaya talk ignores the drug-dealing, terrorist elephant in the room. It is one thing to love your enemy when he is the guy who steals your lunch from the office refrigerator. But what if your enemy actually wants to kill you?

When emphasizing the importance of caring for the immigrant, we cannot overlook the fact that a major obstacle to compassion is *fear*. US Americans are not uneasy about migrants simply because they are often dark-skinned, or culturally other, or linguistically different (although, racism and cultural chauvinism are real drivers for many opponents of immigration). The migrant is also seen as dangerous, both here and abroad. In Colombia, the internally displaced person is feared as a guerilla. In the Europe, the Muslim is feared as a terrorist. In the US, the Mexican migrant is feared as a drug-dealer or a rapist. And setting aside the fact that immigration does *not actually* raise crime levels,[71] the reality is that some immigrants will prove to be dangerous. That is something we cannot control; when Matthew 25 tells us to welcome the ξένος, the alien or foreigner, the exhortation is to welcome them *as* alien, unknown.[72] And that means accepting a degree of danger.

Nonetheless, as Mary Hinkle Shore pointedly inquires, "[W]hen has the avoidance of danger ever been an acceptable reason for Christians not to follow Christ?"[73] Jesus was not just being rhetorically florid when he said, "Whoever does not take up the cross and follow me is not worthy of me. Those who find their life will lose it, and those who lose their life for my sake will find it" (Matt 10:38–39). Any Christian discourse about migration that does not seriously contemplate the real-if-remote possibility of

71. Research belies the notion that immigrants raise the crime rate; Nowrasteh, "By the Numbers"; Martínez and Lee, "On Immigration and Crime," 485–524; Mears, "Immigration and Crime," 284–88; Butcher and Piehl, "Crime, Corrections, and California," 1–23.

72. A point elegantly made by Namli, "Identity and the Stranger," 818.

73. Shore, "Jesus as a Refugee," 6.

death will stagnate in a deadlock between the theological virtue of charity and the cardinal virtue of prudence. But there are other Christian virtues at play in this issue, not least of which are justice and courage. When the Gospels narrate how Jesus's life was marked by displacement in the shadow of danger—migration under Herod the Great, as a child; migration during his ministry when Herod Antipas was trying to kill him; and ultimately migration toward Jerusalem, where his enemies succeeded in murdering him—the Evangelists record these events to call us not only to compassion *for* Christ, but to courage *like* Christ. In spite of the danger, Jesus ministered to personal and national enemies: to occupying military forces, to thieves, to Samaritans, to angry mobs bent on hurling him over a cliff to his death. We would speculate that Jesus could embrace dangerous people because (1) he loved them, and (2) because he was reconciled to the fact that he was going to die. So, if we cannot welcome the foreigner because our fear is too powerful . . . that is understandable. But then let us confess, at least in front of the mirror, that we do not yet love them, and that we have not yet embraced the truth that we are going to die. And then migrate home.

Bibliography

Abbott, Edwin A. *Johannine Grammar*. London: A. & C. Black, 1906.

Adichie, Chimamanda Ngozi. "The Danger of the Single Story." *TEDGlobal 2009* (July 2009). https://www.ted.com/talks/chimamanda_ngozi_adichie_the_danger_of_a_single_story/transcript?language=en.

"Adventurers and Slave Traders." *The National Archives*. http://www.nationalarchives.gov.uk/pathways/blackhistory/early_times/adventurers.htm.

Allen, Michael. *Grounded in Heaven: Recentering Christian Hope and Life on God*. Grand Rapids: Eerdmans, 2018.

Athanasius. *On the Incarnation*. Edited by John Behr. Popular Patristics 44b. Yonkers: St. Vladimir's Seminary, 2012.

Atkinson, Kenneth. *A History of the Hasmonean State: Josephus and Beyond*. London: T. & T. Clark, 2016.

Attridge, Harold W. *The Epistle to the Hebrews*. Hermeneia: A Critical and Historical Commentary on the Bible. Philadelphia: Fortress, 1989.

Augustine. *On the Trinity*. Translated by Edmund Hill, OP. Hyde Park: New City Press, 1991.

———. "Lectures or Tractates on the Gospel According to St. John." In *NPNF1* 7, edited by Philip Schaff; translated by John Gibb and James Innes, 5–776. Grand Rapids: Eerdmans, 1956.

Aymer, Margaret. "Sojourners' Truths: The New Testament as Diaspora Space." *Journal of the Interdenominational Theological Center* 41 (2015) 1–18.

Barth, Karl. *The Humanity of God*. Louisville: Westminster John Knox, 1960.

Bauckham, Richard. "The Divinity of Jesus Christ in the Epistle to the Hebrews." In *The Epistle to the Hebrews and Christian Theology*, edited by Richard Bauckham et al., 15–36. Grand Rapids: Eerdmans, 2009.

———. *Jesus and the God of Israel: God Crucified and Other Studies on the New Testament Christology of Divine Identity*. Grand Rapids: Eerdmans, 2008.

Baur, Ferdinand Christian. *Paul, the Apostle of Jesus Christ: His Life and Work, His Epistles and His Doctrine*. Translated by Eduard Zeller. 2nd ed. Edinburgh: Williams and Norgate, 1876.

Bertrand, Frédéric. *Mystique de Jésus chez Origène*. Théologie 23. Paris: Aubier, 1951.

Bevans, Stephen. "Mission *among* Migrants, Mission *of* Migrants: Mission of the Church." In *A Promised Land, A Perilous Journey: Theological Perspectives on Migration*, edited by Daniel G. Groody and Gioacchino Campese, 89–106. Notre Dame, IN: University of Notre Dame Press, 2008.

Bibliography

Blomberg, Craig. "The Authenticity and Significance of Jesus' Table Fellowship with Sinners." In *Key Events in the Life of the Historical Jesus: A Collaborative Exploration of Context and Coherence*, edited by Darrell L. Bock and Robert L. Webb, 215–50. Tübingen: Mohr Siebeck, 2009.

———. *Contagious Holiness*. Downers Grove, IL: InterVarsity, 2005.

Bloom, Harold. *The American Religion*. New Haven, CT: Yale University Press, 1992.

Bock, Darrell L. *Blasphemy and Exaltation in Judaism and the Final Examination of Jesus*. WUNT 2/106. Tübingen: Mohr Siebeck, 1998.

Bock, Darrell L., with Benjamin I. Simpson. *Jesus According to Scripture: Restoring the Portrait from the Gospels*. 2nd ed. Grand Rapids: Baker, 2017.

Boff, Leonardo. "Cristología a partir del Nazareno, en Bajar de la cruz a los pobres." In *Cristología de la liberación*, 29–34. Comisión Teológica Internacional de la Asociación Ecuménica de Teólogos/as del Tercer Mundo, 2007.

———. *Jesucristo el liberador: ensayo de cristología crítica para nuestro tiempo*. Translated by Maria E. Rodríguez. Bogotá: Indoamerican, 1979.

Booth, Roger. *Jesus and the Laws of Purity: Tradition History and Legal History in Mark 7*. JSNTSup 13. Sheffield: JSOT Press, 1986.

Brock, Sebastian P., and Susan Ashbrook Harvey, trans. *Holy Women of the Syrian Orient*. 2nd ed. Berkley: University of California Press, 1998.

Butcher, Kristin F., and Anne Morrison Piehl. "Crime, Corrections, and California: What Does Immigration Have to Do with It?" *California Counts: Population Trends and Profiles* (2008) 1–23.

Cahill, P. Joseph. "Narrative Art in John IV." *Religious Studies Bulletin* 2 (1982) 41–48.

Calvin, John. *Commentaries on the Catholic Epistles*. Translated by John Owen. Calvin's Commentaries. Grand Rapids: Baker, 1984.

Campana, Oscar. "Jesús, los pobres y la teología, en Bajar de la cruz a los pobres." In *Cristología de la liberación*, 43–52. Comisión Teológica Internacional de la Asociación Ecuménica de Teólogos/as del Tercer Mundo, 2007.

Carroll, M. Daniel. *Christians at the Border: Immigration, the Church, and the Bible*. Grand Rapids: Baker Academic, 2008.

Carson, D. A. *The Gospel According to John*. Pillar New Testament Commentary. Grand Rapids: Eerdmans, 1991.

Castles, Stephen, and Mark J. Miller. *The Age of Migration: International Population Movements in the Modern World*. 5th ed. London: Guilford, 2013.

Cockerill, Gareth Lee. *The Epistle to the Hebrews*. New International Commentary on the New Testament. Grand Rapids: Eerdmans, 2012.

———. "Hebrews 1:6: Source and Significance." *BBR* 9 (1999) 51–64.

Cohick, Lynn H. *Women in the World of the Earliest Christians: Illuminating Ancient Ways of Life*. Grand Rapids: Baker Academic, 2009.

Comblin, José. "Reflexiones sobre la notificación enviada a Jon Sobrino." In *en Bajar de la cruz a los pobres: Cristología de la liberación*, 61–68. Comisión Teológica Internacional de la Asociación Ecuménica de Teólogos/as del Tercer Mundo, 2007.

Cone, James H. *The Cross and the Lynching Tree*. Maryknoll, NY: Orbis, 2011.

Connor, Phillip. "Faith on the Move: The Religious Affiliation of International Migrants." In *The Pew Forum on Religion & Public Life*. Pew Research Center, 2012.

Cortez, Marc. "The Body and the Beatific Vision." In *Being Saved. Explorations in Human Salvation*, edited by Marc Cortez et al., 326–43. London: SCM, 2018.

———. *Theological Anthropology: A Guide for the Perplexed*. New York: T. & T. Clark, 2010.

Cotton, Hannah M., and Jonas C. Greenfield. "Babatha's Property and the Law of Succession in the Babatha Archive." *ZPE* 104 (1994) 211–24.

Crisp, Oliver D., and Fred Sanders, eds. *The Christian Doctrine of Humanity: Explorations in Constructive Dogmatics*. Grand Rapids: Zondervan Academic, 2018.

Cyril of Jerusalem, *Catechetical Lecture*. Translated by Leo P. McCauley. The Works of St. Cyril of Jerusalem. Washington, DC: Catholic University Press, 1969.

Czajkowski, Kimberley. *Living Under Different Laws: The Babatha and Salome Komaise Archives*. Oxford: Oxford University Press, 2014.

Daley, Brian E., SJ. "Origen's De Principiis: A Guide to the `Principles' of Christian Scriptural Interpretation." In *Nova et Vetera: Patristic Studies in Honor of Thomas Patrick Halton*, edited by John Petruccione, 3–21. Washington, DC: Catholic University of America Press, 1998.

Davidson, Jo Ann. "The Well Women of Scripture Revisited." *Journal of the Adventist Theological Society* 49 (2006) 209–28.

Davies, W. D., and Dale C. Allison. *A Critical and Exegetical Commentary on the Gospel According to Saint Matthew*. 3 vols. International Critical Commentary on the Holy Scriptures of the Old and New Testaments. New York: T. & T. Clark, 1997.

Davis, Julie Hirschfield. "Trump to Cap Refugees Allowed into U.S. at 30,000, a Record Low." *New York Times*, September 17, 2018. https://www.nytimes.com/2018/09/17/us/politics/trump-refugees-historic-cuts.html.

Day, Janeth Norfleete. *The Woman at the Well: Interpretation of John 4:1–42*. Leiden: Brill, 2002.

De Boer, Esther A. *The Gospel of Mary: Listening to the Beloved Disciple*. London: Continuum, 2004.

Dixon, Suzanne. "Sex and the Married Woman in Ancient Rome." In *Early Christian Families in Context: An Interdisciplinary Dialogue*, edited by David L. Balch and Carolyn Osiek, 111–29. Grand Rapids: Eerdmans, 2003.

Dobschütz, Ernst von. *Christusbilder: Untersuchungen zur christlichen Legend*. Leipzig: Hinrichs, 1899.

Douglas, Kelly Brown. *The Black Christ*. Maryknoll, NY: Orbis, 1994.

Douglass, Frederick. *Narrative of the Life of Frederick Douglass, An American Slave, Written by Himself*. Boston: The Anti-Slavery Office, 1845.

Du Bois, W. E. B. *The Souls of Black Folks*. New York: Dover, 1994.

Ellingworth, Paul. *The Epistle to the Hebrews*. New International Greek Testament Commentary. Grand Rapids: Eerdmans, 1993.

Emerson, Michael O., and Christian Smith. *Divided by Faith: Evangelical Religion and the Problem of Race in America*. Oxford: Oxford University Press, 2001.

Epiphanius, Letter to the Emperor Theodosius, and Cyril A. Mango. *Art of the Byzantine Empire: 312–1453, Sources and Documents*. Toronto: Toronto University Press, 1997.

Escobar, Samuel. "Refugees: A New Testament Perspective." *Transformation* 35 (2018) 102–8.

Esler, Philip F. *Babatha's Orchard: The Yadin Papyri and an Ancient Jewish Family Tale Retold*. Oxford: Oxford University Press, 2017.

Eusebius. *Letter to Constantia*. Translated by A. Cyril Mango. Toronto: Toronto University Press, 1997.

Evans, Craig. "Exorcisms and the Kingdom: Inaugurating the Kingdom of God and Defeating the Kingdom of Satan." In *Key Events in the Life of the Historical Jesus: A Collaborative Exploration of Context and Coherence*, edited by Darrell L. Bock and Robert L. Webb, 151–79. Tübingen: Mohr Siebeck, 2009.

Farag, Lois. "Beyond Their Gender: Contemporary Coptic Female Monasticism." *Journal of World Christianity* 2 (2009) 111–44.

Ferguson, Everett. "Spiritual Sacrifice in Early Christianity and its Environment." *Aufstieg und Niedergang der römischen Welt* 11 (1980) 1151–89.

Gathercole, Simon. *The Preexistent Son: Recovering the Christologies of Matthew, Mark, and Luke*. Grand Rapids: Eerdmans, 2006.

Goppelt, Leonhard. *Theology of the New Testament*. Edited by Jürgen Roloff. Translated by John E. Alsup. Grand Rapids: Eerdmans, 1981.

Gorman, Michael J. "The Work of Christ in the New Testament." In *The Oxford Handbook of Christology*, edited by Francesca Murphy, 72–84. New York: Oxford University Press, 2015.

Grieb, A.Katherine. "'Time Would Fail Me to Tell . . .': The Identity of Jesus Christ in Hebrews." In *Seeking the Identity of Jesus: A Pilgrimage*, edited by ed Beverly Roberts Gaventa and Richard B. Hays, 200–214. Grand Rapids: Eerdmans, 2008.

Groody, Daniel G. "The Church on the Move: Mission in an Age of Migration." *Mission Studies* 30 (2013) 27–42.

———. "Jesus and the Undocumented Immigrant: A Spiritual Geography of a Crucified People." *Theological Studies* 70 (2009) 298–316.

Guthrie, George H. "Hebrews." In *Commentary on the New Testament Use of the Old Testament*, edited by G. K. Beale and D.A. Carson, 919–96. Grand Rapids: Baker Academic, 2007.

Gutiérrez, Gustavo. "Poverty, Migration, and the Option for the Poor." In *A Promised Land, A Perilous Journey: Theological Perspectives on Migration*, edited by Daniel G. Groody and Gioacchino Campese, 76–86. Notre Dame, IN: University of Notre Dame Press, 2008.

Hagner, Donald. "Jesus and the Synoptic Sabbath Controversies." In *Key Events in the Life of the Historical Jesus: A Collaborative Exploration of Context and Coherence*, edited by Darrell L. Bock and Robert L. Webb, 251–92. Tübingen: Mohr Siebeck, 2009.

———. *Matthew 14–28*. Word Biblical Commentary 33B. Dallas: Word, 1998.

Hansen, Collin, ed. *Our Secular Age: Ten Years of Reading and Applying Charles Taylor*. Deerfield: The Gospel Coalition, 2017.

Hansler, Jennifer. "US Admits Lowest Number of Refugees in More Than 40 years." *CNN*, October 3, 2018. https://www.cnn.com/2018/10/02/politics/us-refugees-fy18/index.html.

Hanson, Ann Ellis. "The Widow Babatha and the Poor Orphan Boy." In *Law in the Documents of the Judaean Desert*, edited by Ranon Katzoff and David Schaps, 85–103. Leiden: Brill, 2005.

Harris, Dana M. "The Eternal Inheritance in Hebrews: The Appropriation of the Old Testament Inheritance Theme by the Author of Hebrews." PhD diss., Trinity Evangelical Divinity School, 2009.

———. *Hebrews*. Exegetical Guide to the Greek New Testament. Nashville: B&H Academic, 2019.

———. "'Today if You Hear My Voice': The Spirit Speaking in Hebrews—Implications for Inerrancy." *Presbyterion* 45 (2019) 112–14.

———. "Typological Trajectories in the Epistle to the Hebrews." In *Interpreting the Old Testament Theologically: Essays in Honor of Willem A. VanGemeren*, edited by Andrew T. Abernethy, 280–92. Grand Rapids: Zondervan, 2018.

Hays, Christopher M., and H.Leonardo Ramírez. *La esperanza económica después del desplazamiento forzoso: manual del facilitador*. Medellín: Publicaciones SBC, 2018.

Hayes, Diana L. "Christology in African American Theology." In *The Oxford Handbook of African American Theology*, edited by Katie G. Cannon and Anthony B. Pinn, 153–61. Oxford: Oxford University Press, 2014.

Heimburger, Robert W., et al. *Iglesia, política y desplazamiento: currículo para personas en situación de desplazamiento*. Medellín: Publicaciones SBC, 2018.

Heimburger, Robert W., Christopher M. Hays, and Guillermo Mejía-Castillo. "Forgiveness and Politics: Reading Matthew 18:21–35 with Survivors of the Armed Conflict in Colombia." *HTS Teologiese Studies/Theological Studies* 75 (2019) 1–9.

Hjelm, Ingrid. "Lost and Found? A non-Jewish Israel from the Merneptah Stele to the Byzantine Period." In *History, Archaeology and the Bible Forty Years After 'Historicity': Changing Perspectives 6*, edited by Ingrid Hjelm and Thomas L. Thompson, 112–29. New York: Routledge, 2016.

Hoshen, Dalia. *Beruria the Tannait: A Theological Reading of a Female Mishnaic Scholar*. Lanham, MD: University Press of America, 2007.

Hoskyns, Edwyn Clement. *The Fourth Gospel*. Edited by Francis Noel Davey. London: Faber & Faber, 1947.

Hoyt, Thomas, Jr. "Interpreting Biblical Scholarship for the Black Church Tradition." In *Stony the Road We Trod: African American Biblical Interpretation*. Edited by Cain Hope Felder, 17–39. Minneapolis: Fortress, 1991.

Huckabee, Tyler. "So, Were Mary and Joseph Actually Refugees or What? Yes and No." *Relevant*, December 27, 2018. https://relevantmagazine.com/god/faith/so-were-mary-and-joseph-actually-refugees-or-what/.

Hunt, James. *The Negro's Place in Nature a Paper Read Before the London Anthropological Society*. New York: Van Evrie, Horton, & Co, 1864.

Ilan, Tal. *Integrating Women into Second Temple History*. Texts and Studies in Ancient Judaism 76. Tübingen: Mohr Siebeck, 1999.

———. "Premarital Cohabitation in Ancient Judea: The Evidence of the Babatha Archive and the Mishnah (Ketubbot 1.4)." *Harvard Theological Review* 85 (1993) 247–64.

International Displacement Monitoring Centre. "Global Report on Internal Displacement." 2018. http://www.internal-displacement.org/global-report/grid2018/.

Irenaeus. *Against the Heresies*. Translated by Alexander Roberts and James Donaldson. ANF 1.

Jacob, R. "Le Martyre, épanouissement du sacerdoce des Chréiens, dans la littérature patristique jusqu' en 258." *Mélanges de Science Religieuse* 24 (1967) 153–72, 177–209.

Jennings, Willie James. *The Christian Imagination: Theology and the Origins of Race*. New Haven, CT: Yale University Press, 2010.

Jensen, Robin M. *Face to Face: Portraits of the Divine in Early Christianity*. Minneapolis: Fortress, 2005.

Jeremias, Joachim. *The Eucharistic Words of Jesus*. Translated by Norman Perrin. 2nd ed. New York: Scribner, 1966.

"Jesus 2000." *National Catholic Reporter*. https://www.ncronline.org/jesus-2000.

"Jim Crow Laws." Compiled by National Park Service, Martin Luther King Jr. Historical Site. https://www.nps.gov/malu/learn/education/jim_crow_laws.htm.

Bibliography

Johnson, Todd. "USA Evangelicals/Evangelicals in a Global Context." Lausanne World Pulse Archives, January 2006. http://www.lausanneworldpulse.com/research-php/196/01–2006.

Jones, Beth Felker. *Practicing Christian Doctrine: An Introduction to Thinking and Living Theologically*. Grand Rapids: Baker Academic, 2014.

Kalantzis, George. *Caesar and the Lamb: Early Christian Attitudes on War and Military Service*. Eugene, OR: Cascade, 2012.

———. *Theodore of Mopsuestia: Commentary on the Gospel of John*. Early Christian Studies 7. Strathfield, NSW: St. Paul's, 2004.

Kapic, Kelly M. *Embodied Hope: A Theological Meditation on Pain and Suffering*. Downers Grove, IL: IVP Academic, 2017.

Kartveit, Magnar. *The Origin of the Samaritans*. Leiden: Brill, 2009.

Keener, Craig S. *The Gospel of Matthew: A Socio-Rhetorical Commentary*. Grand Rapids: Eerdmans, 2009.

Kinman, Brent. "Jesus' Royal Entry into Jerusalem." In *Key Events in the Life of the Historical Jesus: A Collaborative Exploration of Context and Coherence*, edited by Darrell L. Bock and Robert L. Webb, 383–427. Tübingen: Mohr Siebeck, 2009.

Kirk, J. R. Daniel. *A Man Attested by God: The Human Jesus of the Synoptic Gospels*. Grand Rapids: Eerdmans, 2016.

Klawans, Jonathan. "Moral and Ritual Purity." In *The Historical Jesus in Context*, edited by D. C. Allison Jr. et al., 266–84. Princeton: Princeton University Press, 2006.

Kraemer, Ross S. "Jewish Women and Women's Judaism(s) at the Beginning of Christianity." In *Women and Christian Origins*, edited by Ross S. Kraemer and Mary Rose D'Angelo, 50–79. Oxford: Oxford University Press, 1999.

Kraemer, Ross S., and Mary Rose D'Angelo. *Women and Christian Origins*. Oxford: Oxford University Press, 1999.

Kruse, Colin G. *The Gospel According to John*. Tyndale New Testament Commentaries. Grand Rapids: Eerdmans, 2003.

Kriegsman, Alan M. "Martha Graham Her Magical Muse." *The Washington Post*, March 26, 1989. https://www.washingtonpost.com/archive/lifestyle/style/1989/03/26/martha-graham-her-magical-muse/9a779f42-78a1-424d-8935-aab279e59e19/.

Legon, Jeordan. "From Science and Computers, a New Face of Jesus." *CNN*, December 26, 2002. http://www.cnn.com/2002/TECH/science/12/25/face.jesus/index.html.

Levering, Matthew. *Engaging the Doctrine of Creation: Cosmos, Creatures, and the Wise and Good Creator*. Grand Rapids: Baker Academic, 2017.

"Liberation Theology." In *Oxford Dictionary of the Christian Church*, edited by E. A. Livingstone and F. L. Cross, 978–79. Oxford: Oxford University Press, 1997.

Long, D. Stephen. "God is Not Nice." In *God Is Not . . . : Religious, Nice, "One of Us," An American, A Capitalist*, edited by D. Brent Laytham, 39–54. Grand Rapids: Brazos, 2004.

López, Hugo. "El divino migrante." *Apuntes* 4 (1984) 14–19.

Lucie-Smith, Edward. *The Face of Jesus*. New York: Harry Abrams, 2011.

Luther, Martin. "Heidelberg Disputation." *Career of the Reformer: 1*, edited by Harold John Grimm, 333–37. Luther's Works 31. Philadelphia: Muhlenberg, 1957.

Luz, Ulrich. *Matthew 21–28: A Commentary*. Hermenia. Minneapolis: Augsburg Fortress, 2005.

Maccini, Robert Gordon. *Her Testimony is True: Women as Witnesses According to John*. Sheffield: Sheffield Academic, 1996.

————. "A Reassessment of the Woman at the Well in John 4 in Light of the Samaritan Context." *JSNT* 53 (1994) 35–46.

MacGregor, Neil, and Erika Langmuir. *Seeing Salvation: Images of Christ in Art.* New Haven, CT: Yale University Press, 2000.

MacGregor, Neil, and Gabriel Finaldi. *The Image of Christ: The Catalogue of the Exhibition Seeing Salvation.* London: National Gallery, 2000.

Martin, James, SJ. "Were Jesus, Mary and Joseph Refugees? Yes." *America Magazine*, December 27, 2017. https://www.americamagazine.org/faith/2017/12/27/were-jesus-mary-and-joseph-refugees-yes.

Martínez, Ramiro, Jr., and Matthew T. Lee. "On Immigration and Crime." *The Nature of Crime* 1 (2000) 485–524.

McAuliffe, Marie. "Migration and Migrants: A Global Overview." In *World Migration Report 2018*, edited by Marie McAuliffe and Martin Ruhs, 1–47. Geneva: International Organization for Migration, 2018.

McGrath, James F. *The Woman at the Well.* Bible Odyssey. https://www.bibleodyssey.org/en/tools/ask-a-scholar/woman-at-the-well.

Mears, Daniel P. "Immigration and Crime: What's the Connection?" *Federal Sentencing Reporter* 14 (2002) 284–88.

Meyer, Ben. *The Aims of Jesus.* London: SCM, 1979.

Micheli, Jason. *Cancer is Funny: Keeping Faith in Stage-Serious Chemo.* Minneapolis: Fortress, 2016.

Miller, Liam. "Christification of the Least: Potential for Christology and Discipleship." *Studies in World Christianity* 24 (2018) 255–76.

Moore, Stephen D. *Poststructuralism and the New Testament: Derrida and Foucault at the Foot of the Cross.* Minneapolis: Augsburg Fortress, 1994.

Moxnes, Halvor. *The Economy of the Kingdom: Social Conflict and Economic Relations in Luke's Gospel.* Eugene, OR: Wipf & Stock, 1988.

Murphy, Larry G. "Evil and Sin in African American Theology." In *The Oxford Handbook of African American Theology*, edited by Katie G. Cannon and Anthony B. Pinn, 212–27. Oxford: Oxford University Press, 2014.

Myles, Robert. "Echoes of Displacement in Matthew's Genealogy of Jesus." *Colloquium* 45 (2013) 31–41.

Namli, Elena. "Identity and the Stranger: A Christological Critique of Refugee Politics." *Political Theology* 12 (2011) 813–29.

Norton, Allison. "Migrant-Shaped Urban Mission: The Missionary Nature and Initiatives of The Church of Pentecost, USA." *Working Papers of the American Society of Missiology* 2 (2015) 68–88.

Nowrasteh, Alex. "By the Numbers: Do Immigrants Cause Crime?" Foundation for Economic Education (July 13, 2015). https://fee.org/articles/by-the-numbers-do-immigrants-cause-crime/.

O'Day, Gail R., and Susan E. Hylen. *John.* Louisville: Westminster John Knox, 2006.

Origen. *Commentary on John.* Translated by Allan Menzies. ANF 9. Peabody, MA: Hendrickson, 1994.

————. *Contra Celsum.* Translated by Henry Chadwick. Cambridge: Cambridge University Press, 1953.

————. *Homilies on Leviticus: 1–16.* Translated by Gary Wayne Barkley. Fathers of the Church 83. Washington, DC: Catholic University of America Press, 1990.

————. *Homilies on Luke.* Fontes Christiani 4/1. Freiburg: Herder, 1991.

————. *On First Principles*. Translated by W. George Butterworth. London: SPCK, 1936.

Oudshoorn, Jacobine G. *The Relationship between Roman and Local Law in the Babatha and Salome Komaise Archives: General Analysis and Three Case Studies on Law of Succession, Guardianship and Marriage*. Leiden: Brill, 2007.

Peeler, Amy. "With Tears and Joy: The Emotions of Christ in Hebrews." *Koinonia* 20 (2008) 12–26.

Perkins, Judith. *The Suffering Self: Pain and Narrative Representation in Early Christian Era*. London: Routledge, 1995.

Perpetua. "Passio Sanctarum Perpetua et Felicitatis." In *Women in the Early Church, Message of the Fathers of the Church*, edited by Elizabeth A. Clark, 97–105. Collegeville, MN: Liturgical, 1983.

Peterson, David. *Hebrews and Perfection: An Examination of the Concept of Perfection in the 'Epistle to the Hebrew*. SNTSMS 47. Cambridge: Cambridge University Press, 1982.

Phan, Peter C. "Deus Migrator—God the Migrant: Migration of Theology and Theology of Migration." *Theological Studies* 77 (2016) 845–68.

————. "Migration in the Patristic Era: History and Theology." In *A Promised Land, A Perilous Journey: Theological Perspectives on Migration*, edited by Daniel G. Groody and Gioacchino Campese, 35–62. Notre Dame, IN: University of Notre Dame Press, 2008.

Pierce, Madison N. "Divine Discourse in the Epistle to the Hebrews: An Encounter with a God Who Speaks." PhD diss., Durham University, 2017.

Pummer, Reinhard. *The Samaritans: A Profile*. Grand Rapids: Eerdmans, 2016.

"Quinisext Council." In *Art of the Byzantine Empire: 312–1453, Sources and Documents*. Edited and translated by Cyril A. Mango, 139–40. Toronto: Toronto University Press, 1997.

Ratzinger, Joseph. *Instruction on Certain Aspects of the "Theology of Liberation."* https://www.vatican.va/roman_curia/congregations/cfaith/documents/rc_con_cfaith_doc_19840806_theology-liberation_en.html

Rhee, Victor. "Chiasm and the Concept of Faith in Hebrews 12:1–29." *WTJ* 62 (2001) 269–84.

Rogers, Katie. "Whistle-Blower Did the Unexpected: She Returned to Work." *The New York Times*, April 1, 2019. https://www.nytimes.com/2019/04/01/us/politics/tricia-newbold-whistle-blower-white-house.html.

Root, Andrew. *Ministry in a Secular Age*. 3 vols. Grand Rapids: Baker Academic, 2017–Forthcoming.

Rutledge, Fleming. *The Crucifixion: Understanding the Death of Jesus Christ*. Grand Rapids: Eerdmans, 2015.

Satlow, David. *Jewish Marriage in Antiquity*. Princeton: Princeton University Press, 2001.

Sayers, Dorothy. *The Mind of the Maker*. San Francisco: Harper & Row, 1987.

Seelye, Katharine Q. "Tejshree Thapa, Defender of Human Rights in South Asia, Dies at 52." *The New York Times*, April 1, 2019. https://www.nytimes.com/2019/03/29/obituaries/tejshree-thapa-dead.html.

Seneca. "Withdrawing from the World." In *Seneca Epistles 1–65*, translated by Richard M. Gummere, 84–93. Loeb Classical Library 75. 1917.

Senior, Donald. "'Beloved Aliens and Exiles': New Testament Perspectives on Migration." In *A Promised Land, A Perilous Journey: Theological Perspectives on Migration*, edited by Daniel G. Groody and Gioacchino Campese, 20–34. Notre Dame, IN: University of Notre Dame Press, 2008.

Shaw, Brent D. "Body/Power/Identity: Passions of the Martyrs." *Journal of Early Christian Studies* 4 (1996) 269–312.

Shore, Mary Hinkle. "Jesus as a Refugee." *Journal for Preachers* 40 (2016) 2–8.

Sigismund-Nielsen, Hanne. "Vibia Perpetua—An Indecent Woman." In *Perpetua's Passion: Multidisciplinary Approaches to the Passio Perpetuae et Felicitatis*, edited by Jan N. Bremmer and Marco Formisano, 103–17. Oxford: Oxford University Press, 2012.

Smith, Christian, and Melinda Lundquist Denton. *Soul Searching: The Religious and Spiritual Lives of American Teenagers*. New York: Oxford University Press, 2005.

Smith, James K. A. *How (Not) to Be Secular: Reading Charles Taylor*. Grand Rapids: Eerdmans, 2014.

Sobrino, Jon. *Jesucristo liberador: lectura histórico-teológica de Jesús de Nazaret*. México: Universidad Iberoamericana, 1994.

Souetsu, Yanagi. *The Unknown Craftsman: A Japanese Insight into Beauty*. New York: Kodansha America, 2013.

Stein, Robert H. *The Method and Message of Jesus*. Louisville: Westminster John Knox, 1994.

Stenschke, Christoph W. "Migration and Theology." *European Journal of Theology* 26 (2017) 91–97.

Streete, Gail P. C. *Redeemed Bodies: Women Martyrs in Early Christianity*. Louisville: Westminster John Knox, 2009.

Strine, Casey A. "Migration, Dual Identity and Integration: A Christian Approach to Embracing Others Across Enduring Lines of Difference." In *Christian Citizenship in the Middle East: Divided Allegiance or Dual Belonging?*, edited by Mohammed Girma and Cristian Romocea, 103–20. Philadelphia: Jessica Kingsley, 2017.

Taylor, Charles. *A Secular Age*. Cambridge, MA: Harvard University Press, 2007.

Taylor, Joan. *What Did Jesus Look Like?* London: Bloomsbury, 2018.

Tilling, Chris. *Paul's Divine Christology*. Grand Rapids: Eerdmans, 2015.

Tomasi, Lydio F. *The Other Catholics: The Institutional Role of the Church in the Adjustment Process of Metro Toronto's Italians, a Survey Research*. New York: New York University, 1978.

Tov, Emanuel. "Proto-Samaritan Texts and the Samaritan Pentateuch." In *The Samaritans*, edited by Alan D. Crown, 397–407. Tübingen: Mohr Siebeck, 1989.

Tuckett, Christopher. "Jesus and the Sabbath." In *Jesus from Judaism to Christianity: Continuum Approaches to the Historical Jesus*, edited by Tom Holmén, 411–42. LNST. New York, T. & T. Clark, 2007.

Twelftree, Graham H. *Jesus the Miracle Worker: A Historical and Theological Study*. Downers Grove, IL: IVP Academic, 1999.

U.N.H.C.R. "Figures at a Glance." *UNHCR*, June 19, 2019. https://www.unhcr.org/figures-at-a-glance.html.

———. "Resettlement Data." https://www.unhcr.org/resettlement-data.html.

Wallace, Daniel B. *Greek Grammar Beyond the Basics*. Grand Rapids: Zondervan, 1996.

Wilder, Amos. *Early Christian Rhetoric*. Cambridge, MA: Harvard University Press, 1971.

Williams, Jane. *Faces of Christ: Jesus in Art*. Oxford: Lion Hudson, 2011.

Williams, Michael Allen. *Rethinking "Gnosticism": An Argument for Dismantling a Dubious Category*. Princeton: Princeton University Press, 1996.

Williams, Rowan. *Christ The Heart of Creation*. London: Bloomsbury Continuum, 2018.

————. *Why Study the Past?: The Quest for the Historical Church*. Grand Rapids: Eerdmans, 2005.

Witherington, Ben, III. *The Christology of Jesus*. Minneapolis: Fortress, 1991.

"World Birth and Death Rates." *Ecology*. http://www.ecology.com/birth-death-rates/.

Wright, N. T. *The Day the Revolution Began: Reconsidering the Meaning of Jesus's Crucifixion*. San Francisco: HarperOne, 2016.

Yong, Amos. *The Bible, Disability, and the Church: A New Vision of the People of God*. Grand Rapids: Eerdmans, 2011.

Zong, Jie, et al. *Frequently Requested Statistics on Immigrants and Immigration in the United States*. Migration Policy Institute, 2019. https://www.migrationpolicy.org/article/frequently-requested-statistics-immigrants-and-immigration-united-states#Demographic.